T0311651

Post-Growth Work

This book argues that society must rethink the notion of formal employment and instead introduce and spread the notion of "meaningful work" so that societies can become independent of economic growth.

The excessive consumption of natural resources and the immense emissions resulting from our growth-oriented economic system surpass the planetary boundaries. Despite this, society and the economy still strive for economic growth in order to generate jobs, to finance the social security system and to assure tax income. However, these expectations are increasingly unrealistic, not least because technological developments such as digitalisation and robotisation will change and limit formal employment opportunities as well. Against this backdrop, the book introduces the notion of meaningful activities that embrace various kinds of work, paid and unpaid, sequential or in parallel, which are meaningful for the worker as well as society as a whole. At the same time, the authors argue in favour of reduced working time in formal employment. Furthermore, the book also describes the necessary transformations in companies and for consumers, for social and tax systems, for social services and agriculture.

Innovative and timely, this book will be a key resource for professionals and scholars interested in sustainability, economics, work, transformation and post-growth studies.

Irmi Seidl is Head of the Research Unit Economics and Social Sciences, Swiss Federal Institute for Forest, Snow and Landscape Research WSL, Birmensdorf, Switzerland.

Angelika Zahrnt is Honorary Chair of Friends of the Earth Germany and Fellow at the IÖW – Institute for Ecological Economy Research, Berlin.

Post-Growth Work

Employment and Meaningful Activities within Planetary Boundaries

Edited by
Irmi Seidl and Angelika Zahrnt

Translated from German by
Ray Cunningham

LONDON AND NEW YORK

First published 2022
by Routledge
2 Park Square, Milton Park, Abingdon, Oxon OX14 4RN

and by Routledge
605 Third Avenue, New York, NY 10158

Routledge is an imprint of the Taylor & Francis Group, an informa business

© 2022 selection and editorial matter, Irmi Seidl and Angelika
Zahrnt; individual chapters, the contributors

The right of Irmi Seidl and Angelika Zahrnt to be identified as
the authors of the editorial material, and of the authors for their
individual chapters, has been asserted in accordance with sections
77 and 78 of the Copyright, Designs and Patents Act 1988.

Translation from Original German Language Edition
Tätigsein in der Postwachstumsgesellschaft, 2019
Metropolis-Verlag für Ökonomie, Gesellschaft und Politik GmbH
https://www.metropolis-verlag.de
Copyright: Metropolis-Verlag, Marburg
ISBN 978-3-7316-1405-0

British Library Cataloguing-in-Publication Data
A catalogue record for this book is available from the British Library

Library of Congress Cataloging-in-Publication Data
Names: Seidl, Irmi, 1962- editor. | Zahrnt, Angelika, 1944- editor.
Title: Post-growth work : employment and meaningful activities
within planetary boundaries / Irmi Seidl, Angelika Zahrnt.
Description: New York, NY : Routledge, 2021. |
Includes bibliographical references and index.
Identifiers: LCCN 2021008978 (print) | LCCN 2021008979
(ebook) | ISBN 9781032034584 (hbk) | ISBN 9781032034577
(pbk) | ISBN 9781003187370 (ebk)
Subjects: LCSH: Economic development. | Sustainable
development. | Employment (Economic theory)
Classification: LCC HD75 .P675 2021 (print) |
LCC HD75 (ebook) | DDC 331.2—dc23
LC record available at https://lccn.loc.gov/2021008978
LC ebook record available at https://lccn.loc.gov/2021008979

ISBN: 978-1-032-03458-4 (hbk)
ISBN: 978-1-032-03457-7 (pbk)
ISBN: 978-1-003-18737-0 (ebk)

DOI: 10.4324/9781003187370

Typeset in Goudy
by codeMantra

Contents

About the contributors

Corinna Fischer, Dr phil., is a senior researcher in the Products and Material Flows Department at the Oeko-Institut e.V. – Institute for Applied Ecology, Darmstadt, leading the research group on sustainable products and consumption. She studied political science. Her doctoral thesis dealt with environmental motivation and engagement among young people in Eastern Germany. Before joining the Oeko-Institut, Corinna Fischer worked on energy-efficient products and standardisation at the Federation of German Consumer Organisations (vzbv), as a research associate at the Environmental Policy Research Centre of the Freie Universität Berlin and as a freelance consultant, teacher and advisor to environmental activists. Her main areas of work at present are sustainable consumption, energy saving in private households and product policy.

Ernst Fritz-Schubert, Dr phil., is a qualified economist and system therapist now teaching at the SRH-University Heidelberg. He is the author of numerous publications on the subject of happiness and well-being and runs the Fritz-Schubert-Institut named after him, which researches and develops methods of personal development. After studying economics and law in Heidelberg, he joined the teaching profession. He completed his doctorate (Dr phil.) at the University of Kassel on the subject of "Well-being as a learning goal". From 2000 to 2011 he was Principal of the Willy-Hellpach-Schule in Heidelberg, where in 2007 he established Happiness as part of the school curriculum.

Stefanie Gerold, PhD, is a research associate at the Institute of Vocational Education and Work Studies of TU Berlin, in the Department of Economic Education ans Sustainable Consumption. She holds a BA in economics and political science, and master's in socioecological economics and policy. She received her doctorate from the Macroeconomic Policy Institute (IMK) of the Hans Böckler

Foundation and the Institute for Ecological Economics at the Vienna University of Economics and Business (WU). In her PhD she focused on employee preferences for shorter working hours, firm models for working time reduction, as well as inequalities in working hours and income. Her research is currently focused on sustainable work and social-ecological transformation, time wealth and sustainable lifestyles, platform work and critiques of work.

Franz-Theo Gottwald, Dr phil., diploma in theology. He is an organisational and policy consultant, an expert on philanthropic foundations, and a writer and commentator on ethics, sustainable development, corporate responsibility, organic farming, nutrition, consciousness and futurology. He studied Catholic theology, philosophy, social science and Indology. Since 1988 he has been the director of the Schweisfurth Foundation for Sustainable Agriculture and Food in Munich. He researches and teaches as Honorary Professor in Agricultural, Food and Environmental Ethics at the Humboldt University of Berlin. He is a member of several professional organisations such as the Federation of German Scientists, the Deutsche Gesellschaft für Philosophie (German Society for Philosophy), the Gesellschaft für Wirtschafts- und Sozialwissenschaften des Landbaus (GEWISOLA) e.V. (Society for Economic and Social Sciences of Agriculture) and the Global Ecological Integrity Group (GEIG).

Jonas Hagedorn, Dr rer. pol., has been a research associate since 2016 at the Oswald von Nell-Breuning Institute for Business and Social Ethics of the Sankt Georgen Graduate School of Philosophy and Theology. He studied Catholic theology and social sciences in Münster, Innsbruck and San Salvador (El Salvador). He was awarded a doctorate at the TU Darmstadt. He has worked in research projects on home nursing care and on the importance and organisation of social service delivery in (partly) in-patient facilities. In his dissertation on Oswald von Nell-Breuning SJ and his contribution to the understanding of the welfare state in the Weimar Republic, he focused on working conditions in industrial society. Starting from the (implicitly male) "labour question" in German industrial society, his perspective has expanded to embrace the (non-gendered) "labour question" in European service societies, in particular the organisation of formal and informal care work.

Gerrit von Jorck holds a diploma in economics and social sciences and a BA in cultural sciences and philosophy. He is a research associate at the Institute of Vocational Education and Work Studies of TU Berlin, in the Department of Economic Education and Sustainable Consumption. He is a member of the board of the German Society for Ecological Economy Research (VÖW) and fellow of the Institute for Ecological Economy Research (IÖW). His research currently focuses on social-ecological labour policy, post-growth economics, time wealth and time-rebound effects.

Andrea Komlosy is associate professor at the Department of Social and Economic History, University of Vienna. She works on issues of unequal regional development both on a local, a regional and on a global scale. She combines a regional historical approach with a global historical perspective and an understanding of the regions in their global context and interaction. She is part of the management team for global history studies at the University of Vienna. Her study visits abroad include Brest, Paris, Honolulu and Cambridge, where she was Schumpeter Fellow at the Weatherhead Center for International Affairs at Harvard University in 2014/15. She is lecturing at numerous universities at home and abroad, and also engaged in teacher training and adult education. She (co-)curates and consults numerous events and museums, exhibitions and tourism projects. Her most recent book publications include *Grenzen. Räumliche und soziale Trennlinien im Zeitenlauf* (Borders. Spatial and Social Dividing Lines over the Course of Time), Vienna 2018; and *Work. The Last 1,000 Years*, London – New York 2018.

Angela Köppl, Dr rer. soc. oec., was a research associate from 1987 to 1992 in the Department of Economics of the Institute for Advanced Studies (IHS) in Vienna; since October 1992 she has been an environmental economist at the Austrian Institute of Economic Research (WIFO). At WIFO she twice held the position of deputy director and was responsible for scientific coordination. In 2002 she spent a research period at the Massachusetts Institute of Technology in Cambridge. She is vice-president of the Austria Chapter of the Club of Rome and was a member of the board of the Austrian Economic Association. As a member of the board of the Climate Change Center in its early years, she contributed significantly to its establishment. Since June 2020 she has been a member of the Supervisory Board of the Austrian Federal Railways Holding Company (ÖBB Holding AG). Key areas of her research activities are climate change and the restructuring of the energy system and Austrian and EU energy and climate policy.

Bettina-Johanna Krings, Dr phil., is social scientist and works as senior scientist at the Institute for Technology Assessment and Systems Analysis (ITAS) at the Karlsruhe Institute of Technology (KIT). From 2011 to 2019, she was the co-director of the research group on Knowledge society and knowledge policy. Since 2009 she has established and built up the research group on work and technology at ITAS, which takes a variety of research approaches into the consequences of information technologies on work and organisational structures. She is a recognised expert on several bodies looking at digitalisation processes and their social and ethical consequences in different areas (e.g. Village 4.0, and HR strategy at KIT). Her work focuses on the following topics: the relationship between technology and work structures, concepts of human-machine interaction and sociological theories of the modernisation of societies. She publishes and lectures on all three topics. In these areas, she is leading or has led numerous research projects.

Gisela Kubon-Gilke, Prof. Dr rer. pol., has been professor of economics and social policy at the University of Applied Sciences, Darmstadt since 1998. She studied economics at the University of Göttingen. In 1989 she received a doctorate and in 1997 she received habilitation in economics, both at the TU Darmstadt. She is honorary member of the *Gesellschaft für Gestalttheorie und ihre Anwendungen* (Society for Gestalt Theory and Its Applications) and member of the European Academy of Sciences and Arts. She has published on institutional economics, the theory of social policy, educational economics and basic normative questions of economics, among other topics. Her publications include the following books: *Wi(e)der Elitebildung. Bildung aus ökonomischer Perspektive* (2006); *Außer Konkurrenz. Sozialpolitik im Spannungsfeld von Markt, Zentralsteuerung und Traditionssystemen* (2011, third edition 2018); *Gestalten der Sozialpolitik. Theoretische Grundlagen und Anwendungsbeispiele* (2018) together with 32 contributors; *Utopien und Sozialpolitik* (2020) together with Remi Maier-Rigaud; *Sozialethik und Kritik* (2020) together with five co-editors.

Linda Nierling, Dr phil., has been a researcher since 2005 at the Institute for Technology Assessment and Systems Analysis (ITAS) of the Karlsruhe Institute of Technology (KIT), and since 2020 she has been head of the research group "Digital technologies and societal change". She studied environmental sciences and business administration at the University of Lüneburg and ETH Zurich. In 2011, she received the PhD degree in social recognition in extended working contexts at Goethe University, Frankfurt am Main. She had research residencies at Luleå University of Technology, Sweden, and at the Institute for Advanced Studies on Science, Technology and Society (IAS-STS), Graz, Austria. She is also political consultant to the German and European Parliaments. She is a member of the Scientific Advisory Board at the Institut Mensch, Ethik and Wissenschaft, Berlin. Her main current research interests include digitalisation of work, assistive technologies in the field of disability, post-growth and technology, normativity in technology assessment and methods of qualitative social research.

Norbert Reuter, Dr rer. pol., has been head of the Department for collective bargaining policy at the Headquarter of the United Services Union (ver.di) in Berlin since 2016. He studied economics and political science at the Rheinisch-Westfälische Technische Hochschule Aachen (RWTH Aachen University) and the University of York, Great Britain. He obtained a doctorate in 1994, and habilitation in economics in 2000. He was a member of the Enquete Commission "Growth, Prosperity, Quality of Life" of the German Bundestag (2011–2013). He has published on topics such as institutional economics, labour market policy, the problem of growth and the economic development of industrial societies. Among other titles, he published *Wachstumseuphorie und Verteilungsrealität. Wirtschaftspolitische Leitbilder zwischen Gestern und Morgen* (Growth Euphoria and Distributional Reality. Economic Policy Models between Yesterday and Tomorrow) (second ed. 2007), and *Ökonomik der "langen Frist". Zur Evolution der Wachstumsgrundlagen in Industriegesellschaften* (Economics of the "Long Term". On the Evolution of the Basis for Growth in Industrial Societies) (2005).

Ulf Schrader, Prof. Dr. rer. pol., received a diploma in economics and an MA in political science. He is the head of the Department of Economic education and Sustainable Consumption (ALÖNK) at the Technical University of Berlin, and the director of the School of Education at TU Berlin (SETUB). After studying in Göttingen, Dublin and Hanover, he worked mainly as a research associate at the Institute of Marketing and Consumption of Leibniz University Hannover. Since 2008, he has been a lecturer at the TU Berlin in teacher training for the school subject "Economy-Work-Technology". Among other positions, he was a member of the Scientific advisory council on Consumer and food policy at the German Federal Ministry of Food, Agriculture and Consumer Protection. His work focuses on sustainable consumption, consumer education and corporate social responsibility. In these areas, he is leading and has led numerous transdisciplinary research projects.

Margit Schratzenstaller, Dr rer. pol., held a post-doc position at the Graduate College on the Future of the European Social Model of the University of Göttingen, after studying economics at the Universities of Giessen (Dipl.-Oec.) and Milwaukee (MA, Economics). Since April 2003 she has been working at the Austrian Institute of Economic Research (WIFO) Vienna on the EU budget, tax competition and harmonisation, fiscal federalism and family policy and gender budgeting. She was deputy director during 2006–2008 and 2015–2019. She had research residencies at the German Institute for Economic Research Berlin (2012), the Freie Universität Berlin (2012) and the Berlin School of Economics and Law (2015). She is also a member in the Austrian Fiscal Advisory Council. She is lecturer at the University of Economics and Business Vienna, and she was vice coordinator of the EU research project on Welfare, Wealth and Work for Europe (2012–2016), partner in the EU research project on FairTax (2015–2019). She is member of the board of the Austrian Society for European Politics and of the board of trustees of the European Forum Alpbach. She also received Women's Prize of the City of Vienna (2009), Progressive Economy Prize (2016), Mobility Prize of the Austrian Transport Club (2017) and Kurt Rothschild Prize (2018).

Irmi Seidl, Dr oec., adjunct professor at the University of Zurich, Maître ès Science Economiques, is Head of the Research Unit Economics and Social Sciences at the Swiss Federal Institute for Forest, Snow and Landscape Research WSL, Birmensdorf, Switzerland. She teaches Ecological economics at the University of Zurich and ETH Zürich. Since her dissertation at the University of St Gallen, she has been working in inter- and transdisciplinary environmental research. She is a co-publisher of the journal GAIA and together with Angelika Zahrnt she published the book *Postwachstumsgesellschaft: Konzepte für die Zukunft* (Post-Growth Society: Concepts for the Future), 2010, and established the blog *Postwachstum.de*. Her current work focuses on the economics of land use and settlement development, nature conservation and biodiversity, renewable energy and energy cooperatives, and post-growth society.

Immanuel Stieß holds a PhD in political sciences. He has been working at ISOE – Institute for Social-ecological Research for many years as a research scientist and is head of the Research unit energy and climate protection in everyday life. He is a sociologist and planning expert and received his doctorate in Urban planning from the University of Kassel, with a thesis on communication with tenants during housing refurbishment. His research focus is on low-carbon lifestyles and everyday practices, particularly in the fields of housing, energy use and nutrition. His current research includes climate- and generation-friendly housing, housing sufficiency, sustainable consumption and social participation as well as gender justice and climate policy.

Georg Stoll, Dr theol., was – until recently – an expert in the Department of Politics and Global Future Issues of Misereor (German Catholic Bishops' Organisation for Development Cooperation). He studied philosophy (Munich), theology (Frankfurt, Paris, Rome) and religious studies (Paris). After working as a journalist, since 2001 he has been working on cross-cutting development policy issues at Misereor, including debt, civil society, and tax justice; and since 2010, he has been working increasingly on issues of economic growth, sustainability and social-ecological change. He has spent many years working in the expert group on the global economy and social ethics of the German Bishops' Conference and in the ecumenical process *Umkehr zum Leben – Den Wandel gestalten* (Conversion to Life – Shaping Change). He has numerous publications and educational activities on the role of church actors and on North-South relations against the backdrop of social-ecological transformation.

Theo Wehner, Prof. em. Dr phil., Dipl.-Psych., studied (after a vocational training) psychology, sociology and philosophy in Münster and received his doctorate there. He was appointed as a professor in Bremen. From 1989 to 1997 he was teaching as professor for industrial and organizational psychology at TU Hamburg and from 1997 to 2015 he was professor at the ETH Zürich, where he retired in September 2015. Currently, he is visiting professor at the University of Bremen. His scientific work focuses on questions related to "Developing the New" (creativity and innovation), the "Truth of the Error" (error friendliness and work safety) and the "Experience/Knowledge ratio" (cooperation and knowledge exchange). Under the headings of "knowledge-based cooperation" and "work safety through error-friendliness", he has been implementing projects on behalf of a number of companies for many years. For 20 years now, the focus of his work has also been on research projects on volunteering, corporate volunteering and basic income.

Angelika Zahrnt, Prof. Dr, is an economist. She was an employee, first with Siemens and then worked in the Hesse State Chancellery. She then became active in the family, voluntary and freelance work and a research associate at the Institute for Applied Ecology, Freiburg. She was participant in the women's movement, local politics and the environmental movement. From 1990 to 2007, she was first deputy chair, and then chair of Friends of the Earth Germany; she is now honorary chair. From 2001 to 2013, she was also a member of the German Council for Sustainable Development, she is a member of the advisory council of the Institute for Advanced Sustainability Studies (IASS) Postdam and fellow at the Institute for Ecological Economy Research (IÖW), Berlin. She was an initiator of the first comprehensive country-specific study on sustainable development (1996, 2008) (Title: *Sustainable Germany*). She was joint editor (with Irmi Seidl) of *Postwachstumsgesellschaft* (Post-Growth Society), 2010. She was also joint author (with Uwe Schneidewind) of *The Politics of Sufficiency – Making It Easier to Live the Good Life*, 2014. She was awarded the Order of Merit of the Federal Republic of Germany in 2006 and 2013 and the German Environmental Prize of the German Federal Environmental Foundation in 2009.

About the Translator:

Ray Cunningham has a first degree in German and French and a PhD on myth and politics in the writings of Thomas Mann. He was formerly Director of the Anglo-German Foundation and is now a freelance writer, lecturer, consultant and translator, working mainly in bilateral Anglo-German knowledge exchange across the social sciences and humanities. More information at www.raycunningham.eu.

Foreword

Work is more than just the means to a livelihood. It's a vital ingredient in our connection to each other: part of the "glue" that binds society together. Good work carried out under decent conditions sustains our motivation, commands respect from others and offers a sense of fulfilment. It's a vital element in our contribution as individuals to our community. It's one of the means through which we participate in the life of society. In the best case, good work delivers a sense of meaning and a purpose in life.

For too many people, that "best case" has either never been on offer or else it has gone into terminal retreat in recent decades. Even before the coronavirus crisis turned the world of work upside down, the everyday reality was a thousand miles from this happy ideal. Millions were trapped in precarious jobs with insecure wages. Millions more were threatened with long-term unemployment from rapid technological transitions. Paid work had become oppressive and exploitative for many and meaningless for others. Unpaid work – the labours of love that sustain our homes, families and communities – had lost its value in a society driven by productivity, output and profit.

Under the yoke of capitalism, labour has become just a cost to production, to be subsumed away by "efficiency" and replaced by machines. Work is a penance to be avoided, haunted by poor conditions and impossible productivity targets. Livelihoods have turned into a class war between those whose aim was to get rich as fast as possible from the pursuit of profit and those who became ever more dependent on precarious wages. The result is a dystopian paradox. As the economist Fritz Schumacher once pointed out: the ideal for employers is output without workers; the ideal for employees is income without work.

At the heart of this failing lies the uneasy bargain between capital and labour that haunts the modern economy. Growth in what economists call the "productivity" of labour is all that stands between the demands of the stock market and the immiseration of workers. Growth in output is all that stands between the relentless pursuit of productivity and the maintenance of full employment. But growth in output has proved disastrous for the planet on which we all depend. Growth in productivity has eroded the slow and essential economics of care. Ecological loss and social precarity are coded into the dynamics of capitalism. These processes undermine the creativity of the work force and threaten social stability. The long-term implications for society are nothing short of disastrous.

One of the most profound lessons from the global pandemic is that those whose work matters most were those most sorely neglected by society. The doctors and nurses. The teachers and the carers. The farm workers and the food retailers. The delivery drivers and the cleaners. Those on the frontline of the coronavirus crisis were those whose livelihoods had become untenably insecure in the years of austerity that followed the financial crisis. Overworked, poorly recompensed, under-appreciated: these were the people who turned out to matter more than they had ever been given credit for. The ones whose dedication and hard work stood between society and catastrophe when the virus struck.

How did this happen? How was it allowed to happen? How could we have forgotten so many fundamental truths about the value of good work? To address these questions is not just to bemoan lost opportunity or to bewail injustice. It is to begin to understand where recovery must seek redress. The chapters in Irmi Seidl and Angelika Zahrnt's timely and insightful exploration of *Post-Growth Work* represent an essential stepping stone towards that vital task. They address the fundamental dilemmas of work in a post-growth society. They explore the dynamics of different sectors in the economy. They seek remedies for the devaluation of housework and the denigration of care. Above all they serve as the foundation for understanding the transition towards a greener, fairer economy.

Even as it shone a cruel light on the cracks in our society, the indelible experience of the year 2020 offered us an object lesson in this essential transformation. Early in the pandemic, with an alacrity as surprising as it was laudable, governments moved to protect people's incomes through furlough schemes and business grants. Hospitals were built, supply chains were restructured and communities were galvanised. Lockdown curtailed our opportunities. But it sharpened our vision. Growth was set to one side. Health became our priority. The crisis provoked a systemic rethink about the nature of prosperity. But change cannot stop with crisis. Recovery must build on the lessons from this experience. It must learn from the mistakes of the past.

Those lessons are perhaps most profound when it comes to the world of work. Livelihoods matter. Not just for the richest in society. But for all of us. Labour matters. Not just as the means to production but as an investment in the future of society. Work matters. Not just as the means to an income but as the tangible manifestation of our commitment to a collective future. Transforming the world of work must start from these realisations. The contributors to this volume have done us a huge service in setting out the dimensions of that task.

Tim Jackson

Preface

Our economic and social system, which is based on growth, is reaching its limits. The planet can no longer cope with increasing resource consumption and emissions. At the same time, politicians, businesspeople and representatives of other sectors of society continue to call for economic growth. One of their main arguments is the need to maintain employment and create new jobs. Formal gainful employment ensures income and supports consumption, and is the basis for social security contributions and tax payments. Ultimately, everyone has an interest in there being enough jobs, and if growth promises this, then growth policy will enjoy broad support. But the argument that growth creates jobs is flawed:

- for ecological reasons, a structural change needs to take place in the economy. Some sectors, such as the automotive industry, should no longer grow but shrink, while others, such as the fossil energy industry, must be abandoned altogether;
- because consumption markets are increasingly saturated, increases in income are only able to stimulate consumer demand, and thus growth, to a limited extent;
- technical developments such as digitalisation and robotisation are eliminating jobs and it is not yet clear how many new jobs will be created and what they will be;
- high levels of social security contributions and taxes on wages drive the rationalisation of labour.

Just as the role and significance of work changed fundamentally in the transition to an industrial society, so now, in the transition from a growth to a post-growth society, a reorganisation of the world of work and a re-evaluation of formal employment and the associated tax and social security systems are necessary. We need to amend the historically evolved situation we are in so that our economic and social system is no longer dependent on economic growth, remains within planetary boundaries, provides social and economic stability and human well-being, and supplies a sufficient quantity of goods and services produced through various forms of work.

Work – in many forms and fields – is a central component of human life. Our future economic and social system must build on this fact, and on a better balance between paid and unpaid work. This book presents concepts for being meaningfully active in a post-growth society. The individual chapters examine the question of what this means in detail – for companies and consumers, for tax systems, for social services and welfare systems. The starting point for the latter is the forms of social security prevailing in continental Europe.

We would like to thank all those who supported us in the conception and production of this book, in particular the authors, who had the courage to bring together ideas around post-growth, work and other topics, and who invested a lot of patience and work in their discussions with the editors.

We would also like to thank Ray Cunningham for his readable and accurate translation, and the foundations which provided financial support for the book.

Irmi Seidl and Angelika Zahrnt
Zürich and Neckargemünd

Introduction

1 Employment, meaningful activity and the post-growth society

Irmi Seidl and Angelika Zahrnt

Summary

The current economic system is paradoxical: growth is supposed to create jobs, and increasing labour productivity is supposed to contribute to this, but at the same time it results in jobs being lost. So growth must also replace the jobs that have been lost through "rationalisation". This paradox is exacerbated by the social welfare and tax system, which has formal employment as its key source of financing: this drives forward increasing labour productivity. But economic growth cannot continue indefinitely. It is therefore important to diminish the role of formal employment – in social security, and as a source of public revenue, social recognition and integration. At the same time, an understanding needs to be developed of what it means to be meaningfully active, one which includes not only formal employment but also self-determined work, voluntary work, care and community work and other forms of work, and this understanding needs to be promoted and spread by and through our societal institutions.

1 The close link between work and growth

In the last ten years, critical reflection on the constant and at times strong economic growth since the second half of the 20th century has expanded and intensified significantly. The underlying economic and social policies and mechanisms that lead to growth have also come under scrutiny.[1] This criticism is primarily motivated by ecological concerns: economic growth goes hand in hand with high consumption of resources and extensive destruction of the natural foundations of life. This way of organising the economic system has reached or exceeded some of the planetary boundaries. At the same time, the focus on economic growth prevents an effective environmental policy, because any

DOI: 10.4324/9781003187370-1

such policy could slow down or stop economic growth, according to the usual arguments put forward by the defenders of growth.

An important aspect of the critical examination of economic growth is determining what drives it. In their book *Postwachstumsgesellschaft: Konzepte für die Zukunft* (2010) (The Post-Growth Society: Concepts for the Future), Seidl and Zahrnt analysed various factors that drive economic growth and need to be restructured if we are to end the growth dependency of our economies and societies and make the transition to a post-growth society.[2] The present book deals with (paid) work, because work – or more precisely paid work – is a powerful driver of economic growth.

Policies promoting economic growth are very often justified because they are believed to create or maintain (formal) jobs and employment.[3] There is an assumption that economic growth and environmental policy are in conflict because environmental policy slows down growth and thus costs jobs. More recently, it has been argued that "green growth" resolves this conflict and decouples growth from resource use (see Parrique et al. 2019 for a critical analysis). The guidelines for growth policy in Germany are set by the Stability and Growth Act,[4] which enshrines the goal of full employment. There is hardly any critical questioning of this policy because of possible effects on material livelihoods. Since the beginning of the last decade, there has been increasing discussion on "green growth", which is argued to have positive employment effects and at the same time to reduce ecological problems (e.g. OECD 2017). In addition to stimulating growth, the political objective is to increase labour productivity by fostering technological progress and improving the skills of the workforce. This means that more is produced per hour worked, or less labour is required to produce a given quantity of output. This leads to growth and – so it is argued – to increased competitiveness because prices could fall, leading to increased demand and therefore, in turn, to further growth.[5]

Employees as well as the state have an interest in maximising the supply of well-paid formal employment opportunities: such opportunities secure their own livelihoods and those of their families and provide their social security, and the state levies taxes and social security contributions on the basis of earned income. Income taxes account for 22 percent of total tax revenues in Austria, 21 percent in France, 27 percent in Germany, 31 percent in Switzerland and 27 percent in the UK (2018) (on tax rates for different income levels, see Köppl/Schratzenstaller in this book).[6] Social security contributions on employment (employee and employer contributions) amount to 38 percent of total tax revenues in Germany, 35 percent in both France and Austria, 26 percent in Switzerland

and 19 percent in the UK.[7] This means that a large proportion of total tax revenues is dependent on earned income (Germany 65 percent, France 56 percent, Austria 57 percent, Switzerland 56 percent, UK 46 percent).[8] It is understandable that there is widespread support for high labour force participation and high wages under such a tax system.

Employees, employers and the state all have an interest in increasing labour productivity. Employees have the prospect of sharing in productivity gains through wage increases (see Reuter in this book). Employers skim off some of the productivity gains as profit and may improve their market position. The state benefits from higher tax revenues. If increased labour productivity leads to the rationalisation of labour, new work must be created to ensure a high employment rate – in conventional thinking, ideally through economic growth.

The tax system, with its high burden on labour income, means that employers have a standing incentive to increase labour productivity in order to replace "expensive" labour.[9] Consumers shun products and services that involve high labour costs (preferring to buy new shoes rather than having old ones repaired, or buying cheap products from conventional agriculture rather than more expensive, because labour-intensive, organic products). High labour costs are an incentive to reduce the input of human labour; but at the same time society, politicians and the economic system strive for high employment rates. In short, incentives in the tax system, growth policies and increasing labour productivity all encourage or result in a rationalisation of formal employment, which leads to the demand for and promotion of growth in order to create new jobs, which, in turn, are rationalised. And so the spiral continues to turn.

The scientific and political discussion on (paid) work and economic growth as well as on the importance of work for securing livelihoods, the social welfare system and the tax system is just beginning. But there are certainly some debates on reforms that can be built on. Prominent among them are the long debate and extensive theoretical work on an eco-social tax reform (see, among others, Köppl/Schratzenstaller in this book), on new concepts of work (see, among others, Gerold, von Jorck/Schrader, Wehner, Gottwald et al. in this book) and on ways to develop the social welfare system (see, among others, Hagedorn and Kubon-Gilke in this book).

Against this background, this book is guided by the following thesis. If our society is to free itself from its fixation on economic growth and formal employment, the employment system must be restructured. Formal employment cannot continue to be so important that it causes the adverse dynamics described above. This means that the high degree of dependence of the social welfare system on formal employment –

a result of economic and social developments especially since the mid-20th century – must be weakened. At the same time, we need a broader conception of work, one which includes not only formal employment but also care work, self-provisioning, voluntary work and other forms of non-formal employment, and we need structures which make it possible to pursue work in its many different forms.

2 Current challenges in the area of formal employment

Technological, economic and social developments lead to constant changes of work. At present, various such developments are taking place which are relevant to any re-evaluation of work or to an expanded concept of what work is.

– *Digitalisation and robotisation* serve to reduce the total amount of formal employment and the proportion of secure standard employment relations. Internationally, insecure and flexible employment relations are the norm, and they are now also on the increase in Europe (see Stoll in this book). The extent to which these technological developments are replacing formal employment is the subject of controversial debate; in any event, a significant structural change is discernible, in the course of which many jobs may well become redundant (see Nierling/Krings in this book). This development is relevant for any reassessment of work and for expanding the concept of work because it leads to a loss of revenue for the social security and tax system and because the number of people living in precarious circumstances is rising. These technological developments therefore exert great pressure on the established system of formal employment, on social security and on the tax base.

– At the same time, a *value change* is taking place with respect to formal employment. The younger generation in particular is questioning the importance accorded to formal employment and income as a life goal and status symbol; they expect to have and practise greater flexibility, more self-determination and a satisfying work-life balance. They evaluate (formal) work according to whether it is meaningful; a lack of meaningfulness is picked up on and criticised and employers come under pressure to improve the situation (see Gerold in this book). This development is relevant for the reassessment of work and the expansion of our understanding of it because it puts the importance of formal employment in society into perspective and allows a greater variety of activities to evolve.

– A further challenge is *labour shortages* in areas that are labour-intensive and traditionally underpaid and that can only be automated to a limited extent, specifically in social services (especially in health, care, education; see Hagedorn in this book), in agriculture (see Gottwald et al. in this book) and in many crafts and skilled trades.[10] These developments are relevant to any reassessment of work or expansion of the concept of work, as they require incentivisation through the tax and contributions system and innovative work organisation to make these occupations more attractive.

– Finally, we are at the beginning of a *structural change due to ecological factors*, one which primarily impacts on energy- and resource-intensive industries (e.g. the automotive and transport, energy and resource sectors) and favours non-resource-intensive industries (e.g. public transport, renewable energy, reuse and upcycling), and is likely to be based on political choices and green consumer behaviour (on the latter see Walz et al. 2019). Large-scale redundancies can be expected, but so too can the creation of new jobs. This development is relevant because labour market policy measures such as a reduction in working hours and new training schemes may become necessary, and new structures need to be created to enable people to work in sectors where there is a demand for labour, as well as outside formal employment.

3 The concept of work and meaningful activity

The term "work" is usually understood to mean paid employment in a standard employment relation entailing social security. This understanding arose in the transition from the pre-industrial domestic family economy to an industrial society based on the division of labour over the course of the 19th century, in which only paid (male) work outside the home was acknowledged as work (see Komlosy in this book). This occurred in parallel with the devaluation of other activities (mostly associated with women) such as housework, family work and self-provisioning – and thus also of the women who were mainly responsible for this work. The difference in the value accorded to the work of women and men is still widespread, despite the high level of female participation in the labour market and the professionalisation of care work, and despite the fact that family roles and employment biographies have changed considerably.

According to Senghaas-Knobloch (1998, 11ff.), the central role that formal employment holds today is based on four functions: formal employment secures individual income; it confers social recognition and can strengthen mental health;[11] it is an essential entitlement criterion for social welfare systems and it is bound up with civic integration, i.e. the equal involvement of people in the community.

Traditional economics looks at work primarily as a factor of production alongside land and capital. As a cost factor, it influences the competitiveness of companies and economies. This understanding is traditionally linked to a view of human nature which sees humans as rational beings who want to maximise their utility (homo oeconomicus). Work is motivated by wages, which are supposed to enable a high degree of need satisfaction, and in this view of human nature needs are regarded as being unlimited. Even though other concepts of human nature are now finding their way into labour economics, the concept of homo oeconomicus continues to permeate economic and political debates and influences decisions in the sense that a continuous increase in formal employment, goods and services (usually expressed in terms of GDP [Gross Domestic Product]) will increase people's well-being.

Even though this economic understanding of work is dominant today, within the social sciences and humanities, especially history, philosophy, sociology, anthropology and theology, there has been a sometimes long and intensive debate on the concept of work. However, there is no universally accepted definition of work. Rather, the understanding of work depends on intellectual motivation, on the (cultural) historical epoch, on economic life and the necessities of existence, technical possibilities and developments, hierarchies and power structures. Komlosy (2018, 7) describes work as a "chameleon": "Everyone has their own, nuanced definitions, which themselves are in constant flux".

The dominant narrow understanding of work as formal employment does not do justice to the variety of work that has always been and will always be performed in everyday social life and which ensures individual and social life and survival. Hannah Arendt (1958) spoke of "Vita activa or the active life" and thereby formulated an alternative concept to the one-dimensionality of modern (formal) work. It is this diversity of work that we subsume under the concept of meaningful activity.

The women's movement has done a great deal to highlight and politicise unpaid work in the home and family, which is mostly done by women. Against this background, concepts of extended work, mixed work, the "whole of work", regenerative work and others have emerged which go beyond the narrow concept of formal employment (for an overview, see Gerold in this book).

We are using *meaningful activity* here as an overarching concept:

–   (a) for the diversity of possible kinds of work, including formal employment;

- (b) for the fact that people carry out different kinds of work sequentially or in parallel;
- (c) for work which aspires to be meaningful for the person carrying it out and for society as a whole.[12]

(a) Meaningful activity can be paid or unpaid. Unpaid work in particular is extremely diverse: it can be vital (caring for children or the sick, housework, self-determined work or subsistence work), it can satisfy immaterial needs (for social integration, culture, art, etc.) and it can include activities for which no one is able or willing to pay (voluntary work). Unpaid work may have a different quality to paid work, because the act of remunerating work with money excludes reciprocity and asymmetries (Jochimsen 2003). The coordinating mechanism of unpaid work is reciprocity (or unselfishness); for paid work it is the market (on economic coordination mechanisms, see Kubon-Gilke in this book).

(b) Meaningful activity corresponds to the concept of Mischarbeit, or "mixed work" (Brandl/Hildebrandt 2002). Mixed work integrates formal employment, care work, community work and self-determined work and "refers to the simultaneity of different social activities by individuals, the variety of everyday individual combinations of these activities and the changes to these combinations under a biographical perspective" (ibid. 105). This is accompanied by "mixed qualifications, mixed tasks and mixed incomes". Meaningful activity in this way enables work and life to be integrated and overcomes the functional division of labour.

(c) Finally, meaningful activity takes place in a context in which people can realise their abilities, skills and interests, in which they experience their own wider significance and in which social relationships are lived out. In meaningful activity, values can be realised and meaning can be experienced, and through meaningful activity a relationship to everyday life and society is created (Weber 2005).

As central as meaningful activity is for people, there must also be time for doing nothing, for leisure, reflection and contemplation.

4 Starting points for meaningful activity in the post-growth society

While there have been some tentative approaches in politics and economics towards contemplating an end to the growth society (e.g. Seidl/Zahrnt 2010; Artus et al. 2014; Teulings/Baldwin 2014; Petschow 2020; British "All-Party Parliamentary Group on Limits to Growth", limits2growth.org.uk, OECD 2019b), to our knowledge there has so far been no serious thought or research on how the formal employment and social welfare system might be restructured if economic output – whether unintentionally or intentionally – were no longer to grow. In view of the existential importance of the formal employment and social welfare system for the majority of people in our societies, there is an obvious need for wider social debate and research on this topic. This book is intended to make a contribution in this area. In the following section, some central issues for debate, research and transformation are identified.

4.1 Reconsidering the role of formal employment and restructuring the formal employment system

The taxation of labour and other factors of production has a major impact on price relations and thus on factor input. Now the taxes and charges on labour are too high. The tax and social welfare systems that have evolved over time are no longer appropriate for today's social, employment, ecological and financial challenges (see Köppl/Schratzenstaller in this book). There are numerous proposals on how to update the tax system; politicians and the wider society must finally acknowledge the need for a comprehensive reform. However, proposals on how the social welfare system should be reformed if formal employment and growth are declining are lacking.

An overall reduction in working hours would be beneficial for a number of reasons: environmental damage is likely to be reduced, there would be more scope for meaningful activity and a reduction in working hours is in line with current changes in social values (Buhl/Acosta 2016). The central question in this context is: how can working hours be reduced, how can this reduction be cushioned through social security, and is wage compensation necessary (and if so, how much)? (See also Reuter in this book.) At the same time there is a need to (further) develop structures and supporting conditions for forms of work other than formal employment (e.g. for voluntary and self-determined work), to enhance skills for these forms of work and to grant tax and social security benefits for them. Volunteering enriches many people's lives, partly because it provides them with purpose and autonomy. Numerous social tasks can be taken on by volunteers (see Wehner in this book), ideally by a wider cross section of society than was the case in the past. At the same time, structures for self-determined and subsistence work should be promoted so that people can take responsibility for a larger proportion of their daily needs than before.

4.2 Developing and enhancing the social welfare system

Highly developed social welfare systems are extremely complex structures of great economic importance. In 2018, public social welfare spending in Germany amounted to 25 percent of gross domestic product, which is in the upper range for OECD countries (OECD 2019a).[13] As shown above and in the chapter by Köppl/Schratzenstaller in this book, the degree to which fiscal revenues are dependent on formal employment needs to be reduced and financing from other tax sources needs to be increased. In view of demographic change and the labour shortage and often low wages in the health and care sector, the need for funding in the social welfare system will continue to grow (see Hagedorn in this book). However, the social welfare system can be improved by measures which mitigate the financial strain and increase the quality of the services: by preventive social policy and strengthening the reciprocity principle in the provision of services (see Kubon-Gilke in this book), by expanding health provision and personalised services in the health and care sector, and by enhancing services in neighbourhoods and networks.

Possible reforms are being debated in the field of social security that focuses on the quality of different services and their financing, but so far there has been no debate nor research on how the system should evolve when there is less formal employment, when the associated funding is declining and when the economy does not grow anymore.

4.3 Creating the right conditions for the transformation of the social welfare and formal employment system

The restructuring of the social welfare and employment system will affect a wide range of individuals and groups, interests, entitlements and achievements. Such processes are made easier if they are socially just. This can be achieved by measures such as restructuring the tax system towards greater social justice, financial safeguards like basic pensions and minimum income (as well as maximum income, which reduces inequality), and social infrastructure and social practices that make everyday life easier and enable people to provide for themselves in part. Examples include common goods (e.g. buildings and other facilities for public use such as workshops and gardens), close social (support) networks (such as neighbourhoods, self-help initiatives and social services) and structures in which people can practise lifestyles based on sufficiency and subsistence (repair cafés, spaces for self-determined work). There are many different examples of such infrastructures and practices, some of which have now found their way into the mainstream of society (see Schneidewind/Zahrnt 2013; Wackman/Knight 2020, futurzwei.org).

As is emphasised in the current transformation discourse, successful innovations often arise in niche areas (e.g. Geels/Schot 2010; German Advisory Board on Global Change 2011; Schneidewind/Fischedick 2021). This also applies to the fiscal and social welfare system. It is therefore crucial to create and promote scope for experimentation in the field of work and social welfare, and to gain experience in how to simplify and support the spread of innovative practices into the mainstream of society. In such experimental spaces, new values can be created and practised and spread through the transition to the mainstream (see Fritz-Schubert in this book). Such experimentation spaces thrive better in supportive public settings; above all, dissemination requires the financial commitment of the public sector and of relevant institutions and foundations. Public budgets should therefore contain fixed categories which can create conducive conditions for transformations.

5 Conclusion

The (formal) employment and social welfare system has hardly featured in the transformation discourse to date. This is a serious lacuna, because ecologically necessary transformation in the most crucial areas such as mobility, energy, industry and food is being held back by interests which are tied to growth in order to maintain and create jobs and ensure social security. The dominant position of formal employment must therefore be qualified and balanced, and new forms of meaningful activity must be promoted and developed. Following on broadly from Herzog (2018), this requires a pragmatic examination of specific institutional options for improvement on the one hand, and bold visions of a better, though more distant future on the other, whereby both aspects are mutually conditional and complementary. The following chapters will take up both perspectives.

Notes

1 For instance, Parrique (2019) has carried out a comprehensive analysis of recent literature critical of growth.
2 According to Seidl/Zahrnt (2010, 34), a post-growth society is not dependent for its existence on economic growth. It is characterised by the following features: (1) there is no policy aimed at increasing economic growth; (2) growth-dependent and growth-driving sectors, institutions and structures are restructured so that they are independent of economic growth; (3)

energy and resource consumption is reduced to a sustainable level and the loss of biodiversity is stopped.
3 Petschow et al. (2020, 96) confirm the positive correlation between growth and employment, but argue from a mainstream economic perspective that there is no unidirectional causality. Formal employment and ultimately growth could be created if the characteristics of the labour supply, such as skills, flexibility or price, matched the demand for labour.
4 The German Stability and Growth Act was introduced in 1967; however, it lost its importance with the introduction of the European Treaties. In the Treaty on the European Union we read in Art. 3 that the internal market

> shall work for the sustainable development of Europe based on balanced economic growth and price stability, a highly competitive social market economy, aiming at full employment and social progress, and a high level of protection and improvement of the quality of the environment.
> (Version of 2016)

5 For a discussion of different theoretical analyses of the links between work and growth, see Petschow et al. (2020).
6 In addition, there is tax revenue from household expenditure, which is also largely wage-based, such as VAT. This accounts for 28 percent of total tax revenues in Austria, 25 percent in France, 26 percent in Germany, 21 percent in Switzerland, and 32 percent in the UK (2018).
7 The social security contributions in Switzerland and the UK can only be compared with those of the other countries mentioned to a limited extent, because the social, compulsory insurance there is partly provided by non-governmental organisations or is limited.
8 OECD: https://data.oecd.org/tax/social-security-contributions.htm.
9 High taxes on income make work "expensive" because employees or trade unions try to offset part of this burden through higher wages, and because employers also have to make social security contributions based on wages.
10 Predictions of future labour shortages need to be critically examined against the growth figures on which they are based. For example, a study (VBW/Prognos 2019) on ensuring the supply of skilled labour expects the growth rate of German GDP to be 1.6 percent per year from 2016 to 2025 and 1.2 percent per year from 2026 onwards. Over the last ten years, the growth rate of German GDP has averaged around 1.3 percent per year. Over the same period, labour productivity growth has been around 0.7 percent per annum, and has been declining for decades (0.4 percent in France between 2007 and 2016, 0.3 percent in the UK; OECD labour productivity figures). This means that the difference between GDP growth and labour productivity growth is based on the increase in the volume of work performed and/or the expansion of capital investment. However, at the very least, the proportion of growth due to the expansion of labour as a factor of production should be ignored in forecasting the future scarcity of labour.
11 This means that someone who is not in formal employment, for example because of unemployment or protracted illness, not only lacks material opportunities, but also lacks recognition in their professional and social environment, which can also have health consequences.
12 The term *Tätigkeitsgesellschaft* ("society of meaningful activity") has also sometimes been used in the relevant literature (e.g. Senghaas-Knobloch

1998). The Catholic employees' movement (*Katholische Arbeitnehmerbewegung*, KAB) has formulated requirements for such a society and understands it as a future model for successful coexistence, for new forms of work and for a fair economy within the framework of a social and ecological transformation of society. "Work must (...) become liberating work, must become 'meaningful activity'" (KAB 2017). Overall, however, there does not seem to be a consistent understanding of what a "society of meaningful activity" might be. Frayne (2015), a representative of the Post-Work-Movement, sees work as extrinsically motivated and alienated.

13 In Austria the figure is 26 percent, in France 31 percent and in the UK 21 percent. The figure for Switzerland (16 percent) is not comparable because of the extensive private compulsory insurance. The German social security system is financed two-thirds from contributions from employees and employers and one-third from general taxation.

Bibliography

Arendt, H. (1958): *The Human Condition*, Chicago.

Artus, P., García-Peñalosa, C., Mohnen, P. (2014): *Redresser la croissance potentielle de la France*, Conseil d'analyse économique. Les notes du conseil d'analyse économique No. 1, Paris

Brandl, S., Hildebrandt, E. (2002): *Zukunft der Arbeit und soziale Nachhaltigkeit. Zur Transformation der Arbeitsgesellschaft vor dem Hintergrund der Nachhaltigkeitsdebatte*, Opladen

Buhl, J., Acosta, J. (2016): *Work less, do less?* Sustainability Science 11(2), 261–276

Frayne, D. (2015): *The Refusal of Work: Rethinking Post-Work Theory and Practice*, London

Geels, F.W., Schot, J.W. (2010): *The dynamics of transitions: A socio-technical perspective*, in: Grin, J., Rotmans, J., Schot, J. (Eds.): Transitions to Sustainable Development: New Directions in the Study of Long Term Transformative Change, New York, 11–104

German Advisory Board on Global Change (2011): *World in Transition – A Social Contract for Sustainability*, Berlin

Herzog, L. (2018): *Reclaiming the System. Moral Responsibility, Divided Labour, and the Role of Organizations in Society*, Oxford

Jochimsen, M. (2003): *Careful Economics. Integrating Caring Activities and Economic Science*, Boston, Dordrecht, New York

KAB (2017): *Arbeit. Macht. Sinn. Beschluss des 16. Bundesverbandstages der Katholischen Arbeitnehmer-Bewegung (KAB) Deutschlands vom 26.–28. Mai 2017 in Krefeld*, www.kab.de/fileadmin/user_upload/kab_de/Downloads_pdf/leitantrag/Beschluss_Leitantrag_01_09_2017.pdf (accessed 21.01.2021)

Komlosy, Andrea (2018): *Work. The Last 1000 Years*, London, New York

OECD (2017): *Towards Green Growth*, Paris

OECD (2019a): *Social Expenditure Update 2019, Public Social Spending Is High in Many OECD Countries*, Paris, www.oecd.org/social/soc/OECD2019-Social-Expenditure-Update.pdf (accessed 21.01.2021)

OECD (2019b): *Beyond Growth: Towards a New Economic Approach, Report of the Secretary General's Advisory Group on a New Growth Narrative*, Paris

Parrique, T. (2019): *The Political Economy of Degrowth. Economics and Finance*, Université Clermont Auvergne, Stockholms universitet

Parrique, T., Barth, J., Briens, F., Kerschner, C., Kraus-Polk, A., Kuokkanen, A., Spangenberg, J.H. (2019): *Decoupling Debunked. Evidence and Arguments against Green Growth as a Sole Strategy for Sustainability*, European Environmental Bureau

Petschow, U., Aus dem Moore, N., Pissarskoi, E., Korfhage, T., Lange, S., Schoofs, A., Hofmann, D. (2020): *Social Well-Being Within Planetary Boundaries: the Precautionary Post-Growth Approach. Partial Report for the "Approaches to Resource Conservation in the Context of Post-Growth Concepts" Project*, UBA TEXTE 234/2020, Dessau-Roßlau, https://www.umweltbundesamt.de/publikationen/social-well-being-within-planetary-boundaries-the (accessed 24.04.2021)

Schneidewind, U., Fischedik, M. (2021): *Zukunftskunst: The Wuppertal Institute Handbook for Sustainability Transformation*, Berlin, Heidelberg, New York

Schneidewind, U., Zahrnt, A. (2013): *The Politics of Sufficiency. Making It Easier to Live the Good Life*, München

Seidl, I., Zahrnt, A. (Eds.) (2010): *Postwachstumsgesellschaft. Konzepte für die Zukunft*, Marburg

Senghaas-Knobloch, E. (1998): *Von der Arbeits- zur Tätigkeitsgesellschaft. Politikoptionen und Kriterien zu ihrer Abschätzung*, Feministische Studien 2, 9–30

Teulings, C., Baldwin, R. (Eds.) (2014): *Secular Stagnation: Facts, Causes and Cures*, Centre for Economic Policy Research (CEPR), London

VBW (Vereinigung der Bayerischen Wirtschaft e.V.), Prognos (2019): *Arbeitslandschaft 2025*, https://www.vbw-bayern.de/Redaktion/Frei-zugaengliche-Medien/Abteilungen-GS/Sozialpolitik/2019/Downloads/20190221_Arbeitslandschaft-2025_final.docx.pdf (accessed 21.01.2021)

Wackman, J., Knight, E. (2020): *Repair Revolution: How Fixers Are Transforming Our Throwaway Culture*, Novato (CA)

Walz, R., Oldenburg, C., Pfaff, M., Schuler, J., Gotsch, M., Marscheider-Weidemann, F. (2019): *Wider Economic and Social Implications of Sustainable Economy Approaches. Some Insights from a Scenario Exercise*, GAIA 28/S1, 190–197

Weber, P. (2005): *Tätigsein – außerhalb der Erwerbsarbeit*, in: Weber, P. (Ed.): Tätigsein. Jenseits der Erwerbsarbeit, Bonn, 168–174

Part 1
The basics

2 On the historical development of work

Andrea Komlosy

Summary

The narrow understanding of work as paid gainful employment, linked to social security, is from a historical point of view
a recent phenomenon which emerged in Western Europe with
industrial capitalism in the 19th century, became the global
norm in the 20th century, and is now showing some signs of
breaking down with the deregulation and flexibilisation of
global capitalism in the 21st century. In the pre-modern domestic family-based economy, the household was a living and working community. In the industrial system, only paid employment
outside the home was considered work, while unpaid household
work was devalued. In the course of the globalisation of goods
supply chains and of digitalisation, previously secure gainful
employment is also being transformed into flexible, precarious,
informal employment, even in the centres of the world economy. In order to avoid a split in society, we need counter-models
to growthism, extractivism and exploitation. Studying the domestic family-based economy can provide valuable inspiration
to that end.

1 Introduction

This chapter looks at the history of work and demonstrates that the narrow understanding of work as paid employment, excluding all other forms
of work, is a relatively recent phenomenon: it emerged in the course of
the 19th century during the transition from the pre-industrial and family-
based economy to an industrial society based on the division of labour,
in which only paid employment outside the home was regarded as work.
In the process there emerged in the industrialised countries, over several distinct phases during the 20th century, the "standard employment
relationship", with social security. This was – and still is – oriented towards the male wage earner, and does not fit in with the reality of life for

DOI: 10.4324/9781003187370-2

women, small business owners, farmers or home workers. In the global South, industrialisation affected only a small part of the population, if at all, and did not provide wage labourers with comparable income, security and social benefits, so these people were and are dependent on subsistence farming and the activities of their family members in the informal sector for their survival (see the chapter by Stoll in this book).

In recent decades, the "standard employment relationship" has come under pressure from rationalisation and digitalisation, the relocation of industrial mass production to emerging economies and neoliberal reforms of labour and social legislation in the old industrialised countries. In order to provide a sound foundation for the discussion of models for the future, it is worth taking a look at how industrial society has evolved and at the narrow concept of work it has produced (Komlosy 2018).

The chapter begins with a comparison: it contrasts the system of employment outside the home, which separates the concept of work from that of the family household, with the domestic family-based economy, in which the household was a working and living community. The transition from the domestic economy to gainful employment under industrial capitalism triggered criticism and resistance and produced numerous alternative projects and societal blueprints in the 19th and 20th centuries. These all addressed the question of how socially necessary and desirable work should be organised, apportioned and evaluated. Finally, in view of the current crisis of the (paid) work society, the chapter asks to what extent the transition to a post-growth society can be guided by the stability of the cycles in the domestic family-based economy, and to what extent the early counter-models to the growth imperative and wage labour compulsion of industrial capitalism can inspire the necessary transformation of the (paid) work society into a society with a comprehensive understanding of meaningful activity.

2 From the "whole house" to the wage labourer-and-housewife household

The domestic family-based economy, which is also referred to as the "whole house" because of the way people live and work together (Komlosy 2011, 252), has been the basis of economic life throughout the history of humankind, across all social groups, since the establishment of settlements and the introduction of agriculture. This chapter reviews its development since its appearance in the European Middle Ages through early modern times up to the 19th century.

The members of the household produced products and services for their own direct consumption (subsistence), for sale on the market and as dues to their landlords and the state. Whether an activity brought in money or not did not determine how it was perceived or whether it was regarded as work. The division of activities was based on gender, marital or family status, age, chance and necessity, and varied according to regional customs. The "whole house" took on different forms, depending on whether the households were based on farming or trades, rural or urban, settled or nomadic. From the 17th century onwards, those without property and those with little or no land were also able to set up households and, by taking on supply work for the manufactories, to combine such work with subsistence farming (Kriedte et al. 1977; Komlosy 2018). The form of enterprise that emerged from this was called the putting-out system: merchants and manufactory entrepreneurs "put out" individual work activities to rural households. From today's perspective, we can regard such "putting out", which took place on both a small and a large scale, as home-based work. However, there was no such term at that time, as the counterpart to home-based work – centralised and mechanised factory work – did not yet exist. With the expansion of textile production, it was the spinning hands of women and children that brought in the most money, which is why other family members relieved them of their caring duties so that they could devote their time to textile work. Notwithstanding its clear allocation of tasks, the family economy proved itself to be pragmatic, flexible and adaptable (Duden/Hausen 1979).

When, over the course of the 19th century, massive numbers of jobs were created outside the home in factories, mines, construction sites and offices, a clear division was drawn between the work done outside the home and that which remained inside. The former – the external activity – was paid for and was henceforth considered work. The latter – unpaid work in the household – was denied the character of work, even though the specific tasks did not change. The economic driving force behind the transition from the domestic family economy to industrial manufacturing was the demand for wage labourers who were willing to make their labour available on a permanent basis. The prerequisite for this transition was a series of legislative changes that removed the workforce from the family economy. Feudal bondage, corvée work and restrictions in geographical mobility were abolished. The flip side of this development was the loss of one's economic basis, income and essential supplies from within the structures of the family, the household and the village, so that wage labour became the only alternative for more and more people. A particularly stark form of the separation of the rural population from their means of subsistence was the appropriation in England of land used for farming by agricultural entrepreneurs, the so-called enclosures. This was accompanied by the privatisation of communal land (the commons), which drove people to the cities in search of paid work. Since neither the social order of pre-industrial society nor the regulations of the guilds applied in the world of industry, there was no form of protection for wage earners. The result was the unregulated exploitation of early industrial capitalism, the drastic dimensions of which were vividly described by contemporaries such as Charles Dickens and Gerhard Hauptmann.

The ideological accessory to the separation of paid gainful employment from unpaid work in the house was the bourgeois concept of the male breadwinner who brings home the money while the housework is carried out unpaid by the women on account of their role as spouse and mother; indeed, from then on unpaid housework was no longer even regarded as work. It was women's business, and thus devalued on gender grounds – even in situations where men also worked unpaid, such as in subsistence farming, or construction and repairs in the household or in the neighbourhood. As industrial wage labour only became established gradually and unevenly across regions, the domestic family economy by no means disappeared. But in the perspective of political economy, both in its conservative and socialist forms, it was considered backward, unproductive, and in the final analysis not "real work". It is still not reflected today in the gross domestic product (GDP), a measure of economic performance invented later. This also affected – in varying degrees – home-based work, which was paid for but was "worth less" because it was embedded in the household.

The family breadwinner model was only able to establish itself among the propertied middle classes, although here it was not the ladies who did the housework but rather servants. In the families of the industrial workers, women were also forced to take up paid work. The fact that women's wages – even today – are lower than men's is mainly due to the fact that their work was and is regarded as an – often temporary – "additional income", one incapable of providing a foundation for an individual independent existence, because women are primarily assigned to the house. As a result, entire fields of employment and professions associated with women are still paid less today.

When women moved into new fields due to recruitment drives or shifts in demand, they took the wage gap with them in their luggage, so to speak. Modern industrial society thus not only draws a line between paid work and unpaid "non-work", but also extends this line as a gender boundary into the sphere of gainful employment by means of the unequal treatment of women and men (Bock/Duden 1977; Komlosy 2018). In this respect, nothing has fundamentally changed up until the present day.

In several waves – towards the end of the 19th century, in the interwar period and after the Second World War – the concept of work based on gainful employment and the devaluation of the family economy and unpaid work in the home established itself as the norm in Western industrialised countries. The "standard employment relationship" was then secured by the introduction of the employment contract and social security systems for ill health and accidents, old age and unemployment (and, after a long delay, for maternity as well). The commodification of care work increased in parallel as more women entered the labour market in several waves over the 20th century and received correspondingly more education and training. In other words, activities formerly performed unpaid in the household (cleaning, nursing and personal care, bringing up children) became care jobs, which at the lower levels were (and still are) almost exclusively carried out by women.

The involvement of women in formal employment was particularly driven forward during the two world wars, although the jobs were taken up again by men after they returned from the war. Conversely, it was often only the post-war "economic miracle" that enabled women from the lower social strata to live the ideal of the non-working housewife. However, because of the demand for labour but also as a result of emancipation from the old role models, the trend was now towards the nuclear family with two working partners. The increasing use of technology in the household also helped enable women to take up jobs outside the home.

As a result of having their own income, women in employment became more independent from their husbands. The fact that their work was now recognised as "work" again, and offered opportunities for advancement and communication, strengthened their self-esteem. In the 1960s and 1970s, this led to changes in the laws governing marriage and child custody, and in some countries to the legalisation of abortion. However, women remain disadvantaged in terms of pay and career opportunities, as well as by the difficulty of reconciling family and work. Although women were moving into new areas of work, the shadow of "additional income" accompanied them. The "standard employment relationship", subject to proper regulation and eligible for social security, was thus still generally limited to men, whereas female life histories were characterised by shifts between work and the household, by interruptions due to pregnancy, bringing up children and caring for family members at home, and by part-time employment. In domestic and subsistence work, which remained primarily the responsibility of women, the focus shifted from ensuring survival to the intangible areas of care, education and emotional support for husbands and children. Subsistence farming and self-provisioning came into play only when the family income was insufficient. However, even if women earned less than men, women's earned income increased the purchasing power of the household and made it possible for poorer families too to enjoy a relatively high level of consumption.

Since the 1980s, typical employment biographies – differentiated by gender but brought together in the family household – have been destabilised by cyclical crises, ecological problems, technological change and a reorganisation of the international division of labour. The neoliberal restructuring of the economic sphere and of state policy in the course of the globalisation of goods supply chains has ushered in a new phase in the exploitation of capital. The labour and social movements are reacting to this in two ways. By holding on to the rights so far acquired, they are seeking to prevent or hinder this restructuring. At the same time, not least because this tactic often appears to be futile, they are seeking new ways of overcoming neoliberal reforms by abandoning growthism. This latter option could in principle turn the crisis into an opportunity for positive transformation.

The pre-industrial domestic family economy of the "whole house" and the system of formal gainful employment in industrial society based on the wage-earner-housewife couple overlap and complement each other in the course of the transition from the pre-industrial to the factory-industrial age. Table 2.1 serves to differentiate between the two historical systems with regard to key areas of work, supply, consumption and sustainability, social security, co-determination, and the division of labour between the sexes and generations.

The last row of the table, "Capitalism", addresses the question of how the two models relate to capitalism as a system whose economic dynamics are characterised, among other things, by the imperatives of capital valorisation, expansion and growth. Here we follow Fernand Braudel's threefold division of the economy into (a) local subsistence production, (b) regional market economy and (c) supra-regional trade, division of labour and valorisation of capital. Braudel (1992) sees only the third level as capitalist. While the domestic family economy has largely escaped the reach of capitalism, industrial society is entirely subject to its dynamics and constraints. The dynamics of capitalism also influence the state-socialist variants of the industrial system via internal goals such as catch-up development and economic growth (Komlosy 2011, 257).

3 Critique and resistance, alternative visions and practices to the industrial capitalism of the 19th and 20th centuries

The following section illustrates how social movements and socially committed individuals reacted to the new situation on the labour market, the compulsion to work for wages, the lack of labour and social legislation, the misery of industrial labour and the downgrading of unpaid work during the 19th and 20th centuries.

Table 2.1 Comparison between the domestic family economy and the industrial employment system

Issues	Unity of life and work in the "whole house" (13th–19th century)	Separate spheres: wage labour and the home (ca. 1880–1980)
Labour relations	Obligatory participation of all household members in all market and subsistence-oriented activities.	Individual employment contract within the framework of the respective legal requirements as the ideal case; in practice, a living wage and social security are often only accessible to a minority, while the others work in informal relationships under precarious conditions. In addition, employees and relatives perform unpaid work in the household and neighbourhood as well as voluntary political or community work.
Supply and consumption	The family economy is a self-supplying community (via market products and self-provisioning). The quality of supply is dependent on property and status.	Income from work and social benefits determine the consumption patterns of family members on the market. If wages or social benefits are not sufficient or when jobs are lost, unpaid work compensates for the gaps in provision.
Sustainability of consumption	Consumables and capital goods are durable and are repaired when worn out. There is hardly any waste.	As purchasing power increases, the volume of consumption rises, while the proletarian way of life makes repair and re-use in one's own household more difficult.
Social security	Membership of the household guarantees the provision of care in the event of incapacity to work; in the absence of a household and family, community care systems step in.	Social security for dependent employees without their own income or supplies is based on: – insurance systems – assistance to the poor (social assistance) – unpaid activity in the household.
Participation and authority	While the family household is represented externally by its male head, the work is managed by both him and his wife, in their respective areas of activity.	Authority in the nuclear family rests with the male breadwinner, including internal matters.

(Continued)

Issues	Unity of life and work in the "whole house" (13th–19th century)	Separate spheres: wage labour and the home (ca. 1880–1980)
Allocation of responsibilities, gender and inter-generational relations	Work activities are allocated on the basis of gender, age, ability, status and custom. Respon-sibilities vary over the course of a person's life and subject to changing requirements. The closer the family members cooperate, the stronger the position of the housewife within the family.	Gender relations are organised around the ideal of the male breadwinner who provides the income. Additional income-earning married women are under his authority. Unpaid work in the household no longer enjoys the authority-enhancing status that it had in the domestic family economy.
Child-rearing	Education takes place through the children's participation in the activities of the adults. From the middle of the 18th century, compulsory schooling supplements this system of education.	Children have no (legal) place in the world of paid employment. The age at which children can enter the labour market rose over the course of the 19th century from 9 to 14 years. Children continue to help in the household.
Capitalism	According to Braudel, the "whole house" participates in all three levels of economic activity. The focus is on the local and regional levels of the subsistence and market economy, where producer groups have independent power to act and shape their own affairs, while in capitalism they are subordinated under the forces of capital valorisation.	In modern industrial society, all economic activity and work is subject to the requirements of capital valorisation. The valorisation imperative extends to the subsistence and market economies and makes use not only of wage labour, but also of self-employed and unpaid workers.

Deregulation under early capitalism (the overthrow of the pre-industrial social protection arrangements for the peasantry, the servant classes and industrial workers), which put workers at the mercy of the entrepreneurs until they were physically exhausted, left little room for resistance. Criticism of the factory system, but also of the intensified exploitation of agricultural workers in industrialised agriculture, harked back to the "old days" before industrialisation. In vociferous, often downright militant protest movements, rural and urban lower classes demanded a turn away from a capital valorisation economy and back to a "moral economy" (Hobsbawm 1959; Thompson 1963). By this they meant an economy which, despite its divisions into estates and classes, gave the lower classes opportunities to earn a living, social protection and freedom for independent subsistence.

With the growth of wage labour and the introduction of labour legislation in the second half of the 19th century, the focus for social movements and reformers, who came from business circles as well, shifted to the regulation of labour relations and to social security. The first real positive developments applied only to qualified industrial workers, who for the entrepreneurs represented human capital. The great majority of people were in employment sectors where extreme stress, low wages, insecurity of employment and lack of social security remained the norm. Such people – unskilled or day labourers, small tradesmen, harvesters and homeworkers, building labourers and servants – depended on other survival strategies. They took up opportunities for casual work, multiple jobs and charity for the poor, and often slipped into crime in the face of the repressive vagrancy and poor laws. Their activities varied between town and countryside, according to demand and the economic cycle. In the developing labour movement these people were not well regarded and correspondingly played only a marginal role.

In the 1860s and 1870s, the Western industrial states developed constitutions granting workers freedom of assembly and organisation. The future direction of the labour movement was still open: currents concerned primarily with the preservation of the craft trades and their guilds coexisted with others focusing on cooperatives as an alternative to large companies ("self-help"). They were opposed by those who looked to the state as the vehicle for the workers' cause, in German speaking countries called "Staatshilfler", who later formed the social democratic parties. They saw the solution to the social question in state legislation, and within this group there emerged both reform-oriented and revolutionary currents. Anarchist groups, however, put their faith not in the state, but in the free association of workers in a society without any single dominant power (Hautmann/Kropf 1976; Kocka/Breuilly 1983; van der Linden 2008).

Their different visions were articulated in utopian writings, social blueprints and programmes. Charles Fourier, for example, proposed the organisation of society into so-called phalansteries – small living and working communities in which people's basic needs would be collectively provided for (Heyer 2006, 30f.). William Morris advocated the de-construction of the cities and a return to a quasi-medieval economy of craftsmanship and self-sufficiency, in which all activities would enable workers to identify with the products of their labour (ibid., 48ff., Morris 1891). Against this positive view of work, Marx's son-in-law Paul Lafargue proposed a reduction in working time to three hours a day to accommodate "The Right to Be Lazy" (Lafargue 1883).

Practical projects were undertaken as alternatives to exploitation under industrial society. Examples of this in the 19th century include self-organised fraternity funds, corporate social policy such as company health insurance funds and support associations, as well as the introduction of state labour laws, welfare institutions and even compulsory health and accident insurance. Among the projects implemented by or with the help of entrepreneurs, the model workers' settlements of New Lanark and Saltaire in Scotland and Northern England respectively stand out. These were designed – not least because of the paternalistic ideology of the textile manufacturers Robert Owen and Titus Salt – as educational institutions aiming at social reform, in which workers were encouraged from morning till night to achieve self-fulfilment in all areas of life (Davis Bob/O'Hagan 2010). The French early socialist Saint-Simon drove his employees to exercise the utmost working discipline in the belief that they could overcome the opposition between capital and labour by increasing productivity. Such projects required money as well as determination and organisational energy. Workers' social movements were therefore dependent on cooperation with the state administration, with political parties and entrepreneurs who, for whatever reason, considered alternative models of business and work to be advantageous. At the same time, however, workers also experienced resistance to their demands, strikes and protest actions from the state and entrepreneurs, and in many cases physical repression and criminalisation – one reason to set up independent institutions for and of the working class (Tenfelde/Volkmann 1981; Kocka/Breuilly 1983).

Beyond the efforts of the trade unions, the individual projects and model enterprises, socialist social blueprints in the 20th century aimed at a socially just economic and social order in which work was not seen as a source of added value, but as a path to self-realisation. The range of these blueprints extends from the Soviet workers' and peasants' state to the soviet (workers' councils) movements and the social-revolutionary associations which briefly attained power in the political upheavals following the First World War, to militant social-democratic parties which in the revolutionary climate of the time hoped to be able to impose socialist rules on the capitalist system to the benefit of the broad mass of the population. They each laid out their own specific proposals on ownership, decision-making and programmes for all policy areas. They sought to ensure that employment relations could be reshaped and improved. In light of the underprovisioning of the population in the post-war period, a critique of growth was not a prominent feature. However, the fundamental prerequisite for capitalist economic activity – permanent economic growth to make capital valorisation possible – was rejected by socialists on principle.

4 The end of the "work society"?

The end of the "work society", as frequently proclaimed in the media today, is a grave misunderstanding. It is based on a confusion between regulated and secure gainful employment and work (meaningful activity) as such. In fact, gainful employment, as it has existed since the end of the 19th century in the "standard employment relationship" in the industrialised countries, is undergoing a transformation. Since the 1980s it has been transforming into flexible, precarious, informal, unsecured relationships. These conditions do not represent a deviation from normality, but rather – as legislation increasingly legitimises this situation – represent the new norm. For developing countries, this is nothing new. Now, however, this unregulated situation is reappearing in the old industrialised countries. Deregulation and flexibilisation were triggered by the reorganisation of global goods production into goods supply chains, i.e. the outsourcing of individual work stages to the most cost-effective locations (Fischer/Reiner/Staritz 2010). Together with automation and digitalisation, this meant the end of industrial mass production in the old industrialised countries from the 1980s onwards (Komlosy 2018). In the competition for the highest possible level of investment, a worldwide race to the bottom in cost terms is emerging, to which the achievements of the labour movement in the Western world, and ultimately the movements themselves, could well fall victim.

Today, too, there is criticism and resistance and there are visions of what ought to replace the now crumbling order (Kocka 2000). And once again the "old days", i.e. the welfare state of the years 1880–1980, are the reference point that lies nearest to hand. The dominant tenor of the response from the trade unions is that the regulated society of formal employment should be maintained, and that work and income should be distributed if possible to all employees. This demand is not only opposed by the employers, especially the large transnational corporations, but also by social movements searching for alternatives to a society based on acquisition, growth and consumption. Social and economic scientists are in agreement that a return to the "normal working relationship" of the post-war reconstruction boom of the 1960s and 1970s, even if it were desirable, is not feasible. André Gorz formulated this succinctly in 1980 already in his book "Farewell to the Working Class" (Gorz 1982). This demand, it is argued by authors who belong to social movements seeking and testing alternatives to growthism, also reproduces precisely the narrow concept of work which has reduced it to alienated wage labour and led to the exclusion of unpaid and voluntary activities from the understanding of work (Gorz 1989; Haug 2011). It is therefore necessary to use the global upheaval as an opportunity to shape work and life in a completely different way, i.e. to reject the profit and growth imperatives in order to realise life-work models based on solidarity and reciprocity, in experiments and projects combining various forms of work with the aim of creating an alternative, crisis-resistant society. There are so many different ideas, concepts and projects in this area that no literature references are provided here.

5   Can history teach us anything about being meaningfully active in the post-growth society?

The question which introduces this section addresses, on the one hand, the organisation of work in the pre-industrial family economy of the "whole house" and on the other hand the historical exemplars of resistance against industrial capitalism. The review undertaken of pre-industrial life and work shows how diverse and changeable ways of life are. What has emerged is that the narrow concept of formal employment in industrial society is a recent phenomenon in human history, i.e. it is mutable and by no means set in stone. Why, then, should we not return to the combination of different paid and unpaid activities, including the provision of social security and care at the household and community level for all those involved? It goes without saying that the old, feudal and patriarchal patterns must be adapted to today's demands for gender equality, intergenerational equity and new family forms. The household economy could then be converted into a basic cell unit of community self-sufficiency largely independent of supra-regional exchange and immune to economic fluctuations – provided it is able to escape the diktat of the competition rules of international free trade.

There is no recipe for resistance and counter-concepts. The social democratic movements traditionally demand wage increases – and thus consumption increases – from the owners of capital. They have adopted the goal of economic growth on which the valorisation of capital is founded, and their focus is on distributive justice. On closer inspection, however, as briefly indicated above, many ideas, utopias and projects can be identified in the history of the labour movement which can provide inspiration for the conflicts that lie ahead today. What distinguishes today's conditions significantly from those of the 19th and 20th centuries is the global interdependence that characterises our way of life. Our consumption is based on the low wage levels in the factories supplying the world's markets from the global South. There is also a huge gulf between rich and poor in the West and/or North. To ignore these inequalities would be to fall into the same trap as the old labour movement, which did not include in its struggles the plantation workers who supplied the raw materials for the factories, nor the housewives and subsistence workers who were essential to daily survival. Unlike then, in today's industrialised countries in the global South we are dealing with an increasingly self-confident workforce (for example in China: Scherrer 2011; Egger et al. 2013). In many cases, that workforce is oriented towards Western norms of consumption and growth and regards post-capitalist alternatives as an attack on catch-up development and on a fairer share of global wealth for its countries and regions. Here a dialogue between the growth critique in the West and the labour struggles in the global South about the consequences of growth and about ways to achieve global distributive justice is indispensable.

Today we are at the threshold of a radical upheaval, the outcome of which is uncertain. If we do not want society to become further polarised into winners and losers from technological transformation, we must rethink our understanding of work as formal gainful employment. Work, in all its forms of activity, must be recognised as a source of social prosperity. This requires a more equal distribution of paid and unpaid, arduous and agreeable, repetitive and creative activities among all members of society – Which presupposes a significant reduction in formal gainful employment for all people, as well as appropriate remuneration and social security, so that there is enough time for social, cultural and political activity. Examining history with a view to shaping the future can reveal potential options. Moreover, the way it has turned out reminds us that things can change, or can be changed.

Bibliography

Bock, G., Duden, B. (1977): *Arbeit aus Liebe – Liebe als Arbeit: Zur Entstehung der Hausarbeit im Kapitalismus*, in: Gruppe Berliner Dozentinnen (Hrsg.): Frauen und Wissenschaft: Beiträge zur Berliner Sommeruniversität für Frauen 1976, Berlin, 118–199

Braudel, F. (1992): *The Perspective of the World. Vol. 3 of Civilisation and Capitalism 15th–18th Century*, Berkeley, Los Angeles

Davis, B., O'Hagan, F. (2010): *Robert Owen (= Continuum Library of Educational Thought, Vol. 25)*, London

Duden, B., Hausen, K. (1979): *Gesellschaftliche Arbeit, geschlechtsspezifische Arbeitsteilung*, in: Kuhn, A., Schneider, G. (Eds.): *Frauen in der Geschichte*, Düsseldorf, 11–33

Egger, G., Fuchs, D. et al. (Eds.) (2013): *Arbeitskämpfe in China. Berichte von der Werkbank der Welt*, Wien

Fischer, K., Reiner, C., Staritz, C. (Eds.) (2010): *Globale Güterketten. Weltweite Arbeitsteilung und ungleiche Entwicklung*, Wien

Gorz, A. (1982): *Farewell to the Working Class: An Essay on Post-Industrial Socialism*, London

Gorz, A. (1989): *Critique of Economic Reason*, London

Haug, F. (2011): *Die Vier-in-einem-Perspektive: Politik von Frauen für eine neue Linke*, Hamburg

Hautmann, H., Kropf, R. (1976): *Die österreichische Arbeiterbewegung vom Vormärz bis 1945. Sozialökonomische Ursprünge ihrer Ideologie und Politik*, Wien

Heyer, A. (2006): *Die Utopie steht links!* Berlin

Hobsbawm, E.J. (1959). *Primitive Rebels. Studies in Archaic Forms of Social Movements in the 19th and 20th Centuries*, Manchester

Kocka, J. (2000): *Arbeit früher, heute, morgen. Zur Neuartigkeit der Gegenwart*, in: Kocka, J., Offe, C. (Eds.): *Geschichte und Zukunft der Arbeit*, Frankfurt a. M., New York, 476–492

Kocka, J., Breuilly, J. (Eds.) (1983): *Europäische Arbeiterbewegungen im 19. Jahrhundert. Deutschland, Österreich, England und Frankreich im Vergleich*, Göttingen

Komlosy, A. (2011): *Arbeitsverhältnisse und Gesellschaftsformationen*, in: Cerman, M., Eder, F.X., Eigner, P., Komlosy, A., Landsteiner, E. (Eds.): *Wirtschaft und Gesellschaft Europa 1000–2000*, Innsbruck, 244–263

Komlosy, A. (2018): *Work. The Last 1000 Years*, London, New York

Kriedte, P., Medick, H., Schlumbohm, J. (1977): *Industrialisierung vor der Industrialisierung. Gewerbliche Warenproduktion auf dem Land in der Formationsperiode des Kapitalismus*, Göttingen

Lafargue, P. (1883): *The Right to Be Lazy*, Chicago

Morris, W. (1891): *News from Nowhere or an Epoch of Rest*, London

Scherrer, C. (2011): *China's Labor Question*, München

Tenfelde, K., Volkmann, H. (Eds.) (1981): *Zur Geschichte des Arbeitskampfes in Deutschland während der Industrialisierung*, München

Thompson, E.P. (1963): *The Making of the English Working Class*, London

Van der Linden, M. (2008): *Workers of the World. Essays toward a Global Labor History*, Leiden, Boston

3 Value orientation and meaningful activity in the post-growth society

Ernst Fritz-Schubert

Summary

Values are a fundamental motivation for people's activities. They are shaped by people's needs for autonomy, social integration and meaningfulness. Value-oriented action can lead to satisfaction and self-realisation in professional and voluntary work as well as in personal life. There is great potential for social transformation in the value-oriented actions of organisations, companies, social initiatives and individuals. A social discourse of values is needed for a reorientation of politics, business and society. Education must contribute to this value orientation and enable and support action based on values by imparting competences.

1 Introduction

A society that increasingly laments the loss of values, and whose top managers loudly proclaim their search for "purpose, purpose, purpose", gives the impression of a refined form of capitalism. Is this just lip service without any genuine renunciation of the maximisation of profit and growth, or is a sense of economic responsibility for the common good actually increasing? At the very least, these proclamations, initiatives and even legal requirements for corporate responsibility are intensifying the discourse on the necessity of action in society which is based on intangible values (see also Faltin 2018).

At the same time, there is a growing awareness in the population that the ecological limits of material growth have been exceeded and that a reversal is urgently needed. Even international economic organisations such as the Organisation for Economic Co-operation and Development (OECD) have developed ways of measuring a country's quality of life not primarily by its economic performance – expressed in gross domestic

DOI: 10.4324/9781003187370-3

product (GDP) – but by a wide range of indicators. Surveys in industrialised countries show that further GDP growth does not make people happier there.

The current labour market situation enables qualified employees and applicants to increasingly ask not only about wages or salaries, but also about the value and sense of what they do. It is therefore not surprising if immaterial values are increasingly taken into account in personnel management. Perhaps the time is ripe to define one's own actions – whether as an employee or as a consumer – not only in terms of wages and prices, but to become aware of the many ways in which it is possible to act and be active, and to explore underlying and ideal values for oneself and others as a potential source of satisfaction. This requires questioning both the ideal or desired values and the values that are actually lived. The following section therefore clarifies what values are, in order to present their significance for finding meaning, for orientation in this world and for the development of personal competence. Finally, we will discuss what value-based management in companies might look like, and which values shape alternative concepts of living and meaningful activity.

2   Values and value orientation

According to Rokeach (1973), values are conceptions of what is desirable which serve as standards or criteria both for societies and for each individual. Shared *general* values condense human experiences, they have a universal character (cf. Waibel 2011: 11). People feel attracted and directly addressed by general values. *Personal* values refer to a person and a given situation. General and personal values touch people and influence not only their choice of action and their behaviour, but also processes of assessment, attitude formation, argumentation, questioning, rationalisation, and attribution of social status or social role. Values are always pursued and realised in relation to and in connection with other people. Through values people can realise meaning (Rokeach 1973; Waibel 2011).

Frankl clearly distinguishes the meaning *of life* as a universal concept from the meaning *in life* which everyone has to find for themselves. He emphasises the subjective character of value and meaning and points out that value traditions can bring relief to the individual, but that they cannot be made absolute, but can also be changed (Frankl 2005). According to Riemeyer, meaning does not belong to the thing itself, but is given, or discovered or found, by human beings. A thing or an event can be meaningful for one person but meaningless for another, or meaningful for me today and meaningless one year later (Riemeyer 2007, 174).

Individual behaviour is subject to a feedback process which allows us to check whether – measured against general and personal values – we are on the right track. Menninger (1968) sees the evaluation of feedback as a measure of appropriateness that takes into account both the characteristics of the individual and the needs of their environment. In his view, appropriateness must be clearly distinguished from the one-sided adaptation of a flexible individual to a rigid environment. Fromm (1980) describes this as an automata-like adaptation to social and economic trends.

> Since modern man perceives himself simultaneously as a commodity in a market and as a seller of that commodity, his self-esteem is dependent on conditions beyond his control. If he is successful, he is valuable; if not, he is worthless. The resulting feeling of insecurity can hardly be overestimated.
>
> (Fromm 1980, 50)

The multi-option society (Gross 1994) promises modern human being endless possibilities for action and opportunities for happiness and satisfaction. It thus transfers the responsibility for a successful life to each individual. Because failures lead to blame and self-contempt, the focus on success becomes a driver of self-exploitation and self-valorisation, and success becomes a defining value. The economic principle of the maximisation of utility then determines not only the professional sphere, but increasingly also private life. Mobile phones and laptops are the insignia of a success-obsessed society which is increasingly accelerating and condensing and which favours thinking in terms of usability, efficiency and effectiveness. The rise in mental illness is a sign of the alienation processes that lead to people no longer seeing themselves in relation to the world and no longer being touched by their environment. The multi-option society therefore not only promotes diversity in human existence, but at the same time tends to make it simpler and shallower through the one-sided adaptation of the individual to existing economic and social conditions.

A strong personality is needed to avoid one-sided adaptation and hence conformity. In addition to highly developed personal skills (see Section 4), this includes personal (physical, material, cognitive, social and spiritual) resources and a sense of self-efficacy (Rösing 2003). However, the strengthening of personality is not sufficient to promote a cultural change towards sustainable lifestyles, because even strong personalities can follow a focus on material values. The realisation that a focus on immaterial values and sustainable lifestyles can enhance well-being can increase people's willingness to change their ecological behaviour.

3 Values as a source of well-being and a guideline for successful living

On closer inspection, a significant link can be seen between well-being and values. Waibel states:

> Anyone who is unable to stand up for values or who judges everything as being equal, which is tantamount to devaluing values and thus their own person, will sooner or later fall into 'existential frustration' and later perhaps into an 'existential vacuum'.
>
> (Waibel 2011, 105)

According to Waibel, an existential vacuum is not tantamount to an illness, but the resulting feeling of meaninglessness has a negative effect on a person's basic emotional state. The denial of one's own values or indifference towards values, the feeling of life having no meaning and the frustration that arises from this, can be seen as a causal chain at the end of which depressive moods can arise and from which noogenic (mentally or spiritually induced) neuroses can develop. In this respect, well-being, values and an orientation towards them are closely linked.

Humanistic theories of personality regard well-being and an orientation towards values as interdependent. This understanding is taken up in Deci and Ryan's (1993) theory of self-determination. This theory assumes that people try to satisfy their basic psychological needs, to act in a self-determined way and at the same time to feel connected with their environment. The authors identify three basic psychological needs: autonomy, competence and social integration. In their view, the satisfaction of these needs is a prerequisite for the healthy development of the personality, which comes about through personal growth as a coherent self and through integration into the social environment (the satisfaction of these three basic needs also represents a criterion of good work; cf. Wehner in this volume).

In order to satisfy these basic psychological needs, every individual must find out which values are really important to them and how they can contribute to their own well-being. They must also know what they can do and what they need, "what really attracts them, what they want to achieve and experience and what challenges they want to face"; this means that each individual must become aware of "[the] foundation(s) of their aspirations" (Fritz-Schubert/Saalfrank 2015: 20), their values. In Rogers' humanist theory of personality this is described as a tendency to self-actualisation. For Rogers, this tendency is the basic motivation for human activity and contributes to the attainment of autonomy and self-reliance. Self-actualisation in Rogers' (1980) and Maslow's (1954) sense means bringing one's own self in line with what one is currently and what one can be. It is a value orientation that reaches beyond one's own self and that can be seen as an answer to the questions life poses.

According to Frankl, the human needs for security, safety and attachment and the simultaneous desire for self-determination and freedom can only be harmoniously reconciled if they are linked to the search for meaningful life and the connections between the self and the world (Frankl 2015: 100f).

In order to be able to prioritise one' s own values, a basis is needed, an anchor from which the evaluation can be made. This basis is the core of the self, the individual's basic reference point, from which they accept themselves and say "yes" to themselves and their lives. It is the foundation of their striving for a successful life.

It is in activity driven by values – whether in productive work or in relationships with other people and in contemplative experience – that people experience themselves as having meaning and significance. They accept universal values if these promise security, safety and reliability and do not cause a conflict with their personal values, or if any such conflicts seem likely to be tolerable. The evaluation of events is usually carried out via the conscience – which according to Frankl is the sense organ that first feels and perceives. Only then do the cognitive control mechanisms (e.g. checking behaviour against values and knowledge) kick in. The individual thereby becoming self-aware wants to choose the path they feel and recognise to be the right one, and wants to follow it. They do not want to fit in and adapt, but to create and shape and to become active. To do so, however, they need the right framework conditions, ones that are worthy of their engagement and encourage them to take unconventional, perhaps even difficult paths. Well-being is created not simply by being active within one's comfort zone, but more so by overcoming challenges and being rewarded for this by social recognition and appreciation.

4 Competence is more than knowledge

Satisfying one's own needs and overcoming personal challenges is achieved through the use of the necessary competences. According to Erpenbeck and Heyse, "Competences [...] are founded on knowledge, constituted by values, deployed as abilities, consolidated by experience, and realised on the basis of will" (Erpenbeck/Heyse 2007). This requires the communication of knowledge, but it is more difficult to answer the question of how knowledge can be brought into harmony with values.

One answer to this question is provided by Heinrich Roth, who as a member of the German Education Council has had a significant influence on competence research in Germany. On the basis of his pedagogical-anthropological research work, he describes the human capacity to act at various stages of development, from maturity and autonomy to responsible moral decision-making as the highest level of human action. He perceives competence as being embodied in mature and responsible autonomy in three different ways:

1. Self-competence, or the ability to act responsibly for oneself;
2. Technical or specialist competence, or the ability to judge and act in specialist areas and thus to take responsibility for them;
3. Social competence, or the ability to judge, act and be responsible in and for socially, societally and politically relevant areas (Roth 1971, 180).

Roth (ibid.) answers the question of how a person can develop from instinctive rules of behaviour to increasing freedom by positing a step-by-step model of learning. In the course of their development, human beings gradually learn to behave and act in an appropriate and objective manner (professional competence and intellectual maturity), to behave and act in a socially aware manner (social competence and social maturity) and, in the final stage, to behave and act in a value-aware manner (self-competence and moral maturity). The interpretation of competence adopted by the Standing Conference of the Ministers of Education and Cultural Affairs in Germany refers to Roth's concept of competence: "Pupils should be educated to become responsible citizens who are able to manage their professional and private lives responsibly, self-critically and constructively and to participate in political and social life" (Kultusministerkonferenz 2005: 6). Roth's approach to development education also makes clear the connection between personality and competence development, which the Conference of Ministers also recognises: the task of education "is to develop the personality and to provide a focus on values, both of which result from the encounter with key objects of our culture" (ibid.).

These goals were never seriously converted into concrete learning targets and realised because, under the primacy of technical-economic progress, human action was increasingly viewed from a functional perspective. As a consequence, pedagogy has focused on imparting utilisable knowledge and on adaptation. The OECD provides the target benchmarks, and international comparisons show who is among the leaders, and who in the middle ground or among the losers, in the transmission of knowledge.

According to Kuhnle et al. (2011), competence development in the school context is mainly focused on educational, vocational and academic success. This leads to a strong focus on qualifications and to an overvaluation of subject and methodological competences.

The acquisition of personal competences plays a subordinate role. Only if it is possible to prioritise the "responsible citizen", in Heinrich Roth's sense, as a goal of the educational system instead of focusing incessantly on vocational and academic qualifications can schools fulfil one of their most important tasks, namely preparing students for a successful life. To do this, they must formulate concrete learning goals related to happiness and satisfaction and how to achieve them. Motivations and goals can be derived from the individual needs of autonomy, competence and social inclusion as identified by Deci and Ryan which can, in turn, be translated into concrete actions and thus enable new experiences. The newly gained experiences lead to new competences and personal resources needed to master challenges (cf. Fritz-Schubert 2017).

5 Values-based corporate management and meaningful formal employment

Traditionally managed companies tend to be run on a "transactional" basis. Transactional management means the targeted influencing of people within organisations through transparent and rational processes of exchange. Results are rewarded through the exchange of money for performance. The desired motivation should be provided by performance-related salary components, bonus payments or other benefits. The underlying image of human nature is that of a rationally acting employee who gets involved on purely financial grounds – an image of human nature which psychology has long since refuted. The fact that employee management based on this model no longer works can be seen in the decreasing motivation of employees. In 2018, the annual Gallup survey again revealed a major problem with employee satisfaction. Only a fifth of the employees surveyed felt any degree of emotional connection to their own company, while an even smaller proportion (15 percent) felt genuinely happy there.

It is therefore not surprising that more and more companies are reorienting themselves and relying on employees who work more out of inner conviction and attachment than for material reasons. "Transformational leadership" means conveying the importance and meaning of work activities. It aims to address and motivate employees on an emotional level and to help them identify with their work and the company (Babcock-Roberson/Strickland 2010). Companies that manage in this way develop collectively – as a social system – a consensus of values (e.g. in the form of a corporate mission statement) that will guide their actions.

Through the design of work and products, companies can contribute to giving workers and consumers a sense of purpose. They have the potential to create alternatives to dominant production and consumption patterns and to further the process of change towards sustainability and a post-growth society (cf. von Jorck/Schrader in this volume). A focus on values can also motivate people to set up new businesses and participate in the transformation of society as entrepreneurs, and especially as social entrepreneurs.

6 Concepts for a value-oriented development with a diverse range of meaningful activities

Transformation processes towards a post-growth society based on ecological and social values have recently emerged in the form of bottom-up movements in various areas. Alternative forms of work and living such as ecovillages, Findhorn communities[1] and (political) communes are guided by values and life practices such as communal living, ecological housing and consumption, working for one's own subsistence, eliminating the pressure for formal employment and grassroots decision-making. In the field of money and exchange, local currency initiatives seek to enable a healthy coexistence between producers, consumers and the wider community rather than to optimise interest income and profit, and to foster the autonomy of local economies and the actors involved. In this way, the momentum of growth is suppressed, and these economies remain detached from the national monetary system and the globalised economy (Kennedy/Lietaer 2004). Local exchange trading systems, which are based on the value of reciprocity, enable the production and exchange of services that the formal market does not or cannot provide. They can also involve active input from people who otherwise cannot or do not want to participate in the market. One extension of these ideas is so-called timebanking, which makes it possible to recover active time input at a later date as earned time, for example as a retirement pension (Lang/Wintergerst 2011; cf. also Kubon-Gilke in this volume). Modern subsistence activities such as urban gardening/urban farming (Müller 2011), do it yourself and repair and sharing initiatives focus on the frugal use of resources and on securing one's own livelihood. The aim is to meet existential needs even with limited financial resources, and to uncouple from unreliable production and market structures; they are about fostering proximity and participation in local food production, taking a stand against waste, developing personal creativity and freedom from market-determined fashions.

The values of togetherness are central to such grassroots movements: there is a shift taking place from individual to community action, from individual ownership of goods to communal use, including the creation of new commons (common goods). These include not only socialised material goods such as real estate and production facilities, but also immaterial social and cultural goods such as Wikipedia or open source software, which are produced and used partly or entirely for free.

The majority of the input to such movements and activities is either voluntary work (when the common good is the primary concern) or unpaid work for one's own livelihood. Not forgetting the many traditional value-based activities of the 31 million people in Germany active in voluntary associations and honorary political posts, for example in environmental projects and in the social sector (Simonson et al. 2017).

All the activities and voluntary services mentioned above directly or indirectly satisfy the need for autonomy, competence and social inclusion, and are not only of value to the community, but, when the challenges they present are overcome, promote the personal development of the protagonists and contribute to strengthening their resources. Volunteering to help others increases self-esteem, the sense of being effective and significant, and is an excellent means of self-transcendence.

7 Concluding remarks

The transformation to a post-growth society that offers space for a wide diversity of activities opens up opportunities for a good and successful life. However, this requires a greater social awareness of the ecological and social consequences of the current high level of consumption and production, which has led to the transgression of planetary boundaries and demonstrates the limits to economic growth. Insights can only bear fruit if they are based on knowledge that serves to give direction to one's own actions, purposes and goals. On the basis of shared and personal values, knowledge can condense into a knowledge of what is valuable. Such a knowledge is a basis for transformation and requires two things. First, the promotion of universal values that can overcome the current economic growth paradigm. Second, the integration of these values into people's personal value systems, and that these values are reflected in people's attitudes, intentions and actual behaviour.

Whether integration and action on this basis succeeds will depend largely on whether the actions are perceived as beneficial, i.e. rewarded in the broadest sense – whether intrinsically or extrinsically. Initiating a cultural change towards a post-growth society will entail a wide range of political and economic instruments that recognise and reward the values-driven activities of all those involved.

Note

1 Findhorn Ecovillage is an evolving model that is used as a learning environment by a number of academic and school groups, professional associations and communities worldwide to promote and teach sustainability practices.

Bibliography

Babcock-Roberson, M.E., Strickland, O.J. (2010): *The relationship between charismatic leadership, work engagement, and organizational citizenship behaviors*, The Journal of Psychology 144(3), 313–326

Deci, E.L., Ryan, R.M. (1993): *Die Selbstbestimmungstheorie der Motivation und ihre Bedeutung für die Pädagogik*, Zeitschrift für Pädagogik 39(2), 223–238

Erpenbeck, J., Heyse, V. (2007): *Die Kompetenzbiographie*, Münster

Faltin, G. (2018): *Brains versus capital. Entrepreneurship for everyone*, https://david-gegen-goliath.de/shop/brains-versus-capital (accessed 21.01.2021)

Frankl, V.E. (1989): *Das Leiden am sinnlosen Leben*, Freiburg, Basel, Wien

Frankl, V.E. (2005): *Der Wille zum Sinn*, 5, erw. Aufl., Bern

Frankl, V.E. (2015): *Der Mensch vor der Frage nach dem Sinn*, 27. Aufl., München

Fritz-Schubert, E. (2017): *Lernziel Wohlbefinden – Entwicklung des Konzeptes „Schulfach Glück" zur Operationalisierung und Realisierung gesundheits- und bildungsrelevanter Zielkategorien*, Weinheim

Fritz-Schubert, E., Saalfrank, W.-T. (2015): *Schulfach Glück – Skizze und Hintergründe*, in: Fritz-Schubert, E., Saalfrank, W.-T., Leyhausen, M. (Eds.): Praxisbuch Schulfach Glück. GErundlagen und Methoden, Weinheim, 14–39

Fromm, E. (1980): *Gesamtausgabe. Band II: Analytische Charaktertheorie*, Stuttgart

Gross, P. (1994): *Die Multioptionsgesellschaft*, Frankfurt

Kennedy, M., Lietear, B.A. (2004): *Regionalwährungen: Neue Wege zu nachhaltigem Wohlstand*, München

Kuhnle, C., Hofer, M., Kilian B. (2011): *Ein Vorschlag zur Erweiterung des Leistungsbegriffs angesichts multipler Ziele im Jugendalter*, Wiesbaden

Kultusministerkonferenz (2005): *Bildungsstandards der Kultusministerkonferenz. Erläuterungen zur Konzeption und Entwicklung* (Veröffentlichungen der Kultusministerkonferenz, am 16.12.2004), München, Neuwied

Lang, E., Wintergerst, T. (2011): *Am Puls des langen Lebens – Soziale Innovationen für die alternde Gesellschaft*, München

Maslow, A.H. (1954) *Motivation and Personality*, New York

Menninger, K. (1968). *Das Leben als Balance*, München

Müller, C. (2011): *Urban Gardening: Über die Rückkehr der Gärten*, München

Riemeyer, J. (2007): *Die Logotherapie Viktor Frankls und ihre Weiterentwicklungen. Eine Einführung in die sinnorientierte Psychotherapie*, Bern

Robins, R.W., Trzesniewski, K.H., Tracy, J.L., Gosling, S.D., Potter, J. (2002). *Global self-esteem across the life span*. Psychology and Aging 17, 423–434

Rogers, C. (1980). *A Way of Being*, Boston

Rokeach, M. (1973): *The Nature of Human Values*, New York

Rösing, I. (2003): *Ist die Burnoutforschung ausgebrannt. Analyse und Kritik der internationalen Burnoutforschung*, Heidelberg

Roth, H. (1971): *Pädagogische Anthropologie. Bd. 2. Entwicklung und Erziehung, Grundlagen einer Entwicklungspädagogik*, Braunschweig

Simonson, J., Vogel, C., Tesch-Römer, C. (Eds.) (2017): *Freiwilliges Engagement in Deutschland. Der Deutsche Freiwilligensurvey 2014*, Wiesbaden

Waibel, E.-M. (2011): *Erziehung zum Sinn – Sinn der Erziehung. Grundlagen einer existenziellen Pädagogik*, Augsburg

4 Revaluations of work

Enabling and combining a diversity of activities

Stefanie Gerold

Summary

This chapter discusses a range of theoretical concepts and policies that provide valuable pointers for meaningful activity in a post-growth society. Expanded concepts of work call into question an understanding of work that focuses on formal employment, demanding a redistribution and revaluation of activities essential for our society. Debates about unsustainable or meaningless jobs not only imply a drastic reduction of working hours, but also that some jobs must disappear completely. If formal employment loses its central role in society, then new forms of participation and new ways of securing one's livelihood will be needed. Innovative working time policies in recent years offer important starting points on how to arrange living and working time in a sustainable way.

1 Introduction

To counter the worsening ecological crisis, the consumption of energy and materials must be drastically reduced. The structural changes required for this would result in the loss of large numbers of jobs. This would further aggravate the crisis of the "work society", a crisis characterised by the end of full employment and the increase in precarious employment that does not provide a secure livelihood. In addition, digitalisation and automation are giving rise to fears of job losses.

But paradoxically, at the same time as we are supposedly running out of work, core human needs – such as care, social recognition and participation – are not being properly met. Moreover, paid and unpaid activities are very unequally distributed between genders. Although they are essential to society, domestic work and care work, which are predominantly carried out by women, receive less financial and social recognition.

DOI: 10.4324/9781003187370-4

Against this background, this chapter discusses various concepts and demands for new work-life-time arrangements. Expanded concepts of work (Sections 2 and 3) seek to deconstruct an understanding of work that is limited to formal employment and to bring about a redistribution and revaluation of various activities. Debates on the meaningfulness of work (Section 4) challenge societies in which work has become an end in itself. Section 5 discusses options for securing livelihoods and participation emerging from the proposals under discussion. Section 6 looks at working time policies of recent years that allow for new work-life-time arrangements possible.

2   Reducing working hours – expanding the concept of work

Proposals for alternative arrangements of working and leisure time are based on the assumption that working hours must be reduced. Shorter working hours would in fact be the only way to enable people to pursue unpaid activities. Distributing the total work volume among a greater number of people would be fairer and could reduce unemployment, which, in turn, would decrease the pressure for economic growth (Antal 2014). Moreover, a reduction in the total amount of work could lower gross domestic product, and in turn the burden on the environment. Furthermore, it can be assumed that behavioural change at the individual level could have positive ecological effects: if incomes fall along with shorter working hours, resource-intensive consumption may be reduced. A sustainable lifestyle may also require a certain amount of freely disposable time, for example for environmentally friendly (slower) mobility, informed purchasing decisions, repair work or increased self-sufficiency (Knight et al. 2013).

A reduction in formal employment is also an important aspect of expanded concepts of work (Littig 2018). These approaches are critical of an understanding of work that centres on formal employment, advocating the inclusion of activities such as housework, self-determined work or engagement in civil society (see also the chapter by A. Komlosy in this book). Such concepts of work are often based on feminist labour research, which problematises the lack of social recognition given to unpaid care work. At its heart is the call for redistributing and revaluing activities essential for our society. Such a perspective differs from a model of gender equality which primarily aims to integrate women into the labour market without questioning the predominant role of formal employment (Weeks 2011).

A prominent example of a feminist concept of work is Haug's *Four-in-One Perspective* (2009). Haug argues for a way of life in which different areas of human activity are interlinked and of equal importance (in terms of time): formal employment, reproductive work, personal development and leisure, and political participation. In contrast to Haug, advocates of the *caring economy* have an explicit ecological orientation. This approach is critical of the gender-hierarchical separation of productive and reproductive spheres: whereas market-mediated processes are regarded as productive, unpaid activities and natural processes often receive little attention or appreciation, even though they are essential to the functioning of the economic sphere. This approach therefore calls for the understanding of work to be extended to the preservation of natural reproduction processes and the satisfaction of human needs. The concept of *caring work* thus includes not only formal employment but also care, self-determined work and civic engagement, in which women and men should participate equally (Biesecker/Hofmeister 2010; Biesecker/von Winterfeld 2011).

In recent years, expanded concepts of work have also emerged in the context of the sustainability debate. The notion of *mixed work* developed within the framework of the research project "Work and Ecology" (HBS 2000; Littig 2018) takes into account not only formal employment but also private care work, self-determined work and community work. The idea of a *half-day society* is based on the premise that formal employment should be reduced to 20 hours a week, and that work should be drastically redistributed. Schaffer and Stahmer (2005) calculate the reduction in CO_2 emissions that would stem from halving working hours. Their results show only a modest decrease, since the model assumes a large proportion of those previously unemployed to be integrated into the labour market, thus reducing output only marginally. The authors suggest incentives and sanctions to ensure that the time freed up is spent on socially important activities such as bringing up children, caring for the elderly or voluntary work. These incentives and sanctions include remuneration (in the form of a complementary currency), state support for children, greater social prestige for unpaid work and higher tax rates for those contributing less in terms of social engagement (Schaffer/Stahmer 2005). A reduction in working hours to 20 hours is also a key element for Paech (2012). His outline of a *post-growth economy* is predicated on the scaling back of industrial mass production based on the division of labour. Instead, local subsistence work without monetary remuneration would increase in importance.

Self-providing also plays an important role in Bergmann's concept of *New Work* (2019). The time spent on wage labour should be reduced to one-third. Another third is spent on high-tech self-providing, and one-third on work people "really, really want". New Work should thereby enable more autonomous lives and participation in society.

All these concepts problematise any understanding of work limited to formal employment and advocate instead a redistribution and revaluation of socially necessary activities. As important as this project is, however, it brings with it the danger that all human activities will be referred to as "work" (Hoffmann 2018). In her Four-in-One concept, Haug even speaks explicitly of a "workday entailing 16 hours" (Haug 2009, 120). The productivity mindset that dominates formal employment might in turn penetrate even further into our everyday lives. Even now, the term "work" is often used as a kind of quality label intended to raise the status of certain activities, as Liessmann (2018, 17) notes critically of the term "relationship work". Instead of regarding all activities as work, we should also reflect on the important role of non-work, of forms of idleness and contemplation.

3 "Sustainable work" and exnovation

Among the various bodies of the UN, the debate on the link between work and sustainability has so far been restricted mainly to the creation of *Green Jobs* in a *Green Economy*. Even the *Sustainable Development Goals* adopted in 2015 refer exclusively to formal employment when calling for "full and productive employment and decent work for all" (UN 2015).

A much broader understanding of work characterised a report from the United Nations Development Programme (UNDP) in 2015: it explicitly includes domestic work, private care and nursing activities, and voluntary and creative activities (UNDP 2015). *Sustainable work* here means work that promotes human development and at the same time minimises ecological side effects. For sustainable work to be realised, changes would have to take place on three levels: some jobs would terminate, others would be transformed and completely new fields of work would be created (for example in the provision of renewable energy).

The UNDP concept of sustainable work thus explicitly addresses the need to completely abolish certain activities because they are linked to inherently unsustainable production and consumption patterns. This *exnovation* approach – the phasing out of a technology or practice (Kimberly 1981; Hermwille 2017) – has been rather neglected in sustainability debates so far. Instead, the focus in politics and research is on the promotion of innovations in order to achieve a sustainability transformation through energy- and resource-saving production processes and products. However, there is a growing realisation that a "purposive termination of existing (infra)structures, technologies, products and practices" (Heyen et al. 2017, 326) is necessary in order to enable sustainability goals to be achieved.

Alongside various path dependencies and vested corporate interests, the fear of job losses is the main obstacle to exnovation.

4 The Debates on the meaningfulness of work

If environmental policy measures are accompanied by negative employment effects, attempts are usually made to replace the jobs lost with new jobs. However, it is rarely asked how meaningful these new employment opportunities are. In fact, in recent decades numerous jobs have been created under the imperative of full employment without their social usefulness or ecological sustainability ever being doubted. In his book *Bullshit Jobs*, David Graeber (2018) explores the phenomenon whereby more and more activities and jobs are so superfluous that not even the employees themselves regard them as meaningful. The findings are consistent with a YouGov survey in which 37 percent of British employees said that their work did not make a useful contribution to the world (YouGov 2015). Dur and van Lent (2019) analyse a representative survey covering 47 countries, finding that approximately 8 percent of workers think that their jobs are socially useless. Another 17 percent seems undecided about the usefulness of their job.

Such "bullshit jobs" are often well-paid, prestigious positions in middle management and administration. They can be found in both the public and private sectors, often, according to Graeber, in the financial, insurance and real estate sectors. In contrast, socially indispensable activities such as cleaning, care or childcare are often under pressure for rationalisation, poorly paid or not paid at all, and carried out under precarious or stressful working conditions.

Graeber believes that one of the reasons why meaningless work is so widespread is a society in which work has become an end in itself. The enormous productivity advances of the past have not been used to create more free time for everyone; instead, more and more areas of life have been commodified and new jobs created. The deliberate cultivation of "false needs" (Marcuse 2007, 7) made it possible to put in place the hamster wheel of long working hours, high incomes and consumerism (Schor 1993). Social norms and values also contribute to the fact that formal work enjoys such a high status. Whereas in pre-capitalist societies work was usually a necessary evil, the Protestant ethic gave it an unparalleled elevation to the status of a virtuous activity that promised divine salvation (Weber 2008/1920). This work ethic still persists in a modified form, even though religion has less significance in today's society (Weeks 2011). Thus, work is seen as a moral obligation regardless of its economic or social utility, while doing nothing carries the stigma of laziness and uselessness.

This is why André Gorz called for a broad public debate about the purpose of work as well as the amount and distribution of working time. What is needed is a (re)appropriation of living and working time, which is currently determined by others and subjugated to the production process, in order to give everyone greater freedom in the form of autonomous self-development. Linked with this is the right to interrupt working life of one's own volition and to lead a "multi-active life" (Gorz 1999, 73) which combines paid and unpaid activities.

In recent years, discussions about a *post-work society* have increasingly taken up Gorz' critique of the central role of formal employment in our society, and its simultaneous inability to fulfil the promise of material prosperity, meaningfulness and social recognition. Authors such as Weeks (2011), Frayne (2015) and Chamberlain (2018) have developed a vision of a society in which formal employment is no longer seen as the unquestioned source of income, identity and personal success. Among other things, they call for a radical reduction and redistribution of working time as well as an unconditional basic income (UBI) in order to decouple formal employment from material security. In addition, socially necessary work should be organised differently, and more space created for self-determined activities and self-realisation.

5 Livelihoods and participation

If formal employment becomes less important, the question arises how income, social security and participation in society can be assured (see the chapter by G. Kubon-Gilke in this book). Some ideas on this issue have already been discussed in this contribution. The following section provides a summary of the different approaches.

Discussions about a reduction in working time always give rise to the issue of wage compensation (see the chapter by N. Reuter in this book). Full wage compensation usually meets with resistance from the employers' side. However, companies might also benefit from higher productivity and fewer days of sick leave that accompany a cut in working hours. Moreover, the burden on the social security system would be eased by falling unemployment figures.

A possible compromise would be for companies or state subsidies to offset at least a part of the decline in income (Gerold et al. 2017). In addition, from a distribution perspective it would be desirable to differentiate a wage compensation according to income levels (BUND/EED 2008; Krull et al. 2009). Since it is above all high-income earners who have particularly large ecological footprints (Moser/Kleinhückelkotten 2018), a graduated wage compensation would also have ecological benefits.

In order to enable people to be active beyond formal employment, it is at first necessary to reduce the dependence on wage income. This could be achieved in part through an UBI. Work and income would be decoupled by giving each person a state income, regardless of their individual needs or willingness to provide a service in return (Gorz 1999; Weeks 2011; Bregman 2017; Van Parijs/Vanderborght 2017). Advocates of a UBI are to be found not only on the left-progressive camp, but also on the neo-liberal side. Some of the models proposed differ fundamentally from one another, especially with regard to the level of payments or the extent to which the basic income should replace public services. A UBI must be distinguished from models of needs-oriented basic social security (BUND/EED 2008, 449), in which payments are linked to the willingness to engage in formal employment or civic work (on the basic income, see also Reuter's critical view in this book).

Another approach to reducing dependency on earned income is to provide *universal basic services (UBS)* in the form of public goods and services such as housing, health care, transport and information (IGP 2017; Coote/Percy 2020). While a UBI still seeks to meet needs primarily with money, the provision of a social-ecological infrastructure could potentially contribute to overcoming the general fixation on consumption (Parrique 2019). For Gorz, too, the provision and appropriation of public spaces and infrastructure for self-determined activities plays an important role in enabling people to lead a multiactive life.

Frayne (2015), among others, addresses the idea that a reduction in formal employment would of itself reduce dependency on monetary income. Formal employment is often associated with considerable costs for commuting, work clothing or food. If people were to satisfy their needs more through self-determined work, through local supply and social networks, they would be less dependent on market-mediated external supply and thus also on waged work (Paech 2012).

The half-day society model assumes a reduction in state services because public revenues would fall. Voluntary activities would have to fill this gap, which could be rewarded in the form of a time-based currency (Schaffer/Stahmer 2005). Some local networks today already have time banks: household or gardening work done free of charge can be accumulated as time credits and exchanged for services provided by others. The Swiss association KISS offers a special form of time bank for old age provision.[1] Members provide care and support for elderly people in need of help. They can redeem the time credited to them at a later date if and when they become dependent on such help themselves (see also the chapter by Kubon-Gilke in this book).

Finally, alternative forms of living and working should be mentioned here as potential models for ecologically and socially sustainable forms of economic activity and living together. Social experiments in the area of the solidarity economy (Calvo/Morales 2017) and the subsistence economy (Mies/Bennholdt-Thomsen 1999), Transition Towns[2] and Ecovillages[3] are demonstrating how work, economic activity and life can also operate differently. However, the question always arises as to whether such niche projects can be scaled up to generate a critical mass for a socio-ecological transformation. Also, the question of social security for such lifestyles remains unanswered to date.

6 Innovative working time models

Following this overview of the discussion on alternative work-life-time arrangements, the last section will provide an insight into recently implemented working time policy measures that enable better compatibility between formal employment and other areas of life. Such measures include, first, reductions in working hours. This can be achieved not only by reducing the statutory or industry-specific weekly working hours, but also by extending annual holiday entitlements or increasing the number of public holidays. A legal entitlement to a career break allow people to interrupt their working life for specific stages of their lives, including parental, nursing care or educational leave. Measures to reduce dependency on earned income such as those already discussed should also be considered.

While most EU countries have provisions for parental, nursing care and educational leave, legal rights to cut back on or interrupt employment without evidence of "valid" reasons are rare. An exception is the Netherlands, where there has been a legal right to part-time work since 2000. Dutch employees who work part-time must be on an equal footing with their full-time colleagues in terms of pay and career opportunities. Although in the Netherlands, too, it is predominantly women who work part-time, considerably more than one-fifth of men work part-time, which contrasts markedly with the rest of the EU. For a number of years, Dutch employees were also able to benefit from the so-called *Levensloop* regulation: they were able to save up to 12 percent of their annual income on a preferential tax basis in a special account in order to finance unpaid time off at a later date (OECD 2014). The scheme, introduced in 2006, was discontinued in 2012.

Belgium has a similar model – initially for all employees, but since 2017 only for employees with child-rearing or nursing responsibilities. The *Tijdskrediet* allows employees to take a career break of up to one year, in one or more blocks, with a small state subsidy and the right to return to their old job. Alternatively, the Tijdskrediet allows a reduction in working hours of 50 percent for two years, or 80 percent for five years. While the Netherlands and Belgium have since curtailed these models, trade unions in Germany and Austria have developed innovative models for reducing working time in recent years. Since 2013, Austria has had a *Freizeitoption* (leisure option) in certain sectors. It allows employees to choose whether they want more time off in place of the collectively agreed sectoral wage increase. In 2013, for example, a wage increase of 3 percent was negotiated in the collective agreement for the electrical and electronics industry, which employees can instead have credited to their account as a leisure credit of 60 hours per year – provided that the individual company agrees to this. Other industries have since adopted this model. However, it is currently limited to high-wage sectors such as the metal, automotive and paper industries, as the collectively agreed minimum wage may not be undercut (Gerold/Nocker 2018).

A similar elective model was implemented in Germany in the 2016 collective bargaining round of the Railway and Transport Union (EVG). 58 percent of Deutsche Bahn employees decided to take up the 2.6 percent wage increase negotiated for 2018 in the form of more leisure time (Schulten/WSI 2019). Since the reduction in working hours is made possible by ongoing productivity gains, without cutting existing incomes, this model is likely to meet with greater approval among employees. If employees wanted a significant increase in leisure hours, however, they would have to be able to reapeatedly take such options. Due to opposition from employers' representatives, this has so far only been possible to a limited extent (Gerold/Nocker 2015).

Another innovative model for reducing working hours was offered to employees in the metal industry under the 2018 collective agreement. They can reduce their working hours to as little as 28 hours a week for a maximum of two years and then have the right to return to full-time employment. Employees who work shifts, care for relatives or bring up children can take an additional eight days off per year, of which two days are paid by the employer (Schulten/WSI 2019).

By means of these working time models, trade unions have been able to meet the specific individual needs of employees at different stages of their lives. To a certain extent, however, this has also led to an individualisation of working time policy. This is problematic as such solutions are not available to low-wage earners and employees who are not on permanent contracts. Moreover, it remains uncertain whether such individual arrangements can break the prevailing full-time norm.

7 Conclusion

This chapter has considered a number of theoretical models and policy measures that provide valuable ideas for organising work in a post-growth society. Arguments for expanding the concept of work highlight the central importance of socially necessary activities which are currently often associated with low income, lack of social security and little social recognition. As important as it is to redistribute and reassess various activities, the question arises whether it is really desirable to designate all these activities as work.

A sustainable economic and social system should aim to satisfy core human needs while respecting ecological limits. On the one hand, this means that more time must be invested in previously neglected areas such as raising children and nursing. On the other hand, other activities must be abandoned if they are either no longer ecologically justifiable or do not generate any social benefits. Finally, it should also be taken into account that periods of idleness and inactivity are probably precisely those which have the lowest ecological impact.

Notes

1 www.kiss-zeit.ch (retrieved March 25, 2019).
2 https://transitionnetwork.org/ (retrieved March 25, 2019).
3 ecovillage.org (retrieved March 25, 2019).

Bibliography

Antal, M. (2014): *Green goals and full employment: Are they compatible?* Ecological Economics 107, 276–286

Bergman, F. (2019): *New Work New Culture: Work We Want and a Culture That Strengthens Us*, Reprint Edition. Winchester, Washington

Biesecker, A., Hofmeister, S. (2010): *Focus: (Re)productivity: Sustainable relations both between society and nature and between the genders*, Ecological Economics 69, 1703–1711

Biesecker, A., von Winterfeld, U. (2011): *Erwerbsarbeit im Schatten – im Schatten der Erwerbsarbeit? Plädoyer für ein schattenfreies Arbeiten*, Gegenblende 8/2011, https://gegenblende.dgb.de/08-2011 (accessed 21.01.2021)

Bregman, R. (2017): *Utopia for Realists: How We Can Build the Ideal World*, New York

BUND/EED (Bund für Umwelt- und Naturschutz Deutschland/Evangelischer Entwicklungsdienst) "Brot für die Welt") (Ed.) (2008): *Zukunftsfähiges Deutschland in einer globalisierten Welt. Ein Anstoß zur gesellschaftlichen Debatte*, Frankfurt a. M.

Calvo, S., Morales, A. (2017): *Social and Solidarity Economy: The World's Economy with a Social Face*, New York, London

Chamberlain, J.A. (2018): *Undoing Work, Rethinking Community. A Critique of the Social Function of Work*, Ithaca, London

Coote, A., Percy, A. (2020): *The Case for Universal Basic Services*, Cambridge, Medford

Dur, R., van Lent, M. (2019): *Socially useless jobs.* Industrial Relations: A Journal of Economy and Society 58(1), 3–16

Frayne, D. (2015): *The Refusal of Work: The Theory and Practice of Resistance to Work*, London

Gerold, S., Nocker, M. (2015): *Reduction of working time in Austria. A mixed methods study relating a new work time policy to employee preferences*, WWW for Europe Working Paper 97, Vienna

Gerold, S., Nocker, M. (2018): *More leisure or higher pay? A mixed-methods study on reducing working time in Austria*, Ecological Economics 143, 27–36

Gerold, S., Soder, M., Schwendinger, M. (2017): *Arbeitszeitverkürzung in der Praxis. Innovative Modelle in österreichischen Betrieben*, Wirtschaft und Gesellschaft 43(2), 169–196

Gorz, A. (1999): *Reclaiming Work. Beyond the Wage-Based Society*, Cambridge

Graeber, D. (2018): *Bullshit Jobs: A Theory*, New York

Haug, F. (2009): *The "four-in-one perspective": A manifesto for a more just life*, Socialism and Democracy 23(1), 119–123

HBS (Hans-Böckler-Stiftung) (Ed.) (2000): *Wege in eine nachhaltige Zukunft. Ergebnisse aus dem Verbundprojekt Arbeit und Ökologie*, Düsseldorf

Hermwille, L. (2017): *En Route to a Just Global Energy Transformation? The Formative Power of the SDGs and the Paris Agreement*, Friedrich-Ebert-Stiftung, Berlin

Heyen, D.A., Hermwille, L., Wehnert, T. (2017): *Out of the comfort zone! Governing the exnovation of unsustainable technologies and practices*, GAIA 26(4), 326–331

Hoffmann, M. (2018): *Comment on the contribution Komlosy, A., What is work? Socio-historical and discursive approaches*, Research Group Meeting "Critical Perspectives on 'Sustainable Work' and 'Postwork'", 16–17 May 2018, WU Vienna

IGP (Institute for Global Prosperity) (2017): *Social Prosperity for the Future: A Proposal for Universal Basic Services*, University College London

Kimberly, J.R. (1981): *Managerial innovation*, in: Nystrom, P.C., Starbuck, W.H. (Eds.): Handbook of Organizational Design, Vol. 1, New York, 84–104

Knight, K.W., Rosa, E.A., Schor, J.B. (2013): *Could working less reduce pressures on the environment? A cross-national panel analysis of OECD countries, 1970–2007*, Global Environmental Change 23(4), 691–700

Krull, S., Massarrat, M., Steinrücke, M. (Eds.) (2009): *Schritte aus der Krise: Arbeitszeitverkürzung, Mindestlohn, Grundeinkommen. Drei Projekte, die zusammengehören*, Hamburg

Liessmann, K.P. (2018): *Mut zur Faulheit. Die Arbeit und ihr Schicksal*, in: Liessmann K.P. (Ed.): Mut zur Faulheit. Die Arbeit und ihr Schicksal, Wien, 7–19

Littig, B. (2018): *Good work? Sustainable work and sustainable development: A critical gender perspective from the Global North*, Globalizations 15(4), 565–579

Marcuse, H. (2007): *One-Dimensional Man. Studies in the Ideology of Advanced Industrial Society*, London, New York

Mies, M., Bennholdt-Thomsen, V. (1999): *The Subsistence Perspective: Beyond the Globalised Economy*, New York

Moser, S., Kleinhückelkotten, S. (2018): *Good intents, but low impacts: Diverging importance of motivational and socioeconomic determinants explaining pro-environmental behavior, energy use, and carbon footprint*, Environment and Behavior 50(6), 626–656

OECD (2014): *Ageing and Employment Policies: Netherlands 2014: Working Better with Age*, Paris

Paech, N. (2012): *Liberation from Excess: The Road to a Post-growth Economy*, München

Parrique, T. (2019): *The political economy of degrowth*. Economics and Finance. Dissertation, Université Clermont Auvergne; Stockholms universitet, https://tel.archives-ouvertes.fr/tel-02499463/document (accessed 21.01.2021)

Schaffer, A., Stahmer, C. (2005): *Die Halbtagsgesellschaft – ein Konzept für nachhaltigere Produktions- und Konsummuster*, GAIA 14(3), 229–239

Schor, J. (1993): *The Overworked American: The Unexpected Decline Of Leisure*, New York

Schulten, T. and WSI (2019): *Collective bargaining report 2018*. Collective Agreement Archive, Economic and Social Institute (WSI), Düsseldorf, https://www.boeckler.de/pdf/p_ta_jb_2018_english.pdf (accessed 21.01.2021)

UN (United Nations) (2015): *Transforming our world: The 2030 agenda for sustainable development*, A/RES/70/1

UNDP (United Nations Development Program) (Ed.) (2015): *Work for human development*, Human Development Report 2015, New York

Van Parijs, P., Vanderborght, Y. (2017): *Basic Income: A Radical Proposal for a Free Society and a Sane Economy*, Cambridge

Weber, M. (2008/1920): *The Protestant Ethic and the Spirit of Capitalism*, New York

Weeks, K. (2011): *The Problem with Work: Feminism, Marxism, Antiwork Politics, and Postwork Imaginaries*, Durham

YouGov (2015): *37% of British workers think their jobs are meaningless*, August 12, 2015, https://yougov.co.uk/topics/lifestyle/articles-reports/2015/08/12/british-jobs-meaningless (accessed 21.01.2021)

Part 2

Employment and meaningful activities

Actors

5 The role of consumers

Social participation beyond work and the market

Corinna Fischer and Immanuel Stieß

Summary

Limiting and qualitatively changing the level of consumption are key prerequisites for a post-growth society. However, the post-growth debate rarely takes into account that consumption fulfils important social functions such as recognition and social inclusion. This chapter discusses alternative forms and practices of consumption that could enable social participation independent of formal employment, earnings and conventional consumption.

1 Introduction

Growth, employment, income and consumption are linked in many ways (Røpke 2010). Blueprints for a sustainable and less growth-dependent society therefore usually start from two points: a reduction in working hours (Jackson 2009; Hirsch 2016) and corresponding changes in consumption patterns towards sufficiency (Stengel 2011; Linz 2012; Fischer/Grießhammer 2013; Schneidewind/Zahrnt 2014). Sufficiency comprises both a quantitative reduction in the level of consumption and qualitative changes. It is related to a reduction in working time in two ways: first, a lower income from gainful employment requires a more sufficiency-oriented way of life, and second, a reduction in working time makes people time-rich, which, in turn, makes sufficiency-oriented behaviour easier.[1]

But gainful employment and consumption fulfil important social functions. They are discussed under the headings of "social participation" (Kronauer 2010; Bartelheimer/Kädtler 2012), "recognition", "inclusion" (Voswinkel 2008) or "(symbolic) functions of consumption" (Reisch 2002; Jackson 2004). In the following section, we summarise and group together these functions of gainful employment and consumption under the concept of social participation.[2]

DOI: 10.4324/9781003187370-5

Models of society and social practices[3] that focus on reduced working hours and sufficiency must therefore address the question of how they deal with the fact that consumption and gainful employment in many ways make social participation possible, and that reduced working hours and sufficiency could constrain this level of social participation.

There are a number of different answers to this question, which complement each other in a useful way.

One of them is to develop positive visions of holistic lifestyles with less formal work and more sufficiency. These visions are expressed in terms such as "time wealth" (Reisch/Bietz 2016), "de-cluttering, deceleration, disentanglement and decommercialization" (Sachs 1993), trends such as "minimalism" or slogans such as "living well with less" (BUND/Misereor 1996). Such visions are important contributions to the social debate on how we want to live in the future. At the same time, however, they are ridden with prerequisites and have so far proved attractive only to a small minority. The potential and conditions for their upscaling have so far hardly been studied.

A second response is to change the political framework conditions. Non-sustainable, growth-driving forms of work and consumption can be made more difficult, and sufficiency-oriented practices easier; in some cases, enforcement and prohibition are also necessary (e.g. speed limits, product regulations) (Heyen et al. 2013; Schneidewind/Zahrnt 2014; Linz 2015; Kopatz 2016). Such measures challenge citizens and at the same time support them in finding alternative ways of social participation that are compatible with sufficiency. However, a major challenge is to gain acceptance and support for such sufficiency or post-growth policies.

This chapter proposes a third way. It illustrates by way of specific individual practices how social participation can be realised more independently of formal work, income from such work and conventional consumption. Of particular interest here is the extent to which alternative consumption practices can be identified that fulfil important functions of social participation for people in different social situations and with different needs and values and can be integrated into their everyday lives without requiring the adoption of an altogether different lifestyle. If such alternatives were promoted and disseminated, it would probably also be easier to promote positive visions of sufficiency and to find greater acceptance for sufficiency and post-growth policies.

The focus of this chapter is on consumption. Our thesis is that consumption practices exist that are less growth-driving and consume fewer resources than the usual ones, and which at the same time enable social participation and can bring about diverse ways of being meaningfully

active. We call them "alternative consumption practices". In this context, we address the following questions:

- What are the functions – subsumed under the concept of social
  participation – of consumption (and gainful employment)? (Section 2)
- What alternative consumption practices can be distinguished?
  (Section 3)
- In which social groups are such alternative consumption practices
  already established today and how can they enable these groups to
  participate in the wider society? (Section 4)
- What social, structural and personal prerequisites are necessary for
  alternative consumption practices to spread more widely? (Section 5)

2 The functions of consumption (and gainful employment)

In order to more precisely define the functions of consumption and
gainful employment, the concept of *social participation*, which stems
from social inequality research, is useful. In a broad sense, social participation encompasses all activities and relationships through which
actors acquire social options to realise their individual lifestyles (Bar-
telheimer/Kädtler 2012, 51). This means resources for their livelihoods,
competencies, integration into social networks and the like. According
to Kronauer (2010), four basic forms of social participation can be distinguished: gainful employment, close social relationships, participation
through rights and cultural participation.

- *Gainful employment* has a special status because, on the one hand,
  it is a central source of material subsistence and thus influences
  other forms of participation. On the other hand, through the social division of labour, it enables social integration by creating social relationships, structuring everyday life, helping to develop and
  maintain skills and imparting the experience of social usefulness
  (Kronauer 2010).
- However, social integration is determined not only by gainful employment, but also by being embedded in social relationships and
  networks, such as family, circles of friends and acquaintances and
  neighbourhood. *Close social relationships* therefore constitute a second form of social participation.
- *Legal rights* are a third form of participation. These include especially rights relating to social security, but also those that enable

political participation. With regard to consumption, this means that consumer rights are protected, and consumers can purchase goods and services free from discrimination (Voswinkel 2008).

– Finally, integration into society is also achieved through *cultural participation*, which is an important prerequisite for further forms of participation. For example, language competence, professional qualifications and cultural skills (communication, conflict resolution, adaptability) help with social and labour market integration (Bartelheimer 2004, 54).

Beyond these examples, however, Bartelheimer does not define the concept of cultural participation more precisely. A look at cultural sociology will help us to understand it better. Bourdieu (1984) showed that the acquisition of cultural competencies is not limited to high culture or explicit rules of behaviour. Rather, the sovereign and skilled mastery of informal cultural codes is a crucial prerequisite for social distinction and positioning in the social sphere. Following on from this insight, lifestyle research of the 1980s and 1990s[4] as well as studies in cultural anthropology, economic history and the sociology of consumption[5] have shown that consumption does more than just satisfying material needs. It also has significant symbolic functions.

Reisch (2002) organised these functions of consumption systematically. First of all, consumption is a medium that makes it possible to show that one belongs to a certain group or to express a (political) conviction and at the same time to distinguish oneself from other groups (*position function*). Not only group identity, but also personal taste and individuality can be expressed through consumption (*expression function*). Consumption makes it possible to acquire and demonstrate expertise in the selection of products and their use (*competence function*). Furthermore, consumer goods can impart excitement, well-being and pleasure (*hedonism function*). And last but not least, consumption provides relaxation and compensates for negative experiences, frustration or overload (*compensation function*). These concepts from the sociology of culture and consumption overlap with two of the four basic forms of participation mentioned above, but the terms do not completely merge.[6]

In the following section, we refer to all the functions of consumption described and group them together for simplification as "social participation". It emerges that consumption fulfils both material and symbolic functions, and that the symbolic functions are often linked to material ones.

How changes in consumer practices can fulfil these functions of consumption in the post-growth society will be examined in more detail in what follows.

3 A broader concept of consumption and alternative consumption practices

In conventional economic usage, "consumption" refers to the using (up) of goods and services (Schneck 2015), which are usually assumed to be acquired on the market.

In order to understand and describe alternative consumption practices, a broader concept of consumption is needed, as applied in the sociology of consumption (Wiswede 2000), in ecological economics (Røpke/ Reisch 2004) or in consumer research (OECD 2002). Such a broader concept starts from two points:

–   Consumption as a process: "consumption" describes not only the acquisition and/or use or consumption of a good,[7] but a longer-term process of interaction with it. This process begins with a decision about need, continues with the selection or design of the item and with its acquisition or production, includes the phase of use, care and maintenance, and ends with its disposal, further use or recycling (Wiswede 2000, 24).
–   Consumption as co-production ("prosuming"): goods and services are not provided (solely) via the market, but are (co-)designed, produced, transformed or converted by the users, individually or collectively (Toffler 1980).

Such a broader concept of consumption goes hand in hand with a broader concept of work, one that includes care work, work for oneself and service to the community and also includes a larger time budget for such work (see Gerold in this book). While an expanded concept of work extends to meaningful activity in all its many forms, an expanded concept of consumption goes beyond market goods to include co-produced and collectively used services and goods.

Based on this expanded concept of consumption, Table 5.1 provides an overview of alternative consumption practices[8] associated with various forms of consumption and levels of action. The three levels of action are characterised by increasing complexity, but are not to be understood in terms of a logical or temporal progression: joining in with alternative consumption practices is possible on every level.

At the level of *individual consumer behaviour*, this involves individually using existing goods and services or those offered on the market in a different way, or acquiring them through non-commercial channels. At the level of *prosuming*, users also produce or transform goods and services for their own use. At the level of *collaborative consumption*, the production and distribution of goods and services takes place in a community, on the basis of the sharing of tasks and in an organised way.

What these alternative forms and practices of consumption have in common is greater independence from the market and from money. Individuals and communities take a more active role than just buying ready-made goods, and thus more responsibility for their own consumption. This offers opportunities for a post-growth society, since consumption thus enables social participation to be detached to some extent from gainful employment and income (Section 4). This requires suitable social framework conditions (Section 5).

Table 5.1 Overview of levels of action, forms of consumption and consumption practices

Levels of action	*Alternative forms of consumption*	*Alternative consumption practices*
Individual consumer behaviour	Using existing services for exchanging, sharing and lending goods; extending product lifetimes, giving away or selling products after use, buying used products	Using commercial car/bike sharing and clothing subscription schemes, libraries or media libraries; using mobile phones for longer; using flea markets and second-hand platforms on the Internet; passing on goods to friends, etc.
Prosuming	Self-producing, converting, reusing, repairing, upcycling,[a] participating individually in product development	Growing vegetables in the garden, handicrafts, sewing, generating electricity oneself using photovoltaics, programming open software, repairing household appliances, sprucing up clothes, participating in innovation platforms, etc.
Collaborative consumption	Joint design, production, consumption, repair, distribution and networking	Participating in urban gardening, community-supported agriculture, repair cafés, food banks, local exchange trading schemes (LETS); organising car/bike sharing among friends and acquaintances, etc.

a "Upcycling" means the transformation of a used or defective product into a higher quality product.

4 Social participation through alternative forms of consumption in different social groups

4.1 Social participation through alternative forms of consumption

The question arises as to how alternative forms and practices of consumption can contribute to the functions subsumed under "social participation" (see Section 2). In the following section, we show what the opportunities are, but also where obstacles exist – and where they don't.

Collective production, acquisition or use can facilitate *material* access to goods and services. In this case, they expand the opportunities for material participation. However, these opportunities may remain unused if the necessary skills, time or other resources are lacking or if the practices mentioned cannot be reconciled with personal attitudes or norms of the social milieu. If the self-produced, repaired or shared goods are not available in the same abundance and regularity, or have different characteristics from those known and expected from goods acquired on the market, this can lead to greater appreciation – but it can also be perceived as a drawback.

Alternative consumption practices can fulfil *symbolic* functions particularly well. For example, repairing or doing things yourself requires skills that are learned and demonstrated to others through practice. Individually designed products are especially suited to expressing one's personality, and collective action engenders social relationships. But alternative consumption practices can also conflict with established forms of social participation. This is the case, for example, when choosing not to own a car or not to fly jeopardises the symbols of affiliation, status (position function) and individuality (expression function).

Since the conditions of social participation differ according to social situation, social milieu and lifestyle, the respective contribution of alternative consumption practices to social participation (material and symbolic) depends on the following questions:

– Which alternative consumption practices are feasible for whom (in the light of existing resources and competences)? And which are acceptable to whom (in the light of interests and norms)?
– To what extent, and for whom, do these consumption practices fulfil the functions described above?

These questions will be discussed below on the basis of empirical findings. We will refer principally to a secondary analysis of two representative

surveys for the Federal Environment Agency on environmental awareness in Germany (Scholl et al. 2015, 2017) as well as to other studies
(Greenpeace 2015a, b).

4.2 The prevalence of alternative consumption practices

The analysis of the surveys shows that individual alternative consumption practices are quite widespread, especially in the area of *individual
consumer behaviour.* One example is the *extended use* of products, for
example through the repair of defective items. Especially with expensive
devices such as smartphones, repairing can save money, provided it is
possible at all and no complicated spare parts or special tools are needed.

Second-hand practices are also widespread, especially in the field
of clothing: almost half of the population has already bought or sold
used clothing (Greenpeace e.V. 2015b), and this applies particularly to
children's clothing (Greenpeace e.V. 2015a). In addition, it is common
practice to informally pass on clothing to family and friends. However, a
milieu-specific evaluation shows how the diffusion of second-hand practices varies according to social milieu. Members of "young milieus"[9] in
particular buy used textiles in order to obtain expensive clothes at an
affordable price and to create their own personal style from them. People from "elevated" and "precarious milieus" have greater reservations
and tend to reject second-hand clothes for reasons of hygiene (Scholl
et al. 2015).

Sharing (joint use) is also frequently practised – and in different areas
of need. The lending and borrowing of objects free of charge is widespread, especially in the private sphere. Commercial sharing schemes,
for example in the area of mobility (car sharing or bike rental systems,
including e-bikes and cargo bikes), are used much less frequently. In
2016, only 14 percent of the population with a driving licence and access to such schemes used car sharing[10] (Scholl et al. 2017, 67). One
reason for the low take-up of these services is the lack of infrastructure
in rural areas, being mainly limited to large agglomerations. In addition,
such schemes primarily appeal to "critical-creative" and "young milieus",
where car ownership is not important for demonstrating social status or
as a vehicle and symbol of social participation, or where non-ownership
of a car has even become a status symbol.

Collaborative consumption practices are not very common: in a representative survey for the Federal Environment Agency, just under 10
percent of respondents said that they participated in community initiatives and projects such as neighbourhood initiatives, local exchange
and trading systems or repair cafés, either as users or as organisers.

These respondents were predominantly members of "critical-creative milieus", although repair cafés are also attractive for older people from "traditional milieus" (Scholl et al. 2017, 33). In addition to sociability and social contacts, such initiatives offer possibilities for social recognition and for gaining craft skills.

Urban gardening initiatives reach and connect different population groups, and for a variety of reasons. They link to established practices of self-production and self-provisioning (house and allotment gardens) which are widespread in "traditional milieus" and among people who have moved in from rural areas. They offer relaxation and balance to working people, and for young families they open up an opportunity to experience nature together. And working and celebrating together is attractive across all milieus.

4.3 Alternative consumption practices in "young" and "precarious milieus"

Finally, we want to turn to examples of alternative consumption practices among adolescents/young adults and in "precarious milieus". It will become clear how sustainable consumption practices and social participation – depending on the social and biographical situation – can be connected in very different ways.

For "young milieus", alternative consumption practices are attractive if they improve material participation opportunities. This becomes clear from the example of cycling. It enables rapid travel, regardless of the routes and frequency of public transport – and without the cost of a driving licence and car. Sharing schemes are also attractive if they provide access to freight bikes, cars or cheap private accommodation as an alternative to expensive hotels (Scholl et al. 2015). Second-hand schemes can also enable access to high-priced goods such as smartphones or clothing. The example of clothing shows the high symbolic significance of consumption practices and the ambivalence associated with them: while some people associate second-hand goods with expressiveness and demonstrating their own style, for other young people, owning new branded products fulfils this function.

Joint action within one's peer group, such as sharing, urban gardening or joint repair work, has material and symbolic functions. The participants can experience social relationships and self-efficacy (competence function) while having fun (hedonism function).

Alternative consumption practices have so far been less common in "precarious milieus". Such practices can be integrated into one's own lifestyle above all if they expand material participation possibilities, improve one's quality of life or provide reliable and inexpensive access to goods and services. Examples are financial savings through longer use and repair of products, a cheaper diet through sharing or passing on unneeded food, good access to services and social facilities through non-motorised local mobility, use of good and inexpensive community leisure, sport and catering opportunities through the use of public green spaces, sports facilities, libraries and media libraries in the neighbourhood (see Scholl et al. 2017, 75–76). Obstacles arise for three main reasons: either the practices are too expensive (e.g. participation in energy cooperatives), they require special skills (e.g. repairing) or they are experienced as socially stigmatising (e.g. wearing second-hand clothes or not having your own car).

5 Creating the necessary conditions

As we have shown in Section 4, some alternative forms of consumption are already relatively well established in society, especially those based on traditional practices. Other alternative forms of consumption have been less well received – whether because of lack of time, lack of skills or insufficient connection to the familiar and customary forms of social participation. If such forms of consumption are to play a greater role in a post-growth society, and if individual practices are to be developed further towards fully sufficient lifestyles, better conditions must first be created. Second, these consumption practices must become more attractive; and third, they must not be allowed to lead to new social divisions, exclusions and disadvantage.

In the following section, we list some examples of prerequisites for the further diffusion of alternative consumption practices. They are intended to illustrate what kind of social conditions and political framework would be helpful.

- Many alternative forms of consumption require public resources, such as *publicly accessible infrastructure*. This includes libraries and media libraries, transport infrastructure, and access to spaces and areas where self-organisation and self-production can take place.
- It is also necessary to create *free time periods*. A reduction in working hours must be implemented in such a way that sufficient foreseeable periods of time are created for self-determined activities. In addition, such periods of free time must overlap to a sufficient degree with other people's to enable collective organisation.
- Alternative consumption practices require a wide range of skills – manual, technical, organisational and communicative among

others – which may be very unevenly distributed among people from different milieus, backgrounds and social situations. Consumer advice (for example on the environment or nutrition) can strengthen these skills. In addition, the teaching of practical and craft skills should be integrated into school curricula.

– Furthermore, alternative consumption practices must become *known and attractive*. Because it is only if alternative consumption practices and the ways of living based on them are more widely known and accepted that the opportunities for material benefits, social relationships, self-realisation, recognition and distinction can actually be realised.

– In order for people to learn about alternative consumption practices and to connect with them and develop the required skills and motivation, it is important for them to be able to try them out and to discuss them with others. The many guides and personal accounts on topics such as cooking, gardening, sewing or minimalism that can be found on platforms such as YouTube or Facebook, as well as the discussion groups created around them, are an example of this.

– Trusted contacts and credible and well-connected multipliers in the respective target groups play an important role here. For example, strengthening communicative competence, financial support and networking among youth centres, refugee support initiatives, influencers and community groups could help them to disseminate sustainable consumption practices to their target groups.

– *Regulatory and economic instruments for sufficiency policy* cushioned by appropriate social policy measures (Heyen et al. 2013; Schneidewind/Zahrnt 2014; Linz 2015, 2017) can help the shift towards alternative consumption practices by making unsustainable consumption more difficult and promoting sustainable consumption. Such instruments can also help to make undesirable behaviour socially unacceptable and thus to promote the value change needed to ensure that alternative consumption practices are experienced by more people as a means of participating rather than as stigmatising.

– Finally, an important question is how to ensure the *supply of essential goods and services* (e.g. housing, nutrition, mobility). Alternative consumption practices can make a contribution, but they cannot deliver the core supply by themselves. The functions of material participation and security must therefore be guaranteed by the state, especially in a post-growth society which is less able to rely on income-based security (see Kubon-Gilke and Gerold in this book).

6 Conclusions

Alternative consumption practices can help to free social participation from dependence on gainful employment, income and the consumption of market goods. In this way, such consumption practices can support a post-growth society. However, alternative consumption practices do not (yet) appeal to all social groups, they do not cover all consumption practices and do not perform all the functions of consumption. We need a better understanding of which practices can enable participation for which groups and in which ways, and which support and political framework conditions are needed.

For example, research on sustainable consumption, the good life or alternative ways of doing business has so far neglected certain functions of consumption, namely material participation, positioning and compensation. In the research circles mentioned above, these functions are viewed with suspicion as drivers of growth and of unsustainable consumption. As a result, there is hardly any knowledge about how they could be fulfilled by alternative consumption practices – and no open-minded debate about whether they should be fulfilled. It is conceivable that the functions of material participation, positioning and compensation are key to drawing alternative consumption practices out of their niche and making them accessible and attractive to different milieus.

Notes

1 A reduction in working hours is also conceivable with full income compensation and this may also be desirable from a socio-political point of view. However, the ecological benefits are thereby largely dissipated, as current model calculations by Schumacher et al. (2019) demonstrate.
2 These concepts originate from different theoretical and disciplinary contexts. However, there is a considerable degree of overlap, which is why we consider this summation under the one term of social participation justifiable in the interests of reader-friendliness.
3 By the term (social) practice (for example, Spaargaren 2011), we understand a socially established, supra-individual, "typical" way of carrying out a certain activity. We have chosen the term because it places greater emphasis on the social embedding and cultural framing of personal action than the term "behaviour" does and is more specifically related to individual activities than the term "lifestyle".
4 An overview can be found in Götz et al. (2011).
5 Schneider (2000), Wiswede (2000), Reisch (2002) and Voswinkel (2008) provide overviews.
6 "Cultural participation" can be defined more precisely as a combination of positional, expressive and competence functions. Reisch implicitly refers to "close social relationships": she explains that consumer goods play a role in many rituals that shape and strengthen social relationships such as giving,

celebrating, shared meals, sports or games. "Gainful employment" and "legal rights" do not appear explicitly in the sociology of culture and consumption. On the other hand, the sociology of consumption addresses hedonism and compensation functions that do not feature in the literature on participation.

7 The notion of "good", in this context, is meant to include services.

8 This work is based on the ongoing project *"Bürgerbeteiligung und soziale Teilhabe im Rahmen der Umsetzung des Nationalen Programms für Nachhaltigen Konsum: neue Impulse für das bürgerschaftliche Engagement"* (Civic and Social Participation in the Context of Implementing the National Programme for Sustainable Consumption: New Impulses for Civic Engagement).

9 The authors of the environmental awareness study use a milieu model comprising six social milieus (Scholl et al. 2017, 71). Precarious, traditional, critical-creative and elevated milieus each account for 13–15 percent of the population. Young milieus account for 18 percent and middle-class mainstream for 25 percent.

10 In relation to the total population, the proportion is 4 percent (ibid.).

Bibliography

Bartelheimer, P. (2004): *Teilhabe, Gefährdung und Ausgrenzung als Leitbegriffe der Sozialberichterstattung*, SOFI Mitteilungen 32, 47–61

Bartelheimer, P., Kädtler, J. (2012): *Produktion und Teilhabe – Konzepte und Profil sozioökonomischer Berichterstattung*, in: Baethge, M., Bartelheimer, P. (Eds.): Berichterstattung zur sozioökonomischen Entwicklung in Deutschland, Wiesbaden, 41–85

Bourdieu, P. (1984): *Distinction: A Social Critique of the Judgement of Taste*, Cambridge

BUND, Misereor (Ed.) (1996): *Zukunftsfähiges Deutschland: Ein Beitrag zu einer global nachhaltigen Entwicklung*, Studie des Wuppertal Instituts für Klima, Umwelt, Energie, Basel

Fischer, C., Grießhammer, R. (2013): *When less is more – sufficiency: Terminology, rationale and potentials*, in collaboration with Barth, R., Brohmann, B., Brunn, C., Keimeyer, F., Wolff, F. (Working Paper, 2), Oeko-Institut e.V., Freiburg i.B. https://www.oeko.de/oekodoc/1879/2013-007-en.pdf (accessed 21.01.2021)

Götz, K., Deffner, J., Stieß, I. (2011): *Lebensstilansätze in der angewandten Sozialforschung – am Beispiel der transdisziplinären Nachhaltigkeitsforschung*, in: Rössel, J., Otte, G. (Eds.): Lebensstilforschung, KZfSS Special Edition (51), Wiesbaden, 86–112

Greenpeace e.V. (2015a): *Deutsche Eltern und Secondhand-Bekleidung*, Vollständiger Bericht, https://www.greenpeace.de/sites/www.greenpeace.de/files/publications/mode-elternumfrage-winkle-langfassung-24022015.pdf (accessed 21.01.2021)

Greenpeace e.V. (Ed.) (2015b): *Wegwerfware Kleidung, Repräsentative Greenpeace-Umfrage zu Kaufverhalten, Tragedauer und der Entsorgung von Mode*, Hamburg, https://www.greenpeace.de/sites/www.greenpeace.de/files/publications/20151123_greenpeace_modekonsum_flyer.pdf (accessed 21.01.2021)

Heyen, D.A., Fischer, C., Barth, R., Brunn, C., Grießhammer, R., Keimeyer, F., Wolff, F. (2013): *When less is more – sufficiency – need and options for policy action* (Working Paper 3), Oeko-Institut e.V., Freiburg i.B. https://www.oeko.de/oekodoc/1880/2013-008-en.pdf (accessed 21.01.2021)

Hirsch, M. (2016): *Die Überwindung der Arbeitsgesellschaft. Eine politische Philosophie der Arbeit*, Wiesbaden

Jackson, T. (2004): *Consuming paradise? Unsustainable consumption in cultural and social-psychological context*, in: Hubacek, K., Inaba A., Stagl S.: Driving Forces of and Barriers to Sustainable Consumption, Proceedings of an International Workshop, Leeds, 5th–6th March, 9–26

Jackson, T. (2009): *Prosperity without Growth: Economics for a Finite Planet*, London

Kopatz, M. (2016): *Ökoroutine, Damit wir tun, was wir für richtig halten*, 2nd edition, München

Kronauer, M. (2010): *Exklusion. Die Gefährdung des Sozialen im hoch entwickelten Kapitalismus*, 2. upd. and ed, Frankfurt a. M.

Linz, M. (2012): *Weder Mangel noch Übermass, Warum Suffizienz unentbehrlich ist*, München

Linz, M. (2015): *Suffizienz als politische Praxis, Ein Katalog*, Wuppertal Spezial 49, Wuppertal, epub.wupperinst.org (accessed 21.01.2021)

Linz, M. (2017): *Wie Suffizienzpolitiken gelingen. Eine Handreichung* (Wuppertal Spezial 52), epub.wupperinst.org (accessed 21.01.2021)

OECD (2002): *Towards sustainable household consumption? Trends and policies in OECD countries*, www.oecd-ilibrary.org (accessed 21.01.2021)

Reisch, L.A. (2002): *Symbols for sale, Funktionen des symbolischen Konsums*, in: Deutschmann, C. (Ed.): Die gesellschaftliche Macht des Geldes, Wiesbaden, 226–248

Reisch, L.A., Bietz, S. (2016): *Zeit, Wohlstand und Gutes Leben: Was kann Zeitpolitik zur Großen Transformation beitragen?* in: Held, M. (Ed.): Politische Ökonomik großer Transformationen, Marburg, 263–285

Røpke, I. (2010): *Consumption at the core of the growth engine*, Advancing Sustainability in a Time of Crisis, https://vbn.aau.dk/files/75301476/Consumption%20and%20growth%20ISEE%202010.pdf (accessed 21.01.2021)

Røpke, I., Reisch, L.A. (2004): *The Place of Consumption in Ecological Economics*, in: Reisch, L.A., Røpke, I. (Eds.): The Ecological Economics of Consumption, Cheltenham, Northampton, 1–13

Rosenkranz, D., Schneider, N.F. (Eds.) (2000): *Konsum, Soziologische, ökonomische und psychologische Perspektiven*, Wiesbaden

Sachs, W. (1993): *Die vier E's: Merkposten für einen maßvollen Wirtschaftsstil*, Politische Ökologie 11(33), 69–72

Schneck O. (2015): *Lexikon der Betriebswirtschaft*, München, www.finanzen.net/wirtschaftslexikon (accessed 21.01.2021)

Schneider, N.F. (2000): *Konsum und Gesellschaft*, in: Rosenkranz, D., Schneider, N.F. (Eds.): Konsum. Soziologische, ökonomische und psychologische Perspektiven, Wiesbaden, 9–22

Schneidewind, U., Zahrnt, A. (2014): *The Politics of Sufficiency. Making It Easier to Live the Good Life*, München

Scholl, G., Gossen, M., Holzhauer, B., Schipperges, M. (2015): *Umweltbewusstsein in Deutschland 2014. Ergebnisse einer repräsentativen Bevölkerungsumfrage*, Bundesministerium für Umwelt, Naturschutz, Bau und Reaktorsicherheit & Umweltbundesamt, www.umweltbundesamt.de/publikationen (accessed 21.01.2021)

Scholl, G., Gossen, M., Holzhauer, B., Schipperges, M. (2017): *Umweltbewusstsein in Deutschland 2016, Ergebnisse einer repräsentativen Bevölkerungsumfrage*, Bundesministerium für Umwelt, Naturschutz, Bau und Reaktorsicherheit und Umweltbundesamt, www.umweltbundesamt.de/publikationen (accessed 21.01.2021)

Schumacher, K., Wolff, F., Cludius, J., Fries, T., Hünecke, K., Postpischil, R., Steiner, V. (2019): *Arbeitszeitverkürzung – gut für's Klima? Treibhausgasminderung durch Suffizienzpolitiken im Handlungsfeld „Erwerbsarbeit"*, Dessau

Spaargaren, G. (2011): *Theories of practices, agency, technology, and culture*, Global Environmental Change 21(3), 813–822

Stengel, O. (2011): *Suffizienz, Die Konsumgesellschaft in der ökologischen Krise*, München

Toffler, A. (1980): *The Third Wave*, New York

Voswinkel, S. (2008): *Anerkennung durch Konsum?* in: Rehberg, K.-S. (Ed.): Die Natur der Gesellschaft: Verhandlungen des 33. Kongresses der Deutschen Gesellschaft für Soziologie in Kassel 2006, Teilband 1 und 2, Frankfurt a. M., 3962–3972

Wiswede, G. (2000): *Konsumsoziologie – eine vergessene Disziplin*, in: Rosenkranz, D., Schneider, N.F. (Eds.): Konsum. Soziologische, ökonomische und psychologische Perspektiven, Wiesbaden, 23–72

6 The role of businesses in the creation of sustainable work

Gerrit von Jorck and Ulf Schrader[*]

Summary

Businesses can make a significant contribution to the transition to a post-growth society where the dominant position of formal employment and consumption is diminished and other activities become more important. To achieve this, they must make formal employment sustainable. Work is not just an object of any social-ecological transformation: through working time regimes and work organisation, businesses can make an active contribution to a sustainable lifestyle for employees and increase their time wealth.

1 Introduction

Businesses are key players in the formal employment society. They determine the conditions under which formal employment is carried out and have a significant influence on the understanding of work. Businesses therefore play an important role in the transition from a formal employment society to a society based on meaningful activity that is not dependent on growth.

This chapter shows how businesses, as co-creators of sustainable work, can contribute to a social-ecological transformation of society and of the everyday lives of their employees. To this end, we first address the importance of formal employment for sustainable everyday practices before we examine the scope for businesses to make work more sustainable and at the same time less dependent on growth.

2 Work and sustainability

Work is a crucial aspect of a social-ecological transformation (Barth et al. 2019). The United Nations Development Programme defines sustainable work as follows: "Sustainable work promotes human development while

DOI: 10.4324/9781003187370-6

reducing and eliminating negative side effects and unintended consequences. It is critical not only for sustaining the planet, but also for ensuring work for future generations" (UNDP 2015). This concept of work covers both paid and unpaid activities. Sustainable work thus safeguards both the internal nature of human beings – their physical and mental development – and their external nature – the natural foundations of life.

However, work is not merely the passive object of social-ecological transformation, but can also actively contribute to the social-ecological transformation of everyday practices. Marx described work as a metabolic process between humans and nature and refers thereby to its transformative character. Humans, he argued, change their internal nature by acting on external nature through the work process (Marx 1996). If the work process is characterised by the rationale of growth or increase, then the metabolic process between human being and nature, which is mediated through work, is also accelerated. The work process thereby transforms the relationship between humans and nature: an accelerated working method can lead to a subjectively perceived lack of time (internal nature) as well as to a more intensive use of resources (external nature). At the same time, these two effects are in a reciprocal relationship.

In other words, businesses actively influence their employees' everyday practices by organising work and working time. Employers can enable more diverse and sustainable everyday practices (for example by facilitating ways of living which are more subsistence-based and sufficient) and thus reduce the material and immaterial dependency on formal employment and earned income. Businesses that act in this way can become more attractive as employers and can contribute to the resilience of their employees and to their becoming less dependent on growth.

3 Working differently in alternative organisations and businesses

In the so-called alternative economy – alternative platform economy organisations such as Wikipedia or Fairmondo, open workshops, cooperatives or post-growth organisations (Rätzer et al. 2018) – activities beyond traditional formal employment relationships are often tested out and practised. It can be seen there that activities in the various fields of work – formal employment, care work, community work and self-determined work – are often integrated on an equal footing. Since such alternative concepts of economic activity can also provide a stimulus towards a different understanding of work in traditional businesses, we will discuss in the following section the importance of work in alternative economy organisations.

The opportunities that digitalisation offers for alternative ways of working can be observed in the example of Wikipedia, which as a digital public good is largely supplied by unpaid work. Often, however, digitalisation exacerbates social divisions and expands the sphere of paid work. Platforms such as Helpling, Uber and Airbnb create job opportunities beyond traditional employment relationships and thereby enable a diversification of income streams, while at the same time commodifying the most private areas of life and creating a new "service proletariat" (Scholz 2016; Staab/Nachtwey 2016). What has been termed platform cooperativism (Scholz 2016) is developing in a different direction. Cooperatively organised alternative businesses are taking up the opportunities offered by digitalisation to integrate different forms of work. At the same time, they try to reduce the risks of informal work by making the users of the platforms their owners. One example is the Wikitheater (Bauwens/Kostakis 2014), which collaboratively develops plays through unpaid work. The plays are freely available; for commercial performances, the cooperative negotiates a fee. The platform cooperative thus creates freely accessible commons on the one hand and additional income on the other.

Open workshops and centres for (high-tech) self-providing also try out new ways of production and working (Bergmann 2018; Lange/Bürkner 2018). They provide the means of production to satisfy needs outside the market or to develop new ideas that are later made available on the market. According to Schor (2011), in the course of digitalisation, self-providing costs have fallen significantly (e.g. with 3-D printing), while wage development has stagnated in many sectors. As a result, it has become economically rational for many employees to reduce their working hours and to satisfy their own needs directly instead of remaining in the traditional "work-and-spend cycle".[1] Open workshops can thus help people to become more independent of formal employment.

In some energy cooperatives, interactions between paid and unpaid work can be observed, with cooperative members volunteering skills they have acquired during their employment. Conversely, experiences from alternative work contexts are also fed back into formal employment. The social bonds created in the course of voluntary work can also strengthen the participants (Rommel et al. 2018). This empowerment can lead to the creation of new communities in which dependence on formal employment is reduced through the participants initiating further local economy projects (e.g. in solidarity-based agriculture).

So far, alternative organisations have often remained niche players. One reason for this is that many people are involved in these organisations in addition to their regular formal employment (Houtbeckers 2018). This means that involvement in the alternative economy remains dependent on conventional employment and usually has to adapt to its requirements. For one thing, traditional formal employment takes up a large part of our time resources, and second it influences our attitude to formal employment. This attitude – akin to an excessive focus on productivity or performance – must first be actively unlearned by those involved in the alternative economy. Without a substantial change in formal employment in traditional businesses as well, therefore, the general understanding of formal employment will hardly change.

A rethinking of working practices is also taking place outside alternative organisations. It can be triggered when large order numbers lead to a high backlog of work, which has to be continuously redistributed. This can provide the impetus to actively address the drive for growth and the need for stability and to create scope for reflection on the way work and production are organised. This can lead, in turn, to the emergence of post-growth companies that opt for a reduced pace and reserve capacity through collaborative production communities and anti-cyclical personnel policies: in boom periods they hire few new staff and in downturns they hardly lay off anyone, but instead establish lifetime working time accounts (Gebauer/Mewes 2015; Gebauer 2018). Such businesses deliberately refrain from exploiting all growth opportunities. In doing so, they develop a business model based on the closest possible customer and supplier relationships, which are often regional. The cultivation of relationships thus becomes an important part of formal employment.

4 Employees as co-workers and consumers

When companies take into account the dual role of their employees as both co-workers and consumers, innovations in sustainability can arise in two ways. First, when sustainable practices and consumption patterns become possible in the work sphere (e.g. through the provision of a shower for bike commuters), and second, when ideas and experiences from private life are incorporated into the work sphere (e.g. when private sharing practices are incorporated into the design of products or the workplace in the course of open innovation processes).

Employees with an interest in sustainability are often willing and able to combine their outside skills and experience with the circumstances on the inside and to bring about change (Schmidt-Keilich/Schrader 2019). This requires a suitable framework, such as a participatory, sustainability-oriented corporate culture and sufficient scope to initiate action (Schrader/Harrach 2013). Good ideas for the sustainable design of product packaging or break rooms, for example, can also come from "ordinary" employees and not only from professional designers.[2]

Just as what is learned privately can enrich and enhance formal employment, so too can the workplace become a learning environment for sustainable consumption practices (Muster/Schrader 2011; Süßbauer et al. 2019), for example if the employer provides company bicycles or offers sustainably produced meals in the canteen. If companies perceive their employees both as co-workers and as consumers, they can strengthen self-efficacy experiences and increase employee satisfaction (Muster 2012). However, if sustainability practices are perceived as being imposed, it can lead to defensive reactions. So such a demarcation between formal employment and private life through consumption services and the integration of consumption competences requires a degree of "border control".[3] On the one hand, this calls for personal skills on the part of the employees, such as the ability to assess the costs and benefits for their own lifestyles of any boundary-dissolving innovations the employer is offering (consumption options or working time models); and on the other hand it calls for agreements and rules that enable the employees to decide for themselves how far they wish to combine their private lives with their working lives. Time policy instruments can play an important role here.

5 Time policy instruments

Broadly speaking, three types of time policy instruments can be distinguished: working time flexibilisation; internal working time reduction – i.e. a reduction in market-oriented activities within a formally unchanged working time regime; and external working time reduction – i.e. a reduction in absolute terms in working time. While the following discussion of time policy instruments focuses on the quantitative dimension of time, the concept of time wealth also includes the qualitative dimension of time.

5.1 *Working time flexibilisation*

The flexibilisation of working time seems to hold out the promise of better compatibility between different areas of life. Instead of organising life around formal employment, it enables employees to place family, community involvement or leisure at the centre of their lives. In many cases, however, employees in flexible working time regimes which go beyond simple flexitime models tend to work more. This additional work can take the form of either intensification (more work carried out during the same time period) or extensification (paid but often also unpaid overtime) (Kelliher/Anderson 2010; Lott/Chung 2016).

Working time flexibilisation has different effects according to the gender of the employees affected (Chung/van der Lippe 2018; Lott 2018). If flexibilisation is primarily geared to the interests of the company, the resultant problems in planning work processes make it more difficult for women in particular to organise their lives. If, however, employees can largely determine their own working hours, then men are much more likely to increase their work time significantly. Although women also tend to work more, they seem to be better able to distance themselves from the demands of formal employment. Mothers in flexible employment spend significantly more time looking after children, while fathers spend less time doing so the more flexible their working hours are (Lott 2019). Working time flexibilisation can thus consolidate the traditional gender roles.

Businesses can support the demarcation between formal employment and private life for their employees by, among other things, communicating in a time-conscious manner, i.e. by limiting company communications to certain days of the week (Mückenberger 2017). The traditional division of roles between the sexes can be mitigated somewhat if working hours are also documented in flexible working time arrangements and "parental leave" is recognised as conducive to career development (Lott 2019).

5.2 Internal working time reduction

Growth societies tend to transform various forms of unpaid work into formal employment (Barth et al. 2019). This shifts the boundary between different life spheres in favour of formal employment, which often results in too little time to care for relatives, or to devote to community involvement or personal development. The concept of "life courses with room to breathe" (Jurczyk/Mückenberger 2020) takes into account the different time requirements of these life spheres. Employees should be enabled, with social security cover, to pursue other ways of contributing to society. "Time drawing rights" (Mückenberger 2011, 2017) would give employees a legal entitlement to paid and socially secured time off, for example for socially necessary activities or for leisure. This model combines and extends existing rights such as parental allowances and educational leave. Depending on the purpose, the financing would be provided either by the state (parental allowance), the company (educational leave) or the employees themselves (sabbatical). People's life courses would thus become more independent of the prevailing economic and workplace situation.

Such forms of internal working time reduction are not only crucial over the course of one's life, but also for managing everyday life.

Extending the right to reduce working time internally – in a similar way to the right to stay at home with sick children – to other socially necessary and desirable activities may be an important step towards a society focused on meaningful activity rather than work. In this way companies can promote "investing time in the environment" (Rinderspacher 1996), for example by recognising as working time the longer travelling times of employees who cycle to work (Doiber 2018). Other possible options would be time off for harvest weeks in solidarity-based farming or for volunteer work. In Germany, such dispensations already exist for political office and for the voluntary fire brigade or the Federal German Agency for Technical Relief. In principle, such forms of the reallocation of working time are in a trade-off relationship with external working time reduction: the more working time is reduced in absolute terms, the less scope there is for forms of internal working time reduction (Mückenberger 2017).

5.3 External working time reduction

In regard to time-policy instruments, post-growth discourse is dominated by ideas about external reductions in working time (Hayden 1999; Kallis et al. 2013). A reduction in working time is considered an important pathway to a post-growth society, first because, in the absence of economic growth, the remaining formal employment can be distributed among a greater number of people, and second because workers are thereby given more time for sufficient and subsistence-based consumption (repairs, DIY) (Paech 2012). The successful implementation of short-time work in Germany during the last recession has also shown that a reduction in working hours can clearly strengthen resilience to fluctuations in economic growth. The loss of whole working days may also reduce environmental consumption that is directly linked to work, such as through commuting (King/van den Bergh 2017). However, additional commuting can also be generated if the existing formal employment is distributed among more people. A further rebound effect of external working time reductions can arise if additional leisure time is used in a way that is harmful to the environment (Buhl/Acosta 2016) – for example for air travel.

Whether working time reductions should be implemented with or without wage compensation is a controversial issue (see Reuter in this book). It is often assumed that a drop in income has a positive ecological impact (e.g. Hayden 1999). However, a loss of income often cannot be absorbed by low earners. Social policy measures that financially support low earners and families with children can contribute to an equitable expansion of free time (Goodin 2010). But reductions in working time can also be facilitated if the wage gap is narrowed so that low earners can afford to reduce their working hours or if employers compensate for the loss of earnings. From an economic perspective, wage compensation for a reduction in working time would make the input factor labour more expensive. However, it could also lead to better training of employees in order to increase their productivity (Kallis et al. 2013). In both cases, a reduction in working time accompanied by wage compensation would appear to result in an increase in productivity. It can then result in a boost to the economy, further increasing economic growth and resource consumption.

6 Time wealth

Businesses can also increase the time wealth of their employees without reducing working time.[4] Following Rinderspacher (2012) and Reisch (2001), we define time wealth as "sufficient time per activity (pace) with a sufficiently stable horizon of expectation (plannability) and satisfactory coordination of different temporal requirements (synchronisation) under sufficiently self-determined conditions (time sovereignty) and a reasonable amount of freely disposable time (free time)" (Jorck et al. 2019; adjusted translation). Unlike the debate on reducing working time, time wealth refers to both paid and unpaid work.

Time scarcity, as the negative counterpart to time wealth, is a potential driver of resource-intensive consumer habits (Reisch 2001, 2015). The desire to reduce or prevent time scarcity can lead to favouring acceleration technologies such as the car over more environmentally friendly technologies such as the bicycle. The stress caused by time scarcity can lead to compensatory consumption, such as a visit to the spa or a shopping spree. More intensive and more resource-consuming consumption can, in turn, increase the feeling of being pressed for time, as many of the goods purchased function as "time thieves" (Binswanger 2006).

Rosa (2010) calculates the pace of life by the "number of action or experience episodes per unit of time". The number of these action episodes per time unit can be capped by establishing a minimum staffing level, in the care sector for example, thus reducing time scarcity. Ultimately, a reduction in the pace of work equates to a reduction in labour productivity: less output is generated per labour input. However, if we also look at the quality of output, a reduction in the pace of work can actually increase labour productivity – for example, if patients are more satisfied because more time is devoted to them, and they perhaps recover faster. Without accompanying measures such as binding regional collective agreements, a minimum staffing level tends to reduce the competitiveness of businesses. Lower labour productivity can also lead to a decline in economic output if employment is not expanded at the same rate.

Greater co-determination over performance requirements at company level can also slow down the pace of life. "Collective periods of availability", where the operating time structures of a business are taken under review, represent one such measure (Mückenberger 2017). Such review or reflection periods can also reduce the disparity between environmental awareness and environmental behaviour (Chai et al. 2015). Although previous studies have focused on individuals, reflection periods at work could also help to ensure that the general concern for the environment gives rise to new behavioural priorities. Geiger et al. (Geiger et al. 2019) have shown that mindfulness courses within companies can contribute to a stronger prioritisation of social-ecological values.

However, companies determine not only the pace of work but often also their employees' planning horizons. This planning horizon can be shortened in several ways: through temporary employment, through sudden changes in operational procedures or through digital means of communication that make it possible to change deadlines at short notice. A shortening of the planning horizon makes it more difficult to synchronise different system times such as family time, working time, time for community involvement and personal time. There is a power hierarchy among these system times so that, as a rule, the requirements of working hours take precedence over social time, which, in turn, takes precedence over time for community involvement and personal time. By expanding the planning horizon, for example through long-term employment contracts and predictable operating schedules, companies can actively promote an equilibrium between the various system times.

7 Synopsis and conclusion

Businesses can make a significant contribution to sustainable work. Work is not just a passive object of social-ecological transformation; the way it is organised can make an active contribution to a sustainable way of living. Alternative economy organisations can teach us how paid and unpaid activities can mutually enrich each other. However, since engagement in the alternative economy often takes place in addition to traditional formal employment, conventional businesses also help set the framework for the development of new ways of working. Post-growth companies show how a time-sensitive corporate culture can positively influence formal employment. But even beyond these niches, businesses have a wide range of opportunities to organise work in a sustainable way. If they perceive their employees both as co-workers and as consumers, they can become places of learning for sustainable consumption and at the same time benefit from the sustainable consumption practices of their employees.

Businesses can also influence their employees' lives as managers of working time regimes. A flexibilisation of working time embedded in a time-conscious corporate culture can promote the compatibility of different areas of life. Internal working time reduction measures, such as time off for environmental activities, can promote sustainable consumption practices. Similarly, external working time reductions can facilitate time-intensive consumption practices such as repairs and DIY. However, ecological rebound effects from a reduction in working time can occur, for example if the free time gained is invested in more frequent travel.

Businesses influence not only the quantity of their employees' working time, but also its quality, via its speed, predictability and timing. The concept of time wealth integrates the quantitative and qualitative dimensions of time. By creating periods of reflection on time structures, or by enabling their employees to plan more confidently or by reducing the work tempo by setting minimum staffing levels, businesses can actively contribute to the time wealth of their employees.

Taken together, the measures discussed here represent possible paths towards a social-ecological transformation of the way we work and live. They are thus a contribution to the transition to a post-growth society in which the dominant position of formal employment and of consumption is reduced and other activities gain in importance.

Notes

* The authors wish to thank Viola Muster for her valuable comments.
1 Schor (1993) uses the term work-and-spend cycle to describe the phenomenon wherein formal employment serves primarily to satisfy growing consumer needs, which, in turn, motivate people to take up formal employment, so that productivity gains do not translate into more free time.
2 See the project "Integrating Employees as Consumers into Sustainability Innovation Processes", part of the Social-ecological Research programme of the Federal German Ministry of Education and Research (www.nachhaltigkeitsinnovation.de).
3 Jürgens (2009) uses this to mean actively managing the interactions and contradictions between formal employment and other areas of activity.
4 See the project "Time Rebound, Time Wealth and Sustainable Consumption", part of the Social-Ecological Research programme of the Federal German Ministry of Education and Research (www.time-rebound.de).

Bibliography

Barth, T., Jochum, G., Littig, B. (2019): *Transformation of what? Or: The socio-ecological transformation of working society*, IHS Working Paper No. 1, Vienna

Bauwens, M., Kostakis, V. (2014): *From the communism of capital to capital for the commons: Towards an open co-operativism*, TripleC: Communication, Capitalism & Critique, Open Access Journal for a Global Sustainable Information Society 12(1), 356–361

Bergmann, F. (2018): *New Work, New Culture: Work We Want and a Culture That Strengthens Us*, Winchester, Washington

Binswanger, M. (2006): *Why does income growth fail to make us happier?* The Journal of Socio-Economics 35(2), 366–381

Buhl, J., Acosta, J. (2016): *Work less, do less? Working time reductions and rebound effects*, Sustainability Science 11(2), 261–276

Chai, A., Bradley, G., Lo, A., Reser, J. (2015): *What time to adapt? The role of discretionary time in sustaining the climate change value-action gap*, Ecological Economics 116, 95–107

Chung, H., van der Lippe, T. (2018): *Flexible working, work–life balance, and gender equality: Introduction*, Social Indicators Research 151, 365–381

Doiber, M. (2018): *Arbeits- und Mobilitätszeit neu gedacht*, 4 Oktober 2018, Graz

Gebauer, J. (2018): *Towards growth-independent and post-growth-oriented entrepreneurship in the SME sector*, Management Revue 29(3), 230–256

Gebauer, J., Mewes, H. (2015): *Qualität und Suffizienz in stabilitätsorientierten KMU*, uwf UmweltWirtschaftsForum 23(1–2), 33–40

Geiger, S.M., Fischer, D., Schrader, U., Grossman, P. (2019): *Meditating for the planet: Effects of a mindfulness-based intervention on sustainable consumption behaviors*, Environment and Behavior 52(9), 1012–1042

Goodin, R.E. (2010): *Temporal justice*, Journal of Social Policy 39(1), 1–16

Hayden, A. (1999): *Sharing the Work, Sparing the Planet: Work Time, Consumption, & Ecology*, London

Houtbeckers, E. (2018): *Framing social enterprise as post-growth organising in the diverse economy*, Management Revue 29(3), 257–280

Jorck, G. von, Gerold, S., Geiger, S., Schrader, U. (2019): *Time Wealth: Working Paper on the Definition of Time Wealth in the Research Project ReZeitKon*, Berlin

Jurczyk, K., Mückenberger, U. (2020): *Selbstbestimmte Optionszeiten im Erwerbsverlauf: Forschungsprojekt im Rahmen des „Fördernetzwerks Interdisziplinäre Sozialpolitikforschung" (FIS)*, München

Jürgens, K. (2009): *Arbeits- und Lebenskraft: Reproduktion als eigensinnige Grenziehung*, Wiesbaden

Kallis, G., Kalush, M., O.'Flynn, H., Rossiter, J., Ashford, N. (2013): *"Friday off": Reducing working hours in Europe*, Sustainability, 5(12), 1545–1567

Kelliher, C., Anderson, D. (2010): *Doing more with less? Flexible working practices and the intensification of work*, Human Relations 63(1), 83–106

King, L.C., van den Bergh, J. (2017): *Worktime reduction as a solution to climate change: Five scenarios compared for the UK*, Ecological Economics 132, 124–134

Lange, B., Bürkner, H.-J. (2018): *Open workshops as sites of innovative socio-economic practices: approaching urban post-growth by assemblage theory*, Local Environment 23(7), 680–696

Lott, Y. (2018): *Does flexibility help employees switch off from work? Flexible working-time arrangements and cognitive work-to-home spillover for women and men in Germany*, Social Indicators Research 151, 471–494

Lott, Y. (2019): *Weniger Arbeit, mehr Freizeit? Wofür Mütter und Väter flexible Arbeitszeitarrangements nutzen*, WSI Report No. 47

Lott, Y., Chung, H. (2016): *Gender discrepancies in the outcomes of schedule control on overtime hours and income in Germany*, European Sociological Review 32(6), 752–765

Marx, K. (1996): *Capital: Vol. 1*, London

Mückenberger, U. (2011): *Time abstraction, temporal policy and the right to one's own time*, KronoScope 11(1–2), 66–97

Mückenberger, U. (2017): *Rechtliche Beiträge zu einer zeitachtsamen familienfreundlicheren Veränderung der Arbeitskultur*, Berlin

Muster, V. (2012): *Negative influences of working life on sustainable consumption*, International Journal of Consumer Studies 36(2), 166–172

Muster, V., Schrader, U. (2011): *Green Work-life balance: A new perspective for green HRM*, German Journal of Research in Human Resource Management 25(2), 140–156

Paech, N. (2012): *Liberation from Excess: The Road to a Post-growth Economy*, München

Rätzer, M., Hartz, R., Winkler, I. (2018): *Editorial: Post-growth organizations*, Management Revue 29(3), 193–205

Reisch, L.A. (2001): *Time and wealth*, Time & Society 10(2–3), 367–385

Reisch, L.A. (2015): *Time Policies for Sustainable Societies*, Cham

Rinderspacher, J.P. (1996): *Zeitinvestitionen in die Umwelt: Annäherung an ein ökologisches Handlungskonzept*, in: Rinderspacher, J.P. (Ed.): Zeit für die Umwelt Handlungskonzepte für eine ökologische Zeitverwendung, Berlin, 69–129

Rinderspacher, J.P. (2012): *Zeitwohlstand – Kriterien für einen anderen Maßstab von Lebensqualität*, WISO – Wirtschafts- und Sozialpolitische Zeitschrift des ISW 35(1), 11–26

Rommel, J., Radtke, J., Jorck, G. von, Mey, F., Yildiz, Ö. (2018): *Community renewable energy at a crossroads: A think piece on degrowth, technology, and the democratization of the German energy system*, Journal of Cleaner Production 197, 1746–1753

Rosa, H. (2010): *Alienation and Acceleration: Towards a Critical Theory of Late-modern Temporality*, Malmö

Schmidt-Keilich, M., Schrader, U. (2019): *Sustainability innovation by integrating employees: The potential of sustainable embedded lead users*, International Journal of Innovation and Sustainable Development 13(1), 98–115

Scholz, T. (2016): *Platform Cooperativism: Challenging the Corporate Sharing Economy*, New York

Schor, J.B. (1993): *The Overworked American: The Unexpected Decline of Leisure*, New York

Schor, J.B. (2011): *True Wealth: How and Why Millions of Americans Are Creating a Time-rich, Ecologically Light, Small-scale, High-satisfaction Economy*, New York

Schrader, U., Harrach, C. (2013): *Empowering responsible consumers to be sustainable intrapreneurs*, in: Schrader, U., Fricke, V., Doyle, D., Thoresen, V.W. (Eds): Enabling Responsible Living, Berlin, 181–192

Staab, P., Nachtwey, O. (2016): *Market and labour control in digital capitalism*, TripleC: Communication, Capitalism & Critique, Open Access Journal for a Global Sustainable Information Society 14(2), 457–474

Süßbauer, E., Maas-Deipenbrock, R.M., Friedrich, S., Kreß-Ludwig, M., Langen, N., Muster, V. (2019): *Employee roles in sustainability transformation processes: A move away from expertise and towards experience-driven sustainability management*, GAIA 28(1), 210–217

UNDP (2015): *Human Development Report 2015: Work for Human Development*, New York

7 Employment in the tension between ecology and distributive justice

The role of trade unions

Norbert Reuter

Summary

With their regular wage demands, the trade unions are often perceived by ecologically minded people in particular as drivers of economic growth. However, foregoing wage demands is not an option for contributing to lower growth and an ecologically sound economy: only capital would then reap the rewards of productivity gains, in the form of higher profits. One way out of this dilemma is to reduce working hours. This means that productivity gains are not channelled into growth and thus greater environmental damage, but into more leisure time. The recent renaissance of working time policy in collective agreements is therefore also a good sign from an ecological point of view.

1 The basic problem

In market economy or capitalist systems[1] based on private ownership of the means of production, employment, with wages negotiated between employees and employers, in principle secures people's livelihoods. The better the economic performance of a country – usually measured as gross domestic product (GDP)[2] – the higher people's incomes can be. And the higher the growth rate of GDP, the greater the scope for income growth. From this perspective, therefore, growth has an extremely positive effect.

However, this changes dramatically when the ecological dimension is included. Then, any (further) growth in the advanced countries with continually rising incomes is a step towards a foreseeable global ecological catastrophe. The trade unions also recognise the dilemma between "change by design" and "change by disaster" – i.e. the alternative between deliberately designed change and change enforced by (ecological) catastrophes.

DOI: 10.4324/9781003187370-7

2 The socio-ecological dual character of formal employment

2.1 Formal employment to secure income

Under market economy conditions, all income (national income) is divided between compensation of employees (gross wages and salaries, including employers' social security contributions) and profits (corporate and property income). An increase in national income always occurs when the productivity of the labour force increases, i.e. when more value is created per hour worked (so-called "intensive growth").[3] Up to now, all developing countries have been characterised by a persistent increase in productivity, driven primarily by technological development, although it can generally be observed that in the long term productivity decreases and thus growth rates also decline in the course of economic development (for more detail see Reuter 2000).[4]

In the economy as a whole, higher productivity automatically leads to an increase in profits as long as labour income does not increase. However, there is no corresponding mechanism for increasing compensation of employees. It is therefore a central task of trade unions to ensure that employees get their fair share of productivity gains through periodic collective bargaining – via higher incomes, shorter working hours with full wage compensation or a combination of both. Without such (hourly) wage increases, which have to be fought for time and again, the increase in national income resulting from ongoing productivity increases would flow exclusively into profits. For this reason, a crucial benchmark in collective bargaining negotiations is whether and how far it is possible to exploit the so-called "distribution leeway", which is made up of the percentage increase in productivity and the inflation rate, by means of wage increases. Only if this is fully exploited will the distribution of income between labour and capital remain the same. This can be seen over time in the so-called wage share, which shows the percentage share of national income accounted for by the compensation of employees.

In the past – especially between the years 2000 and 2007 – the German trade unions were not always successful in fully exploiting the distribution leeway in collective bargaining negotiations. As a result of the Red-Green Federal Government's "Agenda 2010",[5] which entailed reduced non-wage labour costs, liberalisation of temporary work, extended possibilities for fixed-term employment contracts, mini-jobs and, in particular, the "Hartz IV" approach which shifted the balance from social support towards social obligations, wages and working conditions came under massive pressure in the 2000s. In January 2005, the then Federal Chancellor Gerhard Schröder was able to announce at the

World Economic Forum in Davos: "We have built up one of the best low-wage sectors in Europe" (Schröder 2005). This has not changed to date. The proportion of low-paid workers[6] in Germany rose to around a quarter of all employees by 2008 and has remained at this level ever since. Germany thus has one of the largest low-wage sectors in Europe (Grabka/Schröder 2019).

As a result, the wage share, i.e. the proportion of national income going to wages, fell from just under 72 percent in 2000 to 63.6 percent in 2007. Although it has risen again since then, it is today around 69 percent, still well below the level of the period before 2000. This represents a considerable historical redistribution from wages to profits (for details of redistribution in Germany, see Wehler 2013). This redistribution "from the bottom to the top" is also confirmed by The German Federal Government's 5th Report on Poverty and Wealth. This states that the gap between rich and poor is getting bigger and bigger, which is shown, among other things, by the fact that "households in the lower half of the distribution only own about 1 percent of total net assets, while the 10 percent of households with the highest assets have more than half of total net assets". The share of the wealthiest households in total assets "has continued to rise over time" (Federal Ministry of Labour and Social Affairs 2017).

It is therefore the historical task of the trade unions to ensure that workers receive their fair share of economic growth in the primary distribution of income by implementing a continuous increase in (hourly) wages – at least as long as there is still economic growth. Anything else would contribute to a further redistribution from "labour" to "capital", without this unilateral renunciation having any positive ecological consequences. At the same time, they are using their political influence to push through reforms in the political sphere which, through improved secondary distribution,[7] counteract a growing division in society.

2.2 Formal employment and its environmental consequences

In the course of their economic development, all societies are subject to two fundamental, interwoven trends: the trend towards a service society and the trend towards declining growth rates mentioned above (Reuter 2010). Without these two trends, the ecological situation would undoubtedly be even more dramatic than it already is. Above all, the trend towards a service society[8] could be massively strengthened by a comprehensive expansion of necessary public services – especially in Germany, which lags significantly behind other Western societies in this respect.

From an ecological point of view, the necessity for higher wages in order to redistribute the gains from continued productivity growth is of course problematic – after all, at least at first glance, this corresponds exactly to the consumption and growth logic, involving a commitment to "always more" and "always higher", which is the core of our ecological problems. Ecological activists therefore often perceive the trade unions as growth fetishists and thus as their adversaries. And indeed, economic growth has so far been directly linked to an increase in the "ecological footprint", i.e. the area of land every individual requires to meet their resource needs and neutralise their waste. An absolute decoupling of economic growth from the consumption of natural resources is not in sight. How can this dilemma be resolved?

The ecological footprint of people in the "Global North" is already far too large. We would need two earths for the current development to be sustainable – and the trend is rising. The recent summers, with their extreme weather events and crop failures, have suddenly made it clear that our "imperial way of life" (Brand/Wissen 2021) threatens the lives of billions of people on earth (Tallig 2018). The demand for a massive contraction of GDP,[9] the most obvious response, cannot be one that trade unions can take on board in view of the consequences for jobs. In order to find appropriate solutions, we have to distinguish between, on the one hand, areas which – for ecological reasons – need to grow (e.g. renewable energies) and, on the other hand, areas which need to shrink or disappear (e.g. coal production). In the service sector (e.g. health, education, care), there is in fact an enormous need for growth and thus for jobs, growth which in addition results in comparatively low ecological follow-up costs.[10] This is an area where the state, on behalf of the whole of society, has an obligation to act. An intelligent policy (commandments and prohibitions, tax incentives and tax burdens, exit scenarios, etc.) would have to effectively promote the one and reduce the other.

In any case, trade union restraint in collective bargaining would therefore not be a suitable contribution to an ecological economy, as it would primarily have a redistributive effect. It would not be the environment that would benefit, but instead, as explained above, principally those whose income comes from profits and property, who would then be able to carry on increasing their consumption of luxury goods.

3 The "magic triangle" of socio-ecological transformation

Trade unions consequently face a dilemma. On the one hand, they recognise that the path of continuous economic growth is ecologically disastrous and see the need for a comprehensive restructuring of our economic system. On the other hand, they are not an environmental organisation and their assertiveness depends directly on the number of

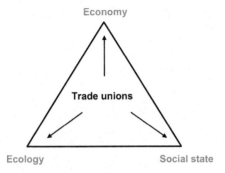

Figure 7.1 The magic triangle of transformation from a trade union perspective

their members. However, joining a trade union is not about saving the environment, but about securing jobs, better pay and improved working conditions (Figure 7.1).

In contrast to environmental associations, which can concentrate primarily on measures that lead to a rapid and massive reduction in ecological damage, trade unions, notwithstanding their sense of ecological responsibility, must consider the economic and above all the social consequences with regard to employees. In a sense, they are operating within a "magic triangle", whereby the adjective "magic", as in the classic "magic square of economic policy",[11] expresses the fact that it is almost impossible to achieve all objectives simultaneously:

- From an economic perspective, the conditions for economic reproduction (above all, profits to secure necessary investments) must be ensured so that ecological restructuring can take place and resource-saving technical developments can be implemented.
- From a social perspective, it is essential to ensure that some social groups (employees, the unemployed, pensioners) do not lose out in the transformation.
- From an ecological perspective, we need to move away from the previous development and (above all) growth models of the global North (which means "degrowth" or "post-growth").

Against this background, it is important from a trade union point of view to develop and pursue strategies that minimise the existing conflicts between objectives, i.e. not to play off jobs, labour income or the welfare state against ecological considerations. Here, the trade unions, as powerful organisations (the German Trade Union Confederation has almost six million members), can exercise their considerable influence on political decision-making and economic developments to support the socio-ecological transformation within the framework of their core business, which is collective bargaining policy.

4 Trade union approaches to socio-ecological transformation

4.1 The political level

Trade unions have never seen themselves merely as a lobby organisation pushing for higher wages, but have always assumed a responsibility for society as a whole. Not least because they represent the interests of millions of employees, they are constantly represented in important state commissions, public hearings and political advisory bodies. Here, together with other civil society organisations, they often work against massive resistance from powerful corporate and profit interests, for example in support of poverty-proof pensions, a fair tax policy or strengthening the welfare state, but also for a socially acceptable exit from the nuclear and coal industries or for setting limits on resource consumption and CO_2 emissions.

One of the major political successes of the trade unions in recent times in Germany was the introduction of the statutory minimum wage at the beginning of 2015. Since 2007, the German trade unions had fought a large-scale campaign for its introduction. This was a way of counteracting increasing income inequality. Tax policy also remains an important area. Time and again, the trade unions have complained that German tax legislation is riddled with injustices and must take much stronger corrective action against the increasingly unequal distribution of both income and (especially) wealth. Measured against their capacity to pay, the super-rich, multinational corporations and top earners contribute far too little to the financing of our society, while dependent employees finance the bulk of the federal, state and local budgets through direct taxes (principally income tax) and indirect taxes (principally VAT). Everywhere, public budgets lack financial resources – be it for education, adequate and efficient infrastructure or ecological restructuring. So public budgets lack the financial means to meet the valid claims of a modern state capable of acting and facing the future. The trade unions try to influence tax policy with their own detailed tax plans (see inter alia ver.di 2014a).

In addition, the trade unions – for example within the framework of the German Federal Parliament's Enquete Commission on "Growth, Well-being and Quality of Life" (2011–2013) – have spoken out in favour of political measures to improve efficiency (higher resource productivity, dematerialisation), consistency (environmental sustainability, quality) and sufficiency (self-limitation, moderation). The addressee here is also the state, which can initiate and strengthen the necessary developments by means of instruments such as taxes and charges and fiscal policy, but also through property policy and through legislation and regulations (see Deutscher Bundestag 2013, 126–189, special vote).

As in the case of the Enquete Commission, trade unions use the opportunities they have to work towards ecological restructuring by making public calls for action from politicians, based on scientific advice. With a view to ecologically necessary changes in energy supply, for example, the German service trade union ver.di demanded several years ago already that firm expansion targets for renewable energies, and clear guidelines for the integration of renewable energies into the electricity market, should be drawn up for Germany and the EU. The federal and state governments were called upon to specify the expansion targets for wind energy and photovoltaics in more concrete terms and at regional level. At the same time, ver.di appealed to the EU to constructively accompany the German path towards an energy transition. To this end, it called for binding targets for the expansion of renewable energies in all EU member states by 2030 (ver.di 2014b).

In order to underpin these demands and their feasibility, ver.di also commissioned a report (Enervis 2016) on how to make the coal phase-out socially fair and acceptable. Using various scenarios, the researchers were able to show that the coal phase-out could be carried out in a socially responsible manner and could be financed through the trading of CO_2 emissions certificates.

4.2 The collective bargaining level

However, the real level of action for trade unions is that of collective bargaining policy (see Reuter/Sterkel 2019). It is the core business of the trade unions, and here their influence is particularly strong and direct because of the right to free collective bargaining enshrined in Article 9 (3) of the German Basic Law. This gives trade unions the right to conclude agreements with employers on working and economic conditions free from state intervention, thus ensuring that employees get their share of the increase in national income (making full use of the distribution leeway). This is traditionally done through wage increases agreed in collective bargaining negotiations.

Another way to ensure a fair share is to reduce working hours with (as far as possible) full wage compensation.[12] Since this increases hourly wages, but reduces working time accordingly, meaning that total income (including profits) does not increase, this way of exploiting the distribution leeway has a growth-dampening effect. In other words, in terms of the "magic triangle" of transformation, a reduction in working time with full wage compensation reduces the conflict between objectives described above when compared with wage increases.

Initially, the trade unions called for a reduction in working hours mainly to combat rampant and long-standing mass unemployment. In 1965, a 40-hour week was introduced in the printing industry, followed by a 38.5-hour week in the metal industry, in wholesale trade and in the public sector between 1984 and 1990. However, the last significant step was taken a long time ago – the introduction of the 35-hour working week in the printing, metal and electrical industries in 1995. Since then, there have been no major steps towards further collective reductions in working time. In fact, there has been a long period of silence around the issue of working time. Other issues were on the agenda due to the decline in the wage share and massive attacks on the collective bargaining system, and environmental topics did not yet carry the weight they do today. To the extent that the issue of working time returned to the agenda at all in collective bargaining disputes, it did so in a sense in the opposite direction: in some sectors, employers were and still are pressing for working hours to be extended again. So just being able to fend off an extension of working time in individual collective bargaining disputes often represented a success.

Against this background, developments in recent years on the working time issue can be regarded as quite positive. Collective bargaining on working time policy has become much more important again alongside the issue of pay. In 2015 a new optional model was introduced in the Austrian electrical and electronics industry for the first time, allowing employees to choose between "more money" and "more holidays". It came as a surprise to all those involved that it was not – as the employers had expected – mainly older employees using the model to enable a smooth transition into retirement, but rather preponderantly younger employees who chose to reduce working hours instead of increasing wages. This is often seen as evidence of the ongoing change in values among the younger generation (Burchardt 2017, see also Gerold in this book).

After the Railway and Transport Union (EVG) and Deutsche Bahn AG agreed on an optional model for the first time in Germany in 2016, and IG Metall succeeded in implementing a similar model for the metal and electrical industry (albeit with the simultaneous option of extending working hours), ver.di was also able to implement a series of collective agreements with options for shorter working hours with full wage compensation – for example with Deutsche Post AG, and with the Bavarian local transport companies. In 2018, a collective bargaining agreement on the reduction of working hours was then successfully concluded once more: in the major operating units of Deutsche Telekom AG, a reduction in weekly working time from 38 to 36 hours with partial wage compensation was negotiated to safeguard jobs.

A common feature of the more recent agreements on reducing working hours is that they are generally not implemented in the form of a weekly reduction in working time, but in the form of additional days off or holidays. This is intended to prevent the reduction in working time from leading to an additional intensification of work, which was often the result of reductions in weekly working time in the past.

The key objective for ver.di therefore remains "short full-time work for all". To this end, a model has been developed which combines a collectively agreed reduction in the working hours of full-time employees with the possibility for employees on (involuntary) part-time contracts to increase their working hours (ver.di 2018). "Short full-time work for all" has also made it easier to reconcile work and private life.

5 The role of the trade unions in "change by design"

Unions recognise that continued economic growth in the developed industrialised countries of the Global North is increasingly creating more problems than it solves. But foregoing wage increases would not be a solution, and would not help to curb the underlying momentum for growth. It would only leave the field even more open to those who receive income from profits and capital assets, to the greater detriment of the broad population who depend on earned income.[13] Existing problems relating to distributive justice would thus already be exacerbated at the level of primary distribution.

This is why trade unions use their influence in society in different ways and at different political levels to achieve a fairer distribution and at the same time to push ahead with the necessary socio-ecological transformation, without this being one-sidedly at the expense of employees, the unemployed and pensioners.

In addition to these important political strategies and initiatives, the unions try to set positive accents in their collective bargaining policy. Recent collective bargaining negotiations, for example, have again been able to focus more strongly on the issue of reducing working hours. New opportunities to take additional days off instead of wage increases reduce some of the strain on employees, but at the same time secure their fair share of productivity gains. Initial experience shows that the majority of the employees concerned, especially the younger ones, make use of and appreciate more leisure time rather than more income and consumption. The trend towards more qualitative elements in collective agreements is therefore likely to continue in future collective bargaining rounds.

Models with options give employees the opportunity to express their changing preferences and therefore reflect an ongoing change in values at an achieved high income level.

As employees in more and more sectors take advantage of the opportunity to have more leisure time instead of higher income, the trade unions are thereby helping to mitigate the conflict between economic, social and ecological objectives in their core area, collective bargaining policy. In this way, productivity gains, which are declining but can be expected to continue at a lower level for the foreseeable future, and which therefore call for continuing redistribution measures, are being channelled not into growth and thus more environmental damage but into less working time. This opens up an opportunity for prosperity no longer to be equated primarily with increased consumption of goods and thus with economic growth, but for a new kind of prosperity to emerge – time prosperity, or time wealth. It is crucial that employees make greater use of this opportunity. This requires supportive political decisions, above all in the areas of tax, social security and fiscal policy, which at the same time need to counteract the growing inequality in distribution (see the chapter by G. Kubon-Gilke in this book).

All collective political strategies – at both the political and the civil society level – for socio-ecological transformation will only be successful, however, if as many people as possible are willing to support them through behaviour that is geared towards reducing their individual ecological footprint.

Notes

1 Capitalist systems are usually understood as a particularly pronounced form of market economy in which the (social) state plays only a subordinate role and "free" market forces can operate largely without restrictions. In this sense, Hall/Soskice (2001, 19f.) distinguish between "liberal market economies" (e.g. the USA) with a weak welfare state and "coordinated market economies" (e.g. Germany) with a strong, regulating welfare state.
2 GDP measures the total value of all goods and services supplied as final products in an economy during a year.
3 Intensive growth must be distinguished from extensive growth, which is not the result of productivity gains, but of the application of more hours worked, for example because of immigration or an extension of working hours.
4 Zinn (2015) assumes that without growth capitalism will also reach its historical end.
5 The "Agenda 2010" was one of the most controversial projects for the reform of the social security system and the labour market in German post-war history. It was implemented between 2003 and 2005 by the federal government formed by the SPD and Bündnis 90/Die Grünen (second Cabinet under Chancellor Gerhard Schröder).

6 "Low wage" is defined as a gross hourly wage of less than two-thirds of the median wage of all employees.

7 Primary distribution becomes secondary distribution through the targeted use of state revenues: the state redistributes parts of its revenues as transfer payments according to social criteria – as a cash benefit (e.g. housing benefit) or as a non-cash benefit (e.g. subsidised places in pre-school nurseries).

8 Jean Fourastié (1949/1969) designated this trend the "great hope of the 20th century" and described it comprehensively at the theoretical level by identifying the driving forces.

9 Matthias Schmelzer and Alexis Passadakis, for example, consider a 25 percent decline in GDP in the industrialised countries necessary (Schmelzer/ Passadakis 2011).

10 Services consume the least energy of all production sectors – for every euro of value added, just one-sixtieth of the primary energy consumption of manufacturing industry (Reuter 2016, p. 123f.).

11 The "magic square" dates back to the German Stability Act of 1967, which describes four economic policy objectives that are in conflict with each other: price stability, high employment rates, an external trade balance and steady and satisfactory economic growth.

12 Without full wage compensation, i.e. with a reduction in labour income, the primary distribution would shift at the expense of the recipients of labour income.

13 Similar problems seem likely to arise from a state-funded Unconditional Basic Income (UBI), which is sometimes discussed in ecological circles as a way of breaking out of the "growth spiral". Daniel Kreutz (2010, 69) rightly pointed out that in the end it only "plays into the hands of the friends of capitalism" because companies would be the ultimate beneficiaries: "Wages then represent (after the introduction of a UBI, N.R.) a less important 'additional income'. A minimum wage would then only have to be high enough to bring about a noticeable and therefore attractive net improvement in income above the UBI. One euro per hour could be quite sufficient for this purpose". A recent publication by Johannes Mosmann (2019, 75) suggests the same thing. The author shows that "an unconditional basic income represents an unprecedented social cost-cutting programme" and thus "would be taking the principle of Agenda 2010 to the extreme".

Bibliography

Brand, U., Wissen, M. (2021): *The Imperial Mode of Living: Everyday Life and the Ecological Crisis of Capitalism*, London

Burchardt, H.-J. (2017): *It's about time, stupid! Die Vermessung des guten Lebens zwischen Status quo und Wertewandel*, Leviathan 45(2), 255–280

Deutscher Bundestag (2013): *Schlussbericht der Enquete-Kommission „Wachstum, Wohlstand, Lebensqualität – Wege zu nachhaltigem Wirtschaften und gesellschaftlichem Fortschritt in der Sozialen Marktwirtschaft"*, Berlin

Enervis (2016): *Sozialverträgliche Ausgestaltung eines Kohlekonsenses*, ver.di – Vereinte Dienstleistungsgewerkschaft, September 2016, ver-und-entsorgung. verdi.de (accessed 21.01.2021)

Federal Ministry of Labour and Social Affairs (Ed.) (2017): *Life situations in Germany, The German Federal Government's 5th Report on Poverty and Wealth.* Executive Summary, Bonn

Fourastié, J. (1949/1969): *Die große Hoffnung des zwanzigsten Jahrhunderts,* 2d ed, Köln (Orig.: Le grand espoir du XXe siècle. Progrès technique, progrès économique, progrès social, Paris, 1949)

Grabka, M.M., Schröder, C. (2019): *The low-wage sector in Germany is larger than previously assumed,* DIW Weekly Report 14, 118–124

Hall, P.A., Soskice, D. (2001): An introduction to varieties of capitalism, in: Hall, P.A., Soskice, D. (Eds.): Varieties of Capitalism – The Institutional Foundations of Comparative Advantage, Oxford, 1–68

Kreutz, D. (2010): *Bedingungslose Freiheit? Warum die Grundeinkommensdebatte den Freunden des Kapitalismus in die Hände spielt,* Blätter für deutsche und internationale Politik 4, 65–77

Mosmann, J. (2019): *Das bedingungslose Grundeinkommen: Pathologie und Wirkung einer sozialen Bewegung,* Berlin

Reuter, N. (2000): *Ökonomik der „Langen Frist". Zur Evolution der Wachstumsgrundlagen in Industriegesellschaften,* Marburg

Reuter, N. (2010): *Der Arbeitsmarkt im Spannungsfeld von Wachstum, Ökologie und Verteilung,* in: Seidl, I., Zahrnt, A. (Eds.): Postwachstumsgesellschaft. Konzepte für die Zukunft, Marburg, 85–102

Reuter, N. (2016): *Der Ausbau von Dienstleistungen als Grundlage einer Postwachstumsgesellschaft,* in: Arbeitskreis Postwachstum. (Ed.): Wachstum – Krise und Kritik. Die Grenzen der kapitalistisch-industriellen Lebensweise, Frankfurt, New York, 115–134

Reuter, N., Sterkel, G. (2019): *Tarifpolitik für ein gutes Leben. Nachholbedarf bei den Löhnen und Initiativen gegen Überlastung und soziale Spaltung,* in: Schröder, L., Urban, H.-J. (Eds.): Transformation der Arbeit – Ein Blick zurück nach vorn (Jahrbuch Gute Arbeit 2019), Frankfurt a. M., 224–239

Schmelzer, M., Passadakis, A. (2011): *Postwachstum. Krise, ökologische Grenzen und soziale Rechte,* Attac Basistexte 36, Hamburg

Schröder, G. (2005): *Rede von Bundeskanzler Gerhard Schröder vor dem world economic forum in Davos,* www.gewerkschaft-von-unten.de/Rede_Davos.pdf (accessed 20.01.2021)

Tallig, J. (2018): *Earth first: Der Preis des Lebens,* Blätter für deutsche und internationale Politik 10, 67–76

ver.di (2014a): *Konzept Steuergerechtigkeit. Ergebnisse der Aktualisierung und Verteilung der Mehreinnahmen auf Bundesländer und ihre Städte und Gemeinden,* Berlin

ver.di (2014b): *Pressemitteilung: ver.di fordert verlässliche Ausbauziele der erneuerbaren Energien für Deutschland und die EU,* www.verdi.de/presse/pressemitteilungen (accessed 20.01.2021)

ver.di (2018): *Mehr Zeit für mich. Das Konzept der Verfügungszeit. Impulse für eine neue Arbeitszeitpolitische Debatte,* 2nd edBerlin

Wehler, H.-U. (2013): *Die neue Umverteilung. Soziale Ungleichheit in Deutschland,* München

Zinn, K.G. (2015): *Vom Kapitalismus ohne Wachstum zur Marktwirtschaft ohne Kapitalismus,* Hamburg

8 Voluntary charitable activity

Motivation, requirements, accomplishments

*Theo Wehner**

Summary

People who engage in voluntary charitable activity are motivated first and foremost at a personal level: they see a need and
a necessity for their volunteering. They get involved for altruistic motives, but can also pursue self-referential goals such as
recognition, social relationships or the acquisition of skills. The
most important criteria for successful or satisfying charitable
engagement are meaningfulness and autonomy in the activity.
Voluntary charitable activity can provide a counterbalance to
externally determined formal employment but does not change
the structure of organised formal employment under capitalism. Voluntary charitable activity, which up to now has been
widespread at the centre of bourgeois society, is facing numerous challenges, which reflect, among other things, the changes
in a society hitherto structured around formal employment.

1 Voluntary charitable activity[1] and its relationship to the "work society"

The unpaid and unassigned giving of help, whether within families, between friends, in the neighbourhood or in the international community, is not the result of clever campaigns and is not an anthropological
constant; nor however is it independent of the society in which it occurs. This applies to philanthropy, honorary posts, work in community
associations and modern forms of voluntary work (online volunteering,
voluntourism). The spontaneous giving of help (such as helping someone who is disabled to cross the street) and so-called ongoing pro-social
behaviour (visiting someone with dementia in their home) must first
and foremost be desired, but not necessarily organised, from the outside:
voluntary charitable activity begins with an individual's recognition of
a need or injustice experienced by individuals or groups – and not with

DOI: 10.4324/9781003187370-8

a socially created organisational framework or incentive structure. Even if the creation of structures is often the result of spontaneous civic involvement, they emerge after people with a shared concern join forces. Two examples: the inhabitants of a village informally agreed on who is to take on the fire watch at night-time; the voluntary fire brigade was only organised as a result of this spontaneous commitment, and today we also encounter it in the form of a professional fire brigade. Today's voluntourism (volunteer work while travelling abroad) was pioneered by individual young people travelling through South America and stopping off to work unpaid on a cooperative coffee plantation, for example.

As a rule, tax breaks and other benefits for voluntary charitable activity were not required for people to get involved, and nor are they now, but are primarily intended to support and promote the involvement of government bodies and non-profit organisations. Such incentives carry the risk that they may undermine the personal motivation of the volunteers.

In short, voluntary charitable activity is primarily dependent on personal interests, needs, attitudes and motivation. The political framework, civil society structures and organisational support from commercial and non-profit organisations all represent a response to voluntary initiatives. In this chapter, we argue that anyone investigating the organisation of voluntary charitable activities must start from a person-centred perspective on the nature of such behaviour – and this is exactly what this chapter does.

Since individual behaviour cannot be understood in isolation from traditions and social relations (Leontjev 1978), the following thesis applies here: anyone who talks about voluntary work or honorary posts is always also talking about the particular "work society" in which such work is carried out.

By looking at voluntary charitable activity in relation to formal employment, research into the labour psychology of voluntary work seeks at the same time to re-evaluate all activities – from work for oneself to housework and formal employment. In this context, the functions served by formal employment "as the linchpin for the life orientation of the individual and for the community" (Senghaas-Knobloch 1999, 119) are of central importance. Formal employment serves not only to secure livelihoods but to provide psycho-social orientation, social security and civic integration. This is the basis for the argument that engagement on behalf of the common good cannot be a refuge or a form of compensation for the experience of alienation, inadequate recognition in labour relations or an unfair social system.

It is well documented that people engaged in voluntary charitable activity often experience their work as self-determined whereas they perceive their formal employment as externally determined (Jaeggi 2014).

Although voluntary charitable activity can thus offer a counterbalance to formal employment, it does not change the structure of a capitalist society organised around formal employment in which that voluntary work is carried out.

2 Voluntary charitable activity: what is it, and what are the underlying motivations and expectations?

The following section presents – in very condensed form – the state of the art in research into volunteering. Many topics have been left out, such as problems of volunteer leadership or cooperation with paid staff in volunteer organisations. These topics have not yet been researched in sufficient depth and generalisations are therefore not possible. Caution is also called for when comparing, for example, timebanking schemes,[2] the European Voluntary Service[3] or voluntourism[4] with traditional voluntary work: there are not only quantitative, but also major qualitative differences between such activities.

2.1 Voluntary charitable activity: definitions and boundaries

Voluntary charitable activity includes unpaid, organised community work; this means a personal, charitable commitment which involves a (regular) expenditure of time, which could in principle also be carried out by another person and which could also be paid if there were a market for it.

This excludes paid work, however poorly paid it may be; it also excludes personal relationships, because although these have a social character, they would not be paid for; it also excludes housework or care within a family, because the family is (still) an element of the community and not itself a community; this of course also applies to hobbies of all kinds. The charitable activities of social welfare recipients or prisoners also do not count as voluntary charitable activity, because they are not sufficiently voluntary; we also exclude donations, because the personal expenditure of time involved can be assumed to be minimal; however, the collecting of donations certainly falls within the scope of voluntary charitable activity.

2.2 What motivates voluntary charitable activity?

It has been demonstrated many times (Bierhoff 2002) that people who engage in voluntary charitable activity exhibit more altruistic personality traits. But there are also other factors that motivate people to engage in volunteering. They may pursue selfish goals, perhaps in order to further their qualifications or to convey their values. It is important to emphasise that they are intrinsically motivated and that excessive positive feedback or (inappropriate) compensation, praise, etc. (i.e. extrinsic incentives) can have a negative influence on their intrinsic motivation: the personal value involved can be undermined by receiving payment, since voluntary charitable activity then sinks into the category of paid or commissioned work.

Clary and Snyder (1999) list a number of other aims and conditions relevant to voluntary charitable activity: willingness to help, fair distribution, experience, skills acquisition and personal values. To these can be added the goal of justice (Jiranek et al. 2013) and – for older people – the enrichment of everyday life (Oostlander et al. 2013).

2.2.1 Enrichment, autonomy, identity

In volunteer surveys (such as Simonson et al. 2016), volunteers are able to select from a list what it is that motivates them to get involved. In first and second place – all over the world – the most common selections are: "I enjoy it"; "I meet people and make friends". There are usually considerably more than two motivations involved: "It is the satisfaction of seeing results"; "It helps me to stay active and healthy"; "It expands my life experience"; "It gives me the opportunity to learn new skills, to win more social recognition and a place in the community, and to maintain and communicate my moral, religious or political principles". Voluntary charitable activity is thus perceived as a multi-faceted enrichment.

Even though those engaged in voluntary charitable activity in civil society are often considered selfless, to put it in simplified terms, the self-referential motive of autonomy is central for those engaged in the activity. It can be heard time and again in interviews and personal statements that self-determination was and is both the decisive initial motivating factor and the reason for continuing in voluntary charitable activity. Other synonyms are independence, freedom of choice and self-reliance. Even closer to the everyday use of the term "autonomy" is the term "autonomous action": this means an attempt to exclude interference by others and to place personal responsibility above determination from the outside.

In interviews with the author, people involved in voluntary charitable activity also always mentioned the desire for identity. In their respective activities, they were able to express very well "who I really am", or "what values I really stand up for". The findings of volunteer research reveal a need to act upon one's own values and communicate them to others, and thereby to gain attention, recognition and self-affirmation.

2.3 Who are the people engaged in voluntary charitable activity?

The majority of volunteers come from the mainstream of middle-class society, are mostly middle-aged, and likely to be well-educated and socially well integrated. People on the fringes of society, the unemployed or migrants rarely engage in voluntary charitable activity. In other words, one has to be able to afford to do unpaid voluntary work.

If we look at the reasons why people do not engage in voluntary charitable activity, the first things that come to light are as follows: 34 percent of the employees surveyed by the Körber Foundation in 2017[5] stated that they were not active in civil society, even though they would get involved if it was compatible with their work. This is in keeping with the findings of the German Volunteer Survey (Simonson et al. 2016) that occupational reasons are the most common grounds for quitting. At the same time, it shows that employers are not a catalyst for involvement in voluntary activity.

2.4 Criteria for good work and their ranking in formal employment and voluntary charitable activity

Industrial and organisational psychology has developed so-called "human-focused" criteria for good work – criteria which can and should also be applied to voluntary charitable activity. These criteria for good (formal) work (Ulich 2001) are social interaction, task diversity, learning and development opportunities, meaningfulness, holistic nature of the task, stress-free management and autonomy.

If people are asked (as in Wehner et al. 2005) about the relative significance of human-focused criteria in their voluntary charitable activities, then meaningfulness comes first and autonomy second, followed by learning and development opportunities, social interaction, a coherent or holistic task, stress-free management and task diversity (Table 8.1).

Classical management methods often fail to take such findings into account when applied in non-profit organisations. They must, however, be taken into account in the organisational support of non-profit organisations in order not to jeopardise the meaningfulness of the activity and the requirement for autonomy, because enforceable quality standards, standardised performance specifications, hierarchies, etc. often make it difficult to gain personal meaningfulness from an activity.

Table 8.1 Human-focused criteria for good work (based on Ulich 2001)

Ranking among voluntary charitable workers	Human-focused criteria for good work	Ranking among formal employees
1	Meaningfulness (concordance of social and individual interests)	4
2	Autonomy (responsibility, sense of self-esteem and professional competence)	7
3	Learning and development opportunities (maintaining and developing mental flexibility and vocational qualifications)	3
4	Social interaction (overcoming difficulties and burdens as a team)	1
5	Holistic nature of the task (being able to see the relevance of one's own work and getting performance feedback)	5
6	Stress-free management (scope for interaction, creativity and input into task design)	6
7	Task diversity (being able to deploy a variety of skills and to avoid one-dimensional tasks)	2

3 Some thoughts on the future of voluntary charitable activity

Discussions of post-growth society (e.g. Seidl/Zahrnt 2010) assume that formal employment will continue to play an important role, but that voluntary charitable activity will become increasingly relevant. The most important motivating factors for voluntary charitable activity, meaningfulness and autonomy will probably continue to remain valid in a post-growth society.

In a post-growth society, more people are likely to have more time for voluntary charitable activity because working hours are likely to be shorter, and more such involvement will be needed because it is likely that fewer state resources from tax revenues will be available for many social and environmental purposes. For this reason, and because increasing and qualitatively changing need and demand can already be perceived and predicted, the development of appropriate structures for voluntary charitable activity should now be planned and initiated.

The challenges for volunteering are manifold:

- Increasing demands on employees' mobility and flexibility make it more difficult for them to find suitable areas for their voluntary charitable activity. One solution is volunteer agencies,[6] which connect and mediate supply and demand.
- It is often very difficult to combine work that secures one's livelihood with charitable activities. Flexible and reduced working hours, among other things, can help here.
- Participation is declining and the number of openings for voluntary engagement is often greater than the number of active participants. Participation can be encouraged by a culture of public recognition (awards, publicity, written acknowledgement of contribution).
- Bureaucratisation affects volunteer work too, but it goes against the aspirations and desires of volunteers. A balance needs to be struck between efficiency and accountability on the one hand and self-determination for volunteers on the other.
- The tendency towards professionalisation, i.e. increasingly specialised knowledge and differentiated organisation, can also reduce the opportunities for volunteering. This can be countered by further training and the recognition and explicit integration of lay, practical and experiential knowledge.

The founder of Migros (Gottlieb Duttweiler)[7] was convinced that "voluntarism is the price of freedom". This freedom is achieved not only through a humanitarian spirit and an interest in the common good, but first and foremost through an income that enables a good living, which brings us back to our starting point: anyone who talks about volunteering is also talking about the "work society" in which it takes place.

It is a challenge for any society to be able to offer individuals and groups the framework conditions that enable them to successfully combine different domains of life. This should be easier to achieve in a post-growth society than in a performance-, success- and growth-oriented "work society".

Notes

* The ideas, concepts and findings presented here were developed in the ETH research group "Frei-Gemeinnützige Tätigkeit" and they could have been formulated by any member of the group. In other words, this text was co-written by authors not mentioned here.
1 Voluntary charitable activity is here taken to mean various forms and definitions of unpaid work, such as civic, civil or community engagement,

honorary posts, volunteering, etc. "Voluntary" refers to free will, independence (see Güntert et al. 2021).

2 Neighbourhood support provided outside the family and relatives can in some countries or places be offset with time credits. These can then be drawn on in case of subsequent need (https://www.moneyland.ch/en/time-banking-currency-switzerland-guide).

3 https://europa.eu/youth/EU/volunteering/european-voluntary-service_en.

4 www.globalteer.org/voluntourism/.

5 www.koerber-stiftung.de/viele-deutsche-wollen-helfen-koennen-aber-nicht-937 (accessed 15.11.20).

6 In Germany, these have been united since 1999 under the umbrella of the Bundesarbeitsgemeinschaft der Freiwilligenagenturen e.V. (Federal Association of Volunteer Agencies, https://bagfa.de/english/).

7 Migros, which is organised as a cooperative, is one of the largest retailers in Switzerland. It was founded in 1925 by the politician Gottlieb Duttweiler (https://en.wikipedia.org/wiki/Gottlieb_Duttweiler?uselang=de,   accessed 15.11.20).

Bibliography

Bierhoff, H.W. (2002): *Prosocial Behavior*, Hove

Clary, E.G., Snyder, M. (1999): *The motivations to volunteer: Theoretical and practical considerations*, Current Directions in Psychological Science, 8(5), 156–159

Jaeggi, R. (2014): *Alienation*, New York

Jiranek, P., Kals, E., Humm, J.S., Strubel, I.T., Wehner, T. (2013): *Volunteering as means to an equal end? The impact of a social justice function on intention to volunteer*, The Journal of Social Psychology 153(5), 520–541

Leontjev, A.N. (1978): *Activity, Consciousness and Personality*, New York

Oostlander, J., Güntert, S.T., Wehner, T. (2013). *Linking autonomy-supportive leadership to volunteer satisfaction: A self-determination theory perspective*, Voluntas: International Journal of Voluntary and Nonprofit Organizations, https://link.springer.com/article/10.1007/s11266-013-9395-0 (accessed 21.01.2021)

Seidl, I., Zahrnt, A. (Eds.) (2010): *Postwachstumsgesellschaft. Konzepte für die Zukunft*, Marburg

Senghaas-Knobloch, E. (1999): *Von der Arbeits- zur Tätigkeitsgesellschaft*, Arbeit 8(2), 117–136

Simonson, J., Vogel, C., Tesch-Römer, C. (Eds.) (2016): *Freiwilliges Engagement in Deutschland – Der Deutsche Freiwilligensurvey 2014*, Wiesbaden

Ulich, E. (2001): *Arbeitspsychologie*, Stuttgart

Wehner, T., Mieg, H., Güntert, S. (2005): *Frei-gemeinnützige Arbeit*, in: Mühlpfordt, S., Richter, P. (Eds.): Ehrenamt und Erwerbsarbeit, München, 19–39

Güntert, S.T., Wehner, T., Mieg, H.A. (2021): *Organizational, motivational, and cultural contexts of volunteering: The European view*, Cham

Part 3

Employment and meaningful activities

Sectors

9 Formal and informal care work[*]

Jonas Hagedorn

Summary

Care work is an umbrella term for many services and activities, both formal and informal, that provide help and advice, healing and nursing, education and training. Such work on and with people, the productivity of which cannot readily be increased, could in future be a significant core area for all human work in post-growth societies. Whether this work will be performed solely through paid services, or whether a mix of care activities will emerge in the course of societal transformation, based on a newly defined relationship between formal and informal care work and a new division of roles between the sexes, is an open question.

1 Introduction

The three largest German-owned private nursing home operators employ a total of 18,300 people. By way of comparison, the number of Opel employees in Germany is around 19,000. While the German public is unlikely to know the home operators by name (they are Pro Seniore, Kursana and Azurit Group), it is very well informed about the fortunes of the Opel Group and the employees working there – a first example of Germany's fixation with manufacturing industries. As a second example, I would like to mention the value of unpaid care work carried out in private households, which, if the data are gathered and quantified in monetary terms, corresponds to almost 40 percent of gross domestic product (GDP) at a conservative estimate (figures from 2013; Statistisches Bundesamt 2017, 245). The two examples illustrate how both formal and informal care work are marginalised in terms of their significance for the division of labour and value creation, but nevertheless underlie all economic activity and should therefore be counted among the core value creation processes (Praetorius 1997, 264).

DOI: 10.4324/9781003187370-9

Although care work is marginalised, the number of people working in social services is growing. Since at least the 1960s and 1970s – the "golden age" of its expansion – the social services infrastructure has been one of the defining features of the German welfare state. Since the 1970s – the social-liberal decade – defining the relationship between formal and informal care work has been an ongoing topic in the debates around the German welfare state and in criticism of it (e.g. Liefmann-Keil 1972; for a discussion of the problem see Kaufmann 1980, 1985). At that time, the debates were ignited by the substitution of unpaid care work by paid services, which some saw as a perverse incentive on the part of the welfare state, which was taking more and more work away from its citizens; and they were also ignited by concern over how social services were to be financed when the economy and tax revenue stagnated. At a time when interest rates are at zero and tax revenues are gushing, economic and fiscal stagnation, a source of great concern in the past, is only a minor issue. As soon as the economy begins to slow down, the question of how to finance the social security system will arise again and, because of declining growth rates, will remain relevant for a long time to come. Today, the debate focuses on growing needs, for example in the area of elderly care, and on the funding required to meet those needs in future in a system basically financed by contributions, but in which there are fewer and fewer paid workers while more and more people are not (or are no longer) employed.

With the expansion of social services from the 1950s onwards, the fear arose that the welfare state and its social policies were weakening the traditional forms of community assistance. A picture was painted of an accelerating spiral in which perfectly good unpaid help work was replaced by expensive, professionalised agencies of the welfare state. There was talk of the state services "*crowding out*" pre-state services (Gross/ Badura 1977, 374). In addition to the predicted danger of the social services becoming unaffordable, the fear was expressed that complex social bureaucracies could emerge which would develop an "unmistakable self-reinforcing momentum" (ibid., 368, 370). In the context of an ageing society and the challenges it poses, there has been a move away from the kind of criticism that was voiced in the 1970s and beyond. For example, the Second Gender Equality Report of the German Federal Government (BMFSFJ 2017, 93) recommends a further expansion of high-quality social services.

Such an expansion has since taken place only to a very limited extent, as the contributions- and tax-financed system remains under persistent financial pressure. If one assumes that growth rates in Western economies are falling and that post-growth societies are emerging (or should be emerging, for ecological reasons), then in the longer term the financing possibilities for social services will reach their limits; neither the state contribution nor the possibilities for private financial provision can increase indefinitely. It is possible, however, that a social transformation will take place in parallel, in which the relationship between formal and informal care work could be rebalanced.

In what follows, I describe as a first step the characteristics of social services (Section 2). Section 3 presents, as a complement to the sociological explanation for the low status accorded to social services, the economic thesis of the *Cost Disease* of personal services, which goes back to William J. Baumol (1922–2017). Section 4 discusses two strategies for reducing the costs of social services: rationalisation and informalisation. The concluding brief reflections address the conditions under which formal and informal care work combine effectively with each other (Section 5).

2 The characteristics of personal social services

Services that help and advise, heal and nurse, and educate and train constitute work "'on' people" (Gross/Badura 1977, 365). One of the core characteristics of such services is that producers and consumers must be present at the same time and must cooperate. The fact that the provision of the service and its consumption are two aspects of a *single* process was described in the early 1970s by Herder-Dorneich/Kötz (1972, 18, 22) as the "uno-actu principle", which has since become the standard criterion for identifying certain personal services. Social services are among the goods that are based on needs or requirements which cannot be standardised and are partly diffuse (Gross/Badura 1977, 363). Social services are accordingly also referred to as *experiential goods*, the quality of which cannot be tested before they are provided and used, but only becomes apparent when someone consumes them. Furthermore, social services are regarded as *trust goods*, where consumers have to trust that they are receiving the right service (e.g. one that is medically or therapeutically indicated) and one that is of good quality. This is particularly true when consumers are restricted in their ability to make decisions or to act (Bäcker et al. 2008, 511f.). In addition, social services usually cannot be stored. Meeting personal needs, which is the core of such services, is generally an urgent matter and can only be postponed to a limited degree. These characteristics mean that social services are difficult to rationalise.

Some care work is unpaid domestic work, mostly done by women. Only over the course of time has such work been partially transformed into a paid service. To this day, many social services are still associated with women, and to this day most social assistance and support services are still provided "not by paid professionals but by lay people in family and social settings" (Bäcker et al. 2008, 507). Not only unpaid care work, but also paid services in the field of formal social services can therefore often still retain in some respects an informal character. Employees in social services are permanently faced with the task of managing "cooperation with the lay system" on the one hand (e.g. the coordination of care professionals with family members providing care), and on the other hand "setting themselves apart from it" (e.g. in order to further their own professional qualifications and to affirm their value) (Mergner 2011, 5).

It was pointed out as early as the 1970s that the importance of the activities and services associated with informal and formal care work for a society based on the division of labour was severely underestimated. In part, this had to do with the fact that a considerable proportion of the activities mentioned – mostly performed by women – were provided free of charge as part of the resilient solidarity network of the family (for example, childcare and care of the elderly). At the same time, on the supply side of social services in Germany, the church welfare organisations (Caritas, Diakonie) for a long time did not reflect the real labour costs, since the use of Protestant and Catholic religious personnel (again mostly women) kept those costs low.

Unlike many goods and corporate services, social services in Germany and other Western countries were for a long time not subject to supply and demand at market prices, and their providers were not in economic competition with each other. This is referred to as a needs-oriented or social economy rationale (Bode et al. 2015). Many social services are still delivered by non-profit private organisations but largely guaranteed by the state and/or subsidised from public funds. In these cases, the public providers form a monopoly of demand which contracts services from municipal, non-profit and – since the introduction of long-term care insurance – private providers. In the case of services in the areas of social work, health and nursing, childcare and education (SAGE),[1] the shift from the principle of cost recovery to standardised models of performance evaluation and pro rata reimbursement has created a service market in which private, profit-oriented actors have squeezed in (Bode 2019; Leiber et al. 2019).

3 William J. Baumol's thesis

The low social recognition accorded to social services is generally attributed to the distinction made between unpaid female care work and paid male industrial work (e.g. BMFSFJ 2017) which emerged in the course of the differentiation between the private family sphere and the public sphere of paid work under industrial capitalism.

The fact that the danger of precarisation often lurks in social services, however, also has an economic cause, which among economists is known as *Baumol's Cost Disease*. It was identified by the economist William J. Baumol (1922–2017), who in various publications (e.g. Baumol 1967) set out his thoughts on the rapid increase in the price of services compared to goods. His central idea can be summarised as follows. If labour productivity in industry increases, i.e. more products are produced per hour, then workers' wages can rise, and their working conditions can also be improved, without the price of goods having to go up. The increased costs per hour worked that result from these improvements are simply spread over more products. Thus, rising labour productivity prevents increased pay and improved working conditions from driving up the cost per product and thus its price. In contrast, productivity in social services can only be increased within narrow limits (Baumol 1967, 416f.; Baumol/ Oates 1972, 46–48; Baumol 1993, 19–21), because social services can be standardised and automated only to a much lesser extent. The nature of the work is such that it does not readily allow for an increase in the number of services that a worker or an employed person can provide in an hour. Ultimately, these are experiential and trust goods, where there is a close connection between production and consumption requiring the co-presence of service providers and service users. Nevertheless, in order for enough people to be willing to work in the social services sector, wages and working conditions must be able to keep pace with wages and conditions in industry (and in other service sectors) over the long term. As a result, the social services sector is experiencing a significant increase in labour costs and rising prices. It is this process that is termed Baumol's cost disease.

In recent years, the euphoric claim has occasionally been made that Baumol's cost disease can be treated, perhaps even cured, by the use of new digital technologies in service work. However, this impression is conveyed above all if the diverse services in the tertiary sector are not viewed in a differentiated way, but instead business-related services are simply lumped together with personal, especially social, services, as if they were all essentially the same. Already Baumol himself has linked his thoughts on cost disease to the production of cultural and social services. The way in which these services are provided has to date only allowed for a very limited degree of technologisation, which would be tantamount to substituting machines for people. As a rule, the growing demand for social services tends to go hand in hand with rising staff numbers and disproportionately rising labour costs.

4 Strategies in the social services sector[2]

In order to reduce or avoid further increases in costs, providers and suppliers of social services rely on two strategies. These can be summed up by the common denominators of rationalisation (in the sense of productivity increases analogous to the productivity increases in industry tried and tested over decades) and informalisation.

4.1 Rationalisation

A distinction is made between organisation-centred and technology-centred rationalisation, depending on the resources used. In what follows, rationalisation is taken to consist of two sets of measures: taylorisation and technologisation.

4.1.1 Taylorisation

Taylorism has been carried over to the organisation of social services work (Knijn 2001; Ranci/Pavolini 2013, 303–305; Bode 2019, 144). This way of organising industrial production, introduced in the early 20th century, breaks up previously connected fields of work into individual tasks in order to reduce the time required for these tasks. Taylorisation means the acceleration, more efficient organisation and "optimisation" of work processes and the standardisation of tasks. This strategy is particularly evident in what is known as minute care (specifications for care tasks defined in precise intervals of minutes).

4.1.2 Technologisation

In the course of technologisation, many work processes in industrial production have seen a considerable reduction in the physical danger to workers and the physical effort required from them, while expectations of their qualifications and concentration have steadily increased. The use of new technology has often improved production processes and saved labour. Today, digitalisation can be regarded as another form of technologisation. The use of new digital technologies in social services is also being discussed and researched (BMG 2013; Ludwig/Evans 2018).

4.2 Informalisation

The second strategy can be termed informalisation. It is sometimes understood as going in the opposite direction to the professionalisation being pursued in various care professions. It involves both low-wage and precarisation strategies as well as personal initiative and the mobilisation of unpaid self-help and external help.

4.2.1 Precarisation

Precarisation is the process of reducing wages and labour costs by lowering standards in working conditions. In Germany, many branches in the tertiary sector – including social services – have become "testing grounds for the introduction of low wages and the expansion of new, often precarious forms of employment" (Bosch/Weinkopf 2011, 439). Precarious workers in social services include, for example, the so-called 24-hour care workers ("live-ins") from Central and Eastern Europe, who have long since ceased to be a marginal phenomenon in Germany. Their number is estimated at well over 200,000. They probably perform one-third of paid elderly care work (in full-time equivalents). Since the eastern enlargement of the EU, many companies have emerged providing Central and Eastern European live-ins to German nursing homes (Leiber et al. 2019). They offer various different working models to elderly care workers, including forms of (apparent) self-employment (Bucher 2018). The central legal and ethical problem of live-in care is the complete removal in most cases of restrictions on working hours (Emunds 2019). An additional ethical problem is the social consequences of the "care drain" caused by the absence of care workers in their home countries (Hochschild 2000; Parreñas 2001).

4.2.2 Personal initiative and mobilisation of others

In the context of personal initiatives and the economic mobilisation of others in care work, two groups of addressees come into focus. One group consists of (self-organising) affected persons, their relatives, and non-family supporters and helpers. They form small social networks (partly based on mutual obligations), take responsibility for each other's care and informally help themselves and/or others. In addition, they may motivate other citizens who are not yet engaged in care work. The motivation behind self-help and external help initiatives and social civic engagement is varied. Some of these initiatives were formed in a conscious attempt to distinguish themselves from so-called expert help and with the aim of strengthening self-competence in order to combat the qualitative shortcomings of the professional help system (Glazer 1988). Some of them are characterised by the emancipatory spirit of the 1968 generation, which led to the establishment of self-help groups in the health sector, private childcare facilities and housing projects as well as initiatives for structural change in the social institutions.

The other group is made up of recipients of social services who are to be mobilised – to participate, for example, in maintaining their own health and avoiding unhealthy behaviour, towards active social inclusion and performing personal tasks and so on. Such activities increase the quality of life, go beyond service provision and encompass people's personal living conditions and circumstances. Behind this, however, there is often also a micro- and macroeconomic calculation. The co-producing patient or client is identified as a "hidden resource" (Gartner/Riessman 1974, 171–196). The aim is to increase their willingness to contribute to reducing costs, for example in the healthcare system, so that overall productivity in the social services increases (Gross/Badura 1977, 377).[3] At the same time, the number of "healthy life years" can be increased.

The tendency towards individual initiative and mobilisation outlined above should be understood in part as a reaction to criticism of the expansion of social services by the welfare state going back to the 1970s, and of possible limits to their affordability. At the peak of rising public expenditure on social services, a broad debate began in which the substitution by formal, publicly financed external services of informal, unpaid work, especially within the family, to satisfy basic needs was problematised and rejected. The talk then of social networks providing not only family services but also extra-familial, non-professional help and support services (Gross/Badura 1977) is today being supplemented by the concept of *caring communities* (Klie 2014). The aim here is to create a "new structure and culture of care", in which "family, neighbourly, civic and professional sources of support function in relation to one another" (ibid., 239), and which is orchestrated by the institutions of social policy and a pluralistic welfare system.[4]

4.2.3 The limits to informalisation, as illustrated by elderly care

If we examine the informal sector using care of the elderly as an example, it becomes clear that, against the background of the German family-based care model, the bulk of domestic care work has so far been performed by relatives – with a sharp increase in the use of live-in carers. However, the German family-based care model is now coming under pressure from several directions. First, families are becoming smaller. The baby boomers of the 1950s and 1960s are having fewer children themselves. As a result, there are fewer people able to assume the responsibility for care as next of kin. In future, therefore, there will not only be more (very old) people in need of care, but they will also tend to have fewer close relatives who can be expected to provide such demanding care. Second, there has been a considerable increase in spatial mobility, which the work society itself has brought about through progressive flexibilisation. Grown-up children often no longer live close to their parents or other relatives. Third, labour force participation and the retirement age are both rising, so that in future, cohorts who give birth later will need to be cared for at a time when their children may themselves still be working. It is obvious that a normal employment model is not compatible in the long term with the difficult and demanding care and support of a relative in need of care (especially when only one person is responsible for that care).

> Today already, families with certain problems, such as domestic care of the elderly, are often stretched to the limit of their capacity. Particularly in the case of long-term commitments [...] the help provided by relatives often comes at the cost of physically and mentally overwhelming them.
>
> (Bäcker et al. 2008, 591)

5 Concluding reflections

The current crisis in social services has so far been perceived primarily as a cost problem, to which the response has been "market-shaped" or "market-compliant" strategies: rationalisation, which has technology-using and labour-dividing ("taylorising") components, and informalisation, which consists of precarisation (for elderly care, for example, live-in employment) together with personal initiative and mobilisation.[5] A possible third, "state-run" strategy, which does not regard cost increases in the social services as an evil which must be avoided, but which instead advocates additional public expenditure per service provided and thus drives both wage increases and improvements in working conditions, has so far lacked support. While rationalising Taylorism and informalising precarisation make social work careers that follow a holistic understanding unattractive, or threaten to undermine their aspirations to professionalism, the consequences of technologisation and of an increase in self-help and voluntary support services for the rising costs of social services are not yet foreseeable. High development and acquisition costs can be expected for technologisation. Personal initiative and mobilisation are also accompanied by the labour costs of a subsidiary infrastructure of professional staff who train and support the patients, relatives and volunteers, but who also provide relief for them when their help and support under acceptable conditions is no longer available.

The strategies of rationalisation and informalisation described above can be understood in a first, as yet undetailed analytical step as part of a trilemma specific to social services (for more detail, see Emunds/ Hagedorn 2020). Similar to a dilemma, which begins with two important goals and asserts that only one of the two can be achieved at any one time, in a trilemma a maximum of two of the three goals can be achieved. For a robust and sustainable social organisation of social services, the following three core goals can be identified. First, wages and working conditions in the social services should keep pace with those in the economy as a whole ("fair social services"). Second, social services should be universally accessible and should therefore remain affordable ("affordable social services"). Third, care work should be of good quality from the perspective of the recipients, and service providers should be able to work to the professional standards they have learnt and in accordance with the rationale and ethos particular to the social services ("good social services") (Figure 9.1).[6]

My initial assumption is that political or organisational measures can be used to pursue a maximum of two of these goals – thus, a trilemma. If pay and working conditions are to keep pace with those in manufacturing industry and if, at the same time, social services are not to become significantly more expensive, there will be increasing pressure to *rationalise* social services in a way that runs counter to their inherent rationale. This leads, for example, to work processes being carved up into chunks timed to the minute, and to activities being fragmented. The result can be a compulsive drive for control and self-optimisation; in addition, the holistic nature of one's hard-earned profession can be lost from view and with it the enjoyment of it. If employees in the social services are to perform their work in a way that corresponds to the demands of the service users and the rationale of these services, and if at the same time a cost explosion is to be avoided, then an informalisation

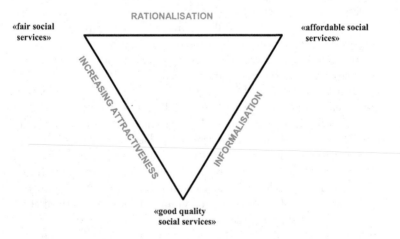

Figure 9.1 The trilemma of social services

of care work has to happen. If we want to give priority neither to rationalisation nor to "unsupervised" informalisation, then society will not be able to avoid allocating more money to social services, i.e. significantly increasing public expenditure per service and thus making the caring professions more attractive. In view of the growing demand for social services, this is a challenge that should not be underestimated. As care work cannot be endlessly further rationalised or informalised, increases in expenditure are inevitable in the longer term.

The strategies of personal initiative and mobilisation, which the present text brings together under the label "informalisation", cannot easily be integrated into the trilemma presented here. This is because they have a far-reaching potential that could help to resolve the conflict between goals. If one understands self-organised care needers, caring relatives, volunteers and active recipients as part of a "resource system" (Brie 2013) in which they perform meaningful, fulfilling work in cooperation with professional actors, then all three goals could be achieved. For a post-growth society strongly characterised by work on and with people, in which formal employment would become less important for all citizens and there would be more time for personal initiative and unpaid care work due to the reduction in working hours, care activities brought together in a hybrid way – in a resource system in which formal and informal care work cooperate – could become a distinguishing feature.[7] It is already possible to identify numerous pioneers who are shaking up the field of essential public services, up until now so permeated by market logic; these are mainly rural initiatives, but also some urban ones, which are reviving intergenerational solidarity and initiating new care arrangements (Lang/Wintergerst 2011). However, these resource systems require a high level of vigilance and protection. Insofar as a post-growth society is likely to be significantly different from today's capitalist economy, there is hope that the resource systems will be able to successfully resist being colonised by any kind of capitalist rationale, which will then presumably be diminished in relevance anyway.

In order to protect these resource systems, it is advisable to pursue the strategies of personal initiative and mobilisation in a supportive way so as to complement the work of professionals, but in no case to replace it. The provision of social services is confronted with at least four challenges that can only be met by a professional subsidiary staff:

–   Social services must guarantee a high degree of predictability, reliability and commitment (including to unpleasant "dirty work"), which volunteers can only to a limited extent be compelled to sign up to.

- Personal initiative and mobilisation must not become mobilisation against one's will (those who volunteer must be able to end their involvement without a guilty conscience, and there must be a "right not to care" [Lewis 1997]).
- Compliance with quality standards, and their supervision and monitoring, must be ensured.
- Unpaid care work must not be used as a pretext for dismantling publicly provided social services, because otherwise only part of the population will bear – unpaid and disproportionately – the burden of care work, which is the responsibility of society as a whole.

The boundaries between self-help, family (self-determined) work or voluntary, social civic engagement on the one hand and formal social services provision on the other have long been fluid (Bäcker et al. 2008, 581). One reason for this is the increasing institutional integration of once pre-institutional family or non-family work.[8] Even if great hopes are attached to unpaid care work and these support activities already interact and overlap with many social services in many different ways, those who do such work for free will increasingly and "fundamentally depend on a public infrastructure" (Heinze 2019, 59) without which the effective practical implementation of the "right to care" (Knijn/Kremer 1997) would not be possible (for example in the care of relatives) and which therefore "contributes significantly to the success of subsidiarity" (Heinze 2019, 59). In this respect, too, the state may, must and can – oblige all citizens to contribute to the financing of formal and informal care work through social security contributions and taxes.

Notes

* This chapter originated as part of the DFG-funded research project "Elderly care work in private households. A question of recognition. Socio-ethical analyses".
1 The differentiation of social services into helping and counselling, healing and nursing, and educating and training services corresponds to the professions that Mergner (2011) abbreviated to SAGE. SAGE stands for (the German terms for) social work, health and nursing, and childcare and education. In the Federal Government's Second Gender Equality Report, the acronym SAGE has been extended to include the field of household-related services (SAHGE). Cf. Hagedorn 2020.
2 This chapter does not discuss new organisational approaches in the outpatient care sector, such as the Buurtzorg model, which rely on a high degree of autonomy among small, decentralised teams of nursing staff and on a patient-centred approach. Patient centeredness refers to the idea that the variable condition of a person in need of care is the focus of attention and that the goal is to help them regain their independence (Monsen/Blok 2013; Kreitzer et al. 2015).

3 Today, co-producing consumers are an integral element not only of the delivery of social services, but also of the production of storable intangible goods. As users, for example, they provide the data volumes and thus feed the algorithms which make sophisticated apps for speech recognition possible and capable of subsequent improvement; their consumption overlaps with the production.

4 The Central Committee of German Catholics however consistently refers to a *caring society* (ZdK 2018), which places greater emphasis on the "provision of care to the population" as "a task for society as a whole" (§ 8 [1] SGB XI).

5 Above all self-help, work undertaken by the family (often for the family), voluntary work or social-civic work undertaken by others.

6 This, too, is an important prerequisite for ensuring that enough people are willing to take on employment in the social services sector in the long term.

7 Lang/Wintergerst (2011) speak in this context of a "complementary economy".

8 The institutional integration and use of volunteer work, for example, is also being questioned. Since the 1990s, the financial value of self-help, family work and voluntary, civic-minded help from others, its relevance to the system and its "excellent economic return" have often been made clear by the commercialisation of social services. The use of such unpaid care work by commercial organisations exposes them to the accusation that they are instrumentalising and "exploiting" such active and activated engagement and using it to gain a competitive advantage (Denninger et al. 2014).

Bibliography

Bäcker, G., Naegele, G., Bispinck, R., Hofemann, K., Neubauer, J. (2008): *Sozialpolitik und soziale Lage in Deutschland*, Vol. 2, Wiesbaden

Baumol, W.J. (1967): *Macroeconomics of unbalanced growth: The anatomy of urban crisis*, American Economic Review 57(3), 415–426

Baumol, W.J. (1993): *Health care, education and the cost disease: A looming crisis for public choice*, Public Choice 77, 17–28

Baumol, W.J., Oates, W.E. (1972): *The cost disease of the personal services and the quality of life*, Skandinaviska Enskilda Banken Quarterly Review (2), 44–54

BMFSFJ (Bundesministerium für Familie, Senioren, Frauen und Jugend) (2017): *Zweiter Gleichstellungsbericht der Bundesregierung*, Deutscher Bundestag: Drucksache 18/12840 vom 21. Juni 2017

BMG (Bundesministerium für Gesundheit) (2013): *Abschlussbericht zur Studie „Unterstützung Pflegebedürftiger durch technische Assistenzsysteme"*, Berlin

Bode, I. (2019): *Let's count and manage – and forget the rest: Understanding numeric rationalization in human service provision*, Historical Social Research 44(2), 131–154

Bode, I., Brandenburg, H., Werner, B. (2015): *Sozial wirtschaften und gut versorgen. Umsteuerungsoptionen für die Wohlfahrtspflege*, Blätter der Wohlfahrtspflege 162(3), 112–116

Bosch, G., Weinkopf, C. (2011): *Arbeitsverhältnisse im Dienstleistungssektor*, WSI-Mitteilungen (9), 439–446

Brie, M. (2013): *Für eine plurale Welt sich selbst organisierender Akteure. Das Forschungsprogramm von Elinor Ostrom*, in: Busch, U., Krause, G. (Eds.): Theorieentwicklung im Kontext der Krise, Abhandlungen der Leibniz-Sozietät der Wissenschaften, Vol. 35, Berlin, 111–136

Bucher, B. (Ed.) (2018): *Rechtliche Ausgestaltung der 24-h-Betreuung durch ausländische Pflegekräfte in deutschen Privathaushalten. Eine kritische Analyse*, Baden-Baden

Denninger, T., van Dyk, S., Lessenich, S., Richter, A. (2014): *Leben im Ruhestand. Zur Neuverhandlung des Alters in der Aktivgesellschaft*, Bielefeld

Emunds, B. (2019): *Überforderte Angehörige – ausgebeutete Live-Ins – Burnout-gefährdete Pflegekräfte. Sozialethische Bemerkungen zur verweigerten sozialen Wertschätzung Pflegender in Deutschland*, in: Fuchs, M., Greiling, D., Rosenberger, M. (Eds.): Gut versorgt? Ökonomie und Ethik im Gesundheits- und Pflegebereich, Baden-Baden, 147–167

Emunds, B., Hagedorn, J. (2020): *Das Trilemma der Pflege. Zu Zielkonflikten und Unzulänglichkeiten verbreiteter pflegepolitischer Strategien*, Amos International 14(2), 3–10

Gartner, A., Riessman, F. (1974): *The Service Society and the Consumer Vanguard*, New York

Glazer, N. (1988): *The Limits of Social Policy*, Cambridge

Gross, P., Badura, B. (1977): *Sozialpolitik und soziale Dienste: Entwurf einer Theorie personenbezogener Dienstleistungen*, in: von Ferber, C., Kaufmann, F.-X. (Eds.): Soziologie und Sozialpolitik, Opladen, 361–385

Hagedorn, J. (2020): *Altenpflege im Spannungsfeld von formeller und informeller Arbeit – sozialethische Anmerkungen zur gesellschaftlichen Organisation der Pflegearbeit*, in: Städtler-Mach, B., Ignatzi, H. (Eds.): Grauer Markt Pflege. 24-Stunden-Unterstützung durch osteuropäische Betreuungskräfte, Göttingen, 129–155

Heinze, R.G. (2019): *Verbandliche Wohlfahrtspflege und Wohlfahrtsmarkt. Neuformulierung der Subsidiarität?* Sozialer Fortschritt 68(1), 45–65

Herder-Dorneich, P., Kötz, W. (1972): *Zur Dienstleistungsökonomik. Systemanalyse und Systempolitik der Krankenhauspflegedienste*, Berlin

Hochschild, A.R. (2000): *Global care chains and emotional surplus value*, in: Hutton, W., Giddens, A. (Eds.): On the Edge. Living with Global Capitalism, London, 130–146

Kaufmann, F.-X. (1980): *Social policy and social services: Some problems of policy formation, program implementation and impact evaluation*, in: Grunow, D., Hegner, F. (Eds.): Welfare or Bureaucracy? Problems of Matching Social Services to Clients' Needs, Cambridge, 29–43

Kaufmann, F.-X. (1985): *Major problems and dimensions of the welfare state*, in: Eisenstadt, S.N., Ahimeir, O. (Eds.): The Welfare State and Its Aftermath, London, 44–56

Klie, T. (2014): *Wen kümmern die Alten? Auf dem Weg in eine sorgende Gesellschaft*, München

Knijn, T. (2001): *Care work: Innovations in the Netherlands*, in: Daly, M. (Ed.): Care Work: The Quest of Security, Geneva: International Labour Office, 159–174

Knijn, T., Kremer, M. (1997): *Gender and the caring dimension of welfare states: Toward inclusive citizenship*, Social Politics 4(3), 328–361

Kreitzer, M.J., Monsen, K.A., Nandram, S., Blok, J.de (2015): *Buurtzorg nederland: A global model of social innovation, change, and whole-systems healing*, Global Advances in Health and Medicine, 4(1), 40–44

Lang, E., Wintergerst, T. (2011): *Am Puls des langen Lebens. Soziale Innovationen für die alternde Gesellschaft*, München

Lewis, J. (1997): *Gender and welfare regimes: Further thoughts*, Social Politics 4(2), 160–177

Liefmann-Keil, E. (1972): *Sozialinvestitionen und Sozialpolitik – Zur Perpetuierung der Sozialpolitik*, Gewerkschaftliche Monatshefte 23(1), 24–38

Ludwig, C., Evans, M. (2018): *Research report: Digitalisierung in der Altenpflege – Gestaltungsoptionen und Gestaltungswege für betriebliche Interessenvertretungen*, Gelsenkirchen

Mergner, U. (2011): *Seien wir SAGE! Wie kann die gesellschaftliche Anerkennung der Disziplinen und Professionen im Bereich der „sozialen Dienstleistungen" erhöht werden?* Bayerische Sozialnachrichten. Mitteilungen der Landesarbeitsgemeinschaft der öffentlichen und freien Wohlfahrtspflege in Bayern, 4, 3–9

Monsen, K.A., Blok, J.de (2013): *Buurtzorg Nederland. A nurse-led model of care has revolutionized home care in the Netherlands*, American Journal of Nursing 113(8), 55–59

Praetorius, I. (1997): *Thinking economy beyond the androcentric order*, in: International Federation for Home Economics (Ed.): Europe – Challenges for Everyday Living. Home Economics as a Vehicle for Social Changes (Publication of an International Workshop, 21.–23. October 1996 in Vienna), Vienna, 261–270

Leiber, S., Matuszczyk, K., Rossow, V. (2019): *Private labor market intermediaries in the Europeanized live-in care market between Germany and Poland: A typology*, Zeitschrift für Sozialreform 65(3), 365–392

Parreñas, R.S. (2001): *Servants of Globalization: Migration and Domestic Work*, Stanford

Ranci, C., Pavolini, E. (2013): *Institutional change in long-term care: Actors, mechanisms and impacts*, in: Ranci, C., Pavolini, E. (Eds.): Reforms in Long-Term Care Policies in Europe. Investigating Institutional Change and Social Impacts, New York, 269–314

Statistisches Bundesamt (Ed.) (2017): *Wie die Zeit vergeht. Analysen zur Zeitverwendung in Deutschland*, Beiträge zur Ergebniskonferenz der Zeitverwendungserhebung 2012/2013 am 5./6. Oktober 2016 in Wiesbaden, Wiesbaden

ZdK (Zentralkomitee der deutschen Katholiken) (2018): *Gerechte Pflege in einer sorgenden Gesellschaft. Zur Zukunft der Pflegearbeit in Deutschland*, Beschlossen von der Vollversammlung des ZdK am 23. November 218

10 Meaningful activities in agriculture

Agro-culture as a guiding principle

Franz-Theo Gottwald, Irmi Seidl and Angelika Zahrnt

Summary

The ecological, economic and social crisis in agriculture is linked to developments in agricultural work since the 1950s. Since that time a rationalisation of agricultural work has been taking place, and redundant labour was taken up in the growing industrial and service sectors. If agriculture is to be practised according to ecological and social principles and thereby to meet societal expectations, more people will have to work in agriculture again. This requires targeted agricultural policy support for work and for organically farmed land. In keeping with the vision of an eco-social agro-culture, a wide range of work opportunities must be created – full-time and part-time work, (partial) subsistence and voluntary work, all year round and seasonal. In a post-growth society where growth is no longer encouraged for the sake of creating further formal employment, this can lead to new, interesting, varied and meaningful activities.

1 The ecological and social crisis in agriculture – a short tour d'horizon

Agriculture is in a deep ecological, economic and social crisis – locally, nationally and globally. Most of the problems have arisen as a result of the industrialisation of agriculture, i.e. the increasing use of agricultural technology and agrochemicals, as well as land consolidation and the focus on global markets. This has also changed agricultural work and the way of life of farming communities.

One of the problems facing agriculture today is its greenhouse gas emissions: in Germany it accounts for 7.3 percent of total emissions, in

DOI: 10.4324/9781003187370-10

Austria 10.3 percent and in Switzerland 13.5 percent. In the EU, the figure is 10 percent (eurostat 2019), globally 10–12 percent (IPPC 2014). Agriculture is the largest contributor to biodiversity loss (Dudley, Alexander 2017). This applies to both the species level and the ecosystem or landscape level: grasslands are becoming increasingly poorer in flora and fauna, and structurally rich cultural landscapes are disappearing. Soil biodiversity is declining, soils are losing humus and soil fertility is dwindling. Liquid manure, synthetic fertilisers and pesticides, which are responsible for many of these problems, also pollute water bodies. Large livestock holdings and poor animal welfare in the EU are also problematic (Stodieck 2018).

Many farms are in a difficult economic situation: many of them are over-indebted and income is low. Only a few farms receive large payments from the billions in EU subsidies: in Germany, 70 percent, and on average across the EU 80 percent of all EU direct payments go to just one-fifth of farms (Heinrich Böll Foundation et al. 2019). From 2003 to 2013, 31 percent of all farms in Germany had to give up, and in the EU as a whole the figure was 28 percent (eurostat 2015). And this development is likely to continue, because in many places no successor is available or willing to take over the farm.

Psycho-social problems are increasing in everyday working life. 32 percent of European farmers are suffering from work-related stress (compared to 22 percent on average for all occupations; Parent-Thirion 2007). Country-specific examples are given as follows: in the federal state of Baden-Württemberg (Germany), 17 percent of all farmers who call in sick are suffering from depression or burnout (Wochenblatt 2017). 12 percent of Swiss farmers experience burnout symptoms (the national average is 6 percent of the population, Reissig 2017). In France, suicide rates among farmers have raised public concern and are being investigated (Bossard et al. 2016). Because no successor can be found for many farms, the traditional intra-family contract between the generations cannot be maintained and many farmers retire into poverty (Stodieck 2018).

2 Agricultural work and business models

Agricultural work has changed considerably since the 1960s with the politically driven structural change in farming. The work force in agriculture has dwindled[1] and the number of family employees continues to decline significantly. Local neighbourhood support is also declining and is increasingly being remunerated in monetary terms. The number of permanently employed workers is increasing slightly and that of seasonal workers is tending to decrease. Informal or undeclared work – above all by foreign workers – is sometimes a topic of public debate, but there are no figures on its extent. The activities carried out in agriculture are increasingly specialised, small-scale, mechanised, determined by agro-chemical inputs and computerised. People often work in isolation and detached from social contexts, alienated from animals and the land.[2] Agricultural work is also generally poorly paid. There is a lack of properly qualified workers in particular.

In Germany there were 275,000 agricultural holdings in 2016, of which 244,000 were independent enterprises[3] (for these and the following statistics see BMEL 2017). 48 percent of these independent enterprises were the full-time operations, 52 percent part-time. The proportion of such part-time farming businesses varies between 40 and 70 percent across the Länder. 90 percent of agricultural production takes place on farms which are full-time businesses, the rest on part-time farms. From the 1960s onwards, the "political model of a growing agricultural sector" (AgrarBündnis 2010, 53) elevated the full-time farm to the ideal model in agricultural policy. Before that period, part-time farms were more widespread than today and were valued for their contribution to food security. Hence, it was common practice until the middle of the 20th century for farmers to secure the livelihood of their families through a variety of activities and thus through various part-time jobs. Simultaneously, the family farm model was propagated from the 1950s onwards. "At that time, labour was needed (…) in industry. So the farming family, getting by solely on the basis of its own labour input (…), became a symbol of efficiency, productivity and competitiveness" (AgrarBündnis 2013).

3 Agricultural work, production and environmental impacts

The undoubtedly higher productivity and increased competitiveness of modern agriculture generate substantial external costs. Research is therefore being carried out to find ways of reducing the negative environmental impact of agriculture. Farmers' associations and other representative bodies are discussing how to bring conventional agriculture closer to EU-certified organic farming and to a new "good farming practice".[4]

For decades now, various ecological alternatives to conventional or industrialised agriculture have been practised in many countries. These have shown that ecologically beneficial agricultural methods are more labour-intensive. Rosa-Schleich et al. (2019) analysed numerous publications and were able to show that organic farming is particularly beneficial due to its lower negative environmental impacts, but is complex and labour-intensive.[5] The overall costs are similar to those of conventional farming – labour costs are higher, but other input costs lower. The higher labour intensity is due to the production of organic fertilisers and compost, weeding, a higher proportion of labour-intensive products such as vegetables and fruit (which generate higher income) and generally smaller farm sizes. The study concludes that no agricultural practice has so far yielded significant environmental benefits without an increase in labour input. So an agricultural system that preserves natural resources must become more labour-intensive again.[6]

Agricultural tasks are heterogeneous. Agricultural work can be physically demanding and monotonous or varied and complex. It often involves high peak workloads, but can also allow a certain flexibility. Craft, commercial, technical, financial and other skills are often required, and there is work at many different qualification levels. Working independently is usually important. This means that there are opportunities for many people from different generations to work in agriculture. For many, the close contact with animals (if animals are kept well and in a manner appropriate to their species), the connection to nature and being embedded locally – whether in natural cycles, communities or clientele – are also a source of satisfaction. Professional and private or social activities often overlap. These characteristics can make part-time and mixed agricultural work, as already practised by many part-time farmers and paid employees, especially interesting.

For post-growth society, where there may be less formal employment and where growth is no longer pursued for the sake of new jobs, organic farming in particular can provide interesting activities – whether paid or in self-provisioning – for many people. The scope for this depends largely on the type of farming and how it is organised, the timeframes in which work can be carried out and how the farm is embedded in its local context. The concept of agro-culture provides a framework for agricultural work with the above-mentioned (positive) characteristics.

4 Agro-culture – a model for eco-social agriculture

Since the 1980s various authors (Glaeser 1986; Groeneveld 1986; Priebe 1990) and institutions (especially the Schweisfurth-Stiftung 1988; Schweisfurth et al. 2002) have worked on agro-culture as a counter-model to industrial agriculture. Agro-culture stands for environmentally sustainable, humane and animal-friendly agriculture and for farming which focuses on the common good. Agro-culture has also become a political term used to describe both traditional rural farming and organic farming. According to Glaeser (1986, 24), agro-culture stands for the "reclaiming of complex cultural contexts and thus of economic, ecological and social diversity". This perspective was intended to lead to a new direction in agricultural practice and agricultural policy. The agro-culture model is now supported by organic farming associations, the German Arbeitsgemeinschaft für bäuerliche Landwirtschaft (Working Group for Farming) and AgrarBündnis (Agricultural Alliance).

The concept of agro-culture is rooted in family-run rural farming, with its own way of life and doing business, but is also characterised by an entrepreneurial self-image. This includes characteristics such as independence, private ownership, self-provisioning as well as being supplied by the market, a long-term perspective, multi-generational and family traditions, multiple skills (arable farming, animal husbandry, craftsmanship and cultural skills) as well as a high level of personal responsibility (Gottwald 2003).

Even though market pressures have increased significantly in recent decades and several waves of structural change, which always mean changes in the way work is done, have washed over rural areas, the basic current of agro-cultural consciousness is still perceptible and identity-forming in farming communities. It is based, among other things, on family ties, ties to the locality, a relationship with nature, intergenerational commitment, permanence and solidarity, and provides a foundation for a wide range of voluntary activities in rural areas (fire brigades, sports clubs, music associations, etc.).

Farms operating wholly or partly in line with the principles of agro-culture display – to varying degrees – characteristics which enable them to carry out a wide range of activities:

- they cover the entire value-creation chain, from tillage to the sale of processed products;
- they involve several generations, whether as family farms or cooperatives;
- they are more labour-intensive, so as to maintain the viability of ecosystems and biodiversity;
- they are often multifunctional (food production, energy production, tourism, education, social integration, etc.) and require a wide range of skills;
- the work is carried out in accordance with natural processes and cycles and the seasons;
- the work on the farms involves household, craft and horticultural tasks as well as plant cultivation and animal husbandry;
- agricultural work, housework and family can overlap and gender-specific role attributions are partially broken down.

The agro-cultural concept together with the related eco-social value system can provide a basis for numerous new and varied working opportunities in post-growth society in the field of agriculture, which can be full-time, part-time, seasonal or self-determined. Agriculture of this kind would promote economic re-localisation, strengthen social networking and promote a long-term orientation on the part of farms.

In order to make such a restructuring of agriculture a reality, society as a whole needs to change its thinking. The current public enthusiasm for rural life can be helpful here, provided that it is not idealised but takes a realistic and critical view of the current social, ecological and economic problems affecting agriculture and rural areas. It is also helpful that the public is aware of the numerous environmental problems to which conventional agriculture contributes. The public has corresponding expectations of agriculture: according to the German Environmental Awareness Study 2018 (BMU/UBA 2020), around 90 percent of the public regard the problems caused by agriculture, such as the decline in biodiversity, environmental pollution caused by pesticides, and the pollution of water bodies and drinking water, as a "very serious" or "fairly serious problem". The contribution to climate change caused by livestock farming is also viewed by 70 percent as a major problem. 59 percent believe that the most important task of agriculture is to protect the environment and nature; 65 percent believe that agriculture must above all ensure the welfare of farm animals. With regard to the future development of agriculture, people believe the most important thing is that it should have as little negative impact as possible on the environment and climate.

The majority of the German public obviously expects a change of direction for agriculture. As the next chapter shows, there are both concepts for political discussion and implementation and practical alternatives which show how agriculture can be further developed in the direction of agro-culturally meaningful activities.

5 Developing agriculture for agro-cultural activities

5.1 Framework conditions

European agricultural policy is currently focused on supporting prices, and allocates payments mainly based on land area. As a result, too much money still goes into area payments which landowners receive without giving much in return (Pe'er et al. 2020). Investment subsidies have a similar effect: they accelerate structural change to the benefit of larger farms. This aspect of agricultural policy is one main reason why only a small proportion of farms, namely the large ones, benefit from agricultural payments. However, the way they manage their land is generally not sustainable and they are far removed from the guiding principles of agro-culture.

In order to make work the starting point for future agricultural support and thus to enable an orientation towards the agro-cultural model, proposals need to be implemented that link direct payments to the labour input required rather than to the land area (Hovorka 2011; Hoppichler 2016). Likewise, the "associations' platform on the CAP" calls for "direct payments to be granted to active farmers who provide public goods and public services" and for "a fair and reasonable ceiling to be set on direct payments to individual farmers … that are a result of a policy based on income levels" (Verbände-Plattform zur GAP 2018, 13).[7] In addition, EU support measures under the second pillar[8] and support programmes at national and regional levels should be linked to ecological and social criteria, thereby increasing support for agricultural services for the common good.

In addition to agricultural payments targeted at the labour force and promoting ecological and social land management, and direct payments for ecological and social services, further combined measures are needed to promote agricultural work, to make it attractive and to encourage an orientation towards the agro-culture model. These include:

- regulatory policy requirements for land management, for example bans on the input of harmful substances (pesticides, fertilisers) or requirements to ensure good working conditions. Above all, however, existing legislation and overarching principles such as the precautionary principle must be enforced;
- a system of taxes and charges based on the ideas put forward by Köppl/Schratzenstaller (in this book), one that reduces the financial burden on labour, makes CO_2 emissions and resource consumption more expensive and reduces social inequalities (this will benefit labour-intensive, organic and small to medium-sized farms);
- social infrastructures in rural areas which ensure a good quality of life and counteract the current dismantling of basic public services. This includes, for example, the local supply of goods and services or local mobility and makes agricultural work and the continuation of farming more attractive. This is where regional policies and financial resources at local and regional levels (financial equalisation, tax collection) are particularly important;
- a simplified procedure for the recognition of the charitable contribution of the agricultural sector. Agriculture – and especially when

it follows agro-cultural principles – often has a non-profit dimension in addition to its income-generating dimension (social work, pedagogical work, consumer advice, education, nature conservation, etc.). This, or some parts of it, can already be recognised as charitable under tax law, although this is complicated (Janitzki 1998). An easier option would be to set up a charitable association covering one or more farms. This could be used to support their non-profit activities. Above all, with the help of such a charitable association, funds could be raised at favourable tax rates.

5.2 Enhancing agricultural practice

Decades of discussion about the negative consequences of agricultural policy and the concrete need for remedies and solutions to problems have led to the development of numerous agricultural methods, activities, projects and forms of organisation which pursue ecological and social goals and in which work is done differently.

First of all, there are agricultural practices which primarily pursue ecological objectives, but which also bring about changes in work (for such practices see endnote 5; another example is permaculture). As discussed in Chapter 3, such methods are often more labour-intensive. In some cases, the employees must be much better qualified and have extensive knowledge of ecological interactions, complex crop rotations or how different segments of a farm complement each other. These methods are spreading – partly because they are promoted by agricultural policy or, for example, by charitable or private foundations, and partly because there is a demand for them. Certified organic farming in particular continues to grow, thanks in part to its well-organised associations and the market expertise it has built up. About 8.1 percent of agricultural land in the EU is farmed organically (FiBL/IFOAM 2021).

For some time now, agricultural consultancies and regional support organisations have been recommending that farms set up so-called para-agricultural operations, i.e. multifunctional farming, in order to improve and diversify their income. Such operations include direct marketing, tourism services such as farm holidays, care, therapeutic, educational and integrative services (farm schools, riding schools, care and support services – also known as "care farming") and energy production. The activities involved sometimes require additional qualifications. For Switzerland, Chandrapalan et al. (2018) were able to show that such activities are attractive compared to the average hourly wage in agriculture. However, these new branches of farms often mean additional work pressure, especially for women farmers.

Cooperation can strengthen agriculture and thus sometimes also change the character of work on and between farms (Gottwald/Boergen 2012). Horizontal cooperation, e.g. in the form of agricultural cooperatives, purchasing groups or producer groups, is one way of adapting to or getting around structural change in agriculture. It reduces the workload and allows greater flexibility, strengthens mutual support and shares out risks.

Vertical cooperation brings in the processors and consumers. The example of community-supported agriculture shows that work thereby takes on a different shape: agricultural producers are linked in a partnership with consumers. Production is geared to their wishes, so the variety of products generally increases. The consumers share the production risk and receive a share of the harvest in return. They are given an insight into the farms, have a say in some decisions (especially if they are cooperatives) and participate in the work – usually voluntarily, but in some arrangements even on a compulsory basis (O'Hara/ Stagl 2001; Siegenthaler 2016).

In Switzerland, the cooperative Les jardins de Cocagne has been operating according to these principles since 1978, the Buschberghof in Schleswig-Holstein in Germany since 1988. Especially since the turn of the millennium, this form of producer-consumer solidarity has been spreading in Europe and worldwide.

A possible extension would be direct cooperation between urban neighbourhoods and their "land base", i.e. with farms in the region, which could provide a large proportion of their basic supplies – produced organically and regionally. Cooperation between neighbourhoods, regional processing and depots, and neighbourhood kitchens are further elements of the food supply for "another city" (Eichenberger 2017).[9]

From the 1950s onwards, much of the agricultural labour force moved to the industrial and service sectors and made their growth possible. However, now that these sectors are experiencing hardly any growth at all, and need less labour as a result of technological progress, one obvious option is to reorient the agricultural sector and make it attractive for diverse and meaningful activities.

Notes

1 Some numbers for Germany: whereas in 1960 there were 3.7 million people working in agriculture in West Germany, in 2016 only 940,000 people were still employed in agriculture as a full- or part-time occupation in Germany (East and West) (of which 449,000 were family members, 206,000 permanent foreign workers and 286,000 seasonal workers) (BMEL 2017).

2 For a more comprehensive description of the "changes in work in agriculture", see Hentschel/Fock (2015). Hentschel/Fock also note that agricultural work in Germany is not adequately recorded in the official statistics.

3 In addition to independent enterprises, there are businesses that are partnerships or other legal forms. Their number is constantly increasing, that of individual enterprises decreasing.

4 According to EU Regulation 1750/1999, Art. 28, "good farming practice" describes the "the standard of farming which a reasonable farmer would follow". This standard refers to conventional farming.

5 The other practices are land cover and green manure, crop rotation, reduced tillage, mixed crops, agroforestry, structural elements, conservation agriculture and diversified animal-plant systems.

6 It is not yet possible to assess whether and to what extent the further digitalisation of agriculture can make part of such labour intensification superfluous; this is currently being investigated and assessed, including through research on organic farming.

7 Binswanger et al. (1979, 294) called for direct income payments to farmers as early as the late 1970s. As criteria they proposed the safeguarding of farmers' livelihoods and organic farming.

8 The first pillar relates to direct payments, the second to rural development.

9 In the book "Die Andere Stadt", the author draws up detailed area and production calculations and comes to the conclusion that such a supply system is feasible.

Bibliography

AgrarBündnis (2010): *Nebenerwerb hat Zukunft. Gegenwart und Potenziale einer unterschätzten Betriebs- und Lebensform*, in: AgrarBündnis (Ed.): Der kritische Agrarbericht 2010, Konstanz/Hamm, 51–56

AgrarBündnis (2013): *Wandel und Zukunft der Arbeit in der Landwirtschaft. Ein Thesenpapier*, https://www.agrarbuendnis.de/Wandel-und-Zukunft-der-Arbeit.286.0.html (accessed 21.01.2021)

Binswanger, H.C., Geissberger, W., Ginsburg, T. (1979): *Der NAWU-Report: Strategien gegen Arbeitslosigkeit und Umweltkrise*, Frankfurt a. M.

BMU (Federal Ministry for the Environment, Nature Conservation and Nuclear Safety), UBA (Federal Environment Agency) (Ed.) (2020): *Environmental Awareness in Germany 2018*, Results of a representative survey, Dessau-Roßlau

BMEL (Bundesministerium für Ernährung und Landwirtschaft) (2017): *Daten und Fakten. Land-, Forst- und Ernährungswirtschaft mit Fischerei und Wein- und Gartenbau*, Rostock

Bossard, C., Santin, G., Guseva Canu, I. (2016): *Suicide among farmers in France: Occupational factors and recent trends*, Journal of Agromedicine 21(4), 310–315

Chandrapalan, R., Zorn, A., Lips, M. (2018): *Wirtschaftlichkeit paralandwirtschaftlicher Betriebszweige*, Agrarforschung Schweiz 9(11–12), 384–391

Dudley, N., Alexander, S. (2017): *Agriculture and biodiversity: A review*, Biodiversity 18(2–3), 45–49.

Eichenberger, U. (2017): *Vom Acker auf den Teller. Die andere Nahrungsmittelversorgung*, in: Widmer, H. (Ed.): Die Andere Stadt, Zürich

eurostat (2015): *While area used for agriculture remained stable, over 1 out of 4 farms disappeared between 2003 and 2013 in the EU*, News Release November 26, 2015

eurostat (2019): *Agri-environmental indicator – greenhouse gas emissions*, Statistics Explained, November 5, 2019

FiBL, IFOAM (2021): *The World of Organic Agriculture. Statistics and Emerging Trends 2021*, Frick and Bonn

Glaeser, B. (Ed.) (1986): *Die Krise der Landwirtschaft. Zur Renaissance von Agrarkulturen*, Frankfurt a. M.

Gottwald, F.-Th. (2003): *Der Bauer als Unternehmer. Perspektiven agrarkulturellen Wirtschaftens auf und mit dem Lande*, in: AgrarBündnis (Ed.): Der Kritische Agrarbericht 2003, Rheda-Wiedenbrück, Hamm, 270–276

Gottwald, F.-Th., Boergen, I. (2012): *Ein neues Miteinander. Erfolgsprinzipien für gute Kooperationen in und mit der Landwirtschaft*, in: AgrarBündnis (Ed.): Der kritische Agrarbericht 2012, Konstanz, Hamm, 255–260

Groeneveld, S. (1986): *Agrarkulturen statt Landwirtschaft: Entwurf einer Perspektive*, in: Glaeser, B. (Ed.): Die Krise der Landwirtschaft. Zur Renaissance von Agrarkulturen, Frankfurt a. M., 165–186

Hentschel, T., Fock, T. (2015): *Wandel der Arbeit in der Landwirtschaft. Über die zunehmende Industrialisierung der Landwirtschaft und ihre Folgen*, in: Agrar-Bündnis (Ed.): Der kritische Agrarbericht 2012, Konstanz, Hamm, 69–74

Heinrich Böll Foundation, Friends of the Earth Europe, Bird Life Europe & Central Asia (2019): *Agriculture Atlas. Facts and Figures on EU Farming Policy*, Berlin

Hoppichler, J. (2016): *Bäuerliche Ökonomie. Wiederentdeckung eines Erfolgsmodells*, in: AgrarBündnis (Ed.): Der Kritische Agrarbericht 2016, Konstanz, Hamm, 283–289

Hovorka, G. (2011): *Die Reform der Agrarpolitik der EU aus Sicht der Berggebiete*, in: Ländlicher Raum 01/2011, Online-Fachzeitschrift des Bundesministeriums für Land- und Forstwirtschaft, Umwelt und Wasserwirtschaft

IPPC (2014): Climate Change (2014): *Mitigation of climate change*, Contribution of Working Group III to the Fifth Assessment Report of the Intergovernmental Panel on Climate Change, Chapter 11, New York

Janitzki, A. (1998): *Ist Landwirtschaft gemeinnützig?* in: AgrarBündnis (Ed.): Der kritische Agrarbericht 1998, Rheda-Wiedenbrück, 189ff.

O'Hara, S.U., Stagl, S. (2001): *Global food markets and their local alternatives: A socio-ecological economic perspective*, Population and Environment 22, 533–554

Parent-Thirion, A. (2007): *Fourth European Working Conditions Survey: European Foundation for the Improvement of Living and Working Conditions*, Luxembourg

Pe'er, G., Bonn, A., Bruelheide, H., et al. (2020): *Action needed for the EU common agricultural policy to address sustainability challenges*, People and Nature 2, 305–316

Priebe, H. (1990): *Die subventionierte Naturzerstörung. Plädoyer für eine neue Agrarkultur*, München

Reissig, L. (2017): *Häufigkeit von Burnouts in der Schweizer Landwirtschaft*, Agrarforschung Schweiz 8(10), 402–409

Rosa-Schleich, J., Loos, J., Mußhoff, O., Tscharntke, T. (2019): *Ecological-economic trade-offs of diversified farming systems – a review*, Ecological Economics 160, 251–263

Schweisfurth-Stiftung (1988): *Jahresbericht*, München

Schweisfurth, K.L., Gottwald, F.-Th., Dierkes, M. (2002): *Wege zu einer nachhaltigen Agrar- und Ernährungskultur. Leitbild für eine zukunftsfähige Lebensmittelerzeugung, -verarbeitung und -vermarktung*, München

Siegenthaler, T. (2016): *Modelle der solidarischen Landwirtschaft: eine Übersicht*, Kultur und Politik: Zeitschrift für ökologische, soziale und wirtschaftliche Zusammenhänge 1, 18–19

Stodieck, F. (2018): *Entwicklung und Trends 2017 – Ein „Weiter so" ist keine Option – jetzt wird sondiert*, in: AgrarBündnis (Ed.): Der Kritische Agrarbericht 2018, Konstanz, 21–33

Verbände-Plattform zur GAP (2018): *Die EU-Agrarpolitik muss gesellschaftlichen Mehrwert bringen. Für Umwelt, biologische Vielfalt, Tierschutz und wirtschaftliche Perspektiven für bäuerliche Betriebe und ländliche Gemeinschaften*, Berlin

Wochenblatt (2017): *Burnout: Bauern in der Krise*, 10.11.2017

11 Digitalisation and concepts of extended work

Linda Nierling and Bettina-Johanna Krings[*]

Summary

The following chapter addresses the question of how the digitalisation of the world of work can affect concepts of extended work, i.e. an extended spectrum of forms of human work. This question is discussed using three thematic areas as illustrative examples, namely developments with regard to the volume of work, to working time and to new digital forms of work. It emerges that current transformation processes due to digitalisation are in principle compatible with concepts of extended work and could even facilitate their implementation. However, in order for this potential to be realised, current digital developments and their use in the world of work need to be subject to social deliberation and action.

1 Introduction

The beginning of the "Internet Age" (Huws 2003) and the subsequent widespread introduction of digital technologies in almost all working environments are regarded as a historical caesura in the evolution of formal employment (Castells 1996; Baukrowitz et al. 2006; Börner et al. 2017). In the last two to three decades, technical – and above all, digital – innovations have significantly changed the institutional, operational and individual framework conditions of work. "Digital and networked working is now the norm in virtually all sectors of the economy" (Schwemmle/Wedde 2012, 16). On the basis of these innovations, a "socio-technical scope for action" (Rammert/Schulz-Schäfer 2002; Huws 2003) has now emerged which in terms of its momentum and potential is almost unprecedented in the world of work (Fisher 2008; Poutanen et al. 2020).

The "concepts of extended work" (see e.g. Nierling 2012 on concepts of extended work and see the chapter by Gerold in this book) which have emerged in the context of the post-growth debate seek to broaden

DOI: 10.4324/9781003187370-11

the spectrum of forms of human work compared to the previous narrow definition of work as gainful employment, and to include not only paid work but volunteer work, care and family work and self-determined work. In this book, the term "meaningful activity" is used to cover this spectrum.

The debate on the digitalisation of work and the debate on concepts of extended work have so far only rarely been brought together: the former addresses "good digital work", but not against the background of a concept of extended work. And the debate on extended work concepts has not yet systematically integrated the influence of digital technologies or the structural changes brought about by digitalisation. Rather, there is a tendency in debates about the digitalisation of work to regard technical developments as a normative orientation and to align the organisation of (paid) work with the supposed requirements of technical-rational logic. The automatisation of work is generally assumed to result in an increase in efficiency and the acceleration and increasing standardisation of work processes. This perspective is at odds with notions of extended work, which seek in a normative way to set out a model balance of work and life leading to a higher quality of both (Nierling 2012).

In what follows, we first outline the development of the debate on the "digitalisation of work" since the 1990s (Section 2). Section 3 then reviews the dominant debates in the digitalisation discourse regarding the volume of work, working time and forms of work, and relates them critically to the normative model of extended work. Finally, Section 4 identifies challenges for the organisation of extended work in the course of digitalisation.

2 The digitalisation of work as a continuous process

The use of digital technologies in the world of work was described early on under the general heading of the "informatisation of work" (Schmiede 1996; Huws 2003). "Informatised work" refers to "all activities in which the processing of information is the central element and information technologies are used" (Baukrowitz et al. 2006, 45). The increase in digital forms of work and in labour markets networked by information technology was subject to a critical analysis undertaken by labour sociologists which had a wide impact, in particular the term "Entgrenzung" (Kratzer 2003), meaning the blurring of boundaries. "Entgrenzung" is understood as the "erosion of temporal, spatial, content-related, motivational and other boundaries between currently prevalent forms of the deployment and use of labour" (ibid., 44) and describes the transformation of the standard employment relationship to flexible and open forms of work organisation (Sennett 1998; Krings 2011).

Scientific analyses are in agreement that (digital) mechanisation in the world of work must be considered in its respective context, and that general statements about its effects are not possible. However, there is a consensus that processes of digitalisation will significantly change work organisation, work processes and occupational profiles in the future (Noon et al. 2013; Huws 2013). Completely new forms of work have also emerged, such as work coordinated via digital platforms. Some of these have met with great approval from (mostly young) users and have inspired visionary ideas about future forms of work, but they are also being discussed critically because they present major challenges for trade union negotiations and social security systems (De Stefano 2016).

In the debates about a post-growth society, the "relationship *between* post-growth and digitalisation" is still an "empty space" (Schmelzer/ Vetter 2019, 233, emphasis in source). There is no doubt that digitalisation is also driving visions of a post-growth society in which a broad understanding of work, with a reduced importance for gainful employment, is key (Mason 2015). How digitalisation processes may affect work in its extended understanding will be discussed in the following section.

3 Extended work and starting points for digitalisation

In accordance with the goals of the socio-ecological transformation, the primacy of formal employment is to be countered by a broader understanding of work and the pervasive commodification of human activities, i.e. the degree to which human work has "become a tradable good" is to be scaled back (Brandl/Hildebrandt 2002; Nierling 2012).[1] This is linked to the idea that having a wide range of activities promotes a self-determined lifestyle and creates sustainable working and living conditions that involve the whole person and their social environment. The revaluation and redistribution of work thus represents a significant "crystallisation point in the post-growth debate" (Schmelzer/Vetter 2019, 30; see also Gerold in this book).

Concepts of extended work developed from the 1970s onwards in parallel with the structural change from an industrial to a service society (Illich 1978). The powerful significance of gainful employment was relativised, and other forms of work were recognised and accorded value as such, and thus as necessary for social cohesion and individual wellbeing. Many proposals for implementing this changed perception emerged (for an overview see Nierling 2012). However, these concepts have found only limited wider resonance in public debate. This was mainly due to the fact that recognition mechanisms such as social security systems, income and organisational integration provide considerable support for paid work, while other – unpaid – forms of work receive far less recognition (Braverman 1974).

So far, digitalisation has hardly played a role in the debate on concepts of extended work. Today, however, the question arises – also in view of digitalisation programmes as policy – of how social visions of concepts of extended work and digitalisation can be combined. What opportunities could digitalisation of the world of work open up for concepts of extended work? And where might the main pitfalls leading to failure lie?

Three areas can be identified (Nierling 2018):

1. Volume of work: possible job losses through the substitution of human labour;
2. Working time: ways in which the boundaries between work and life are being blurred;
3. Forms of work: the emergence of new digital forms of work through platform work and sharing models.

3.1 Volume of work

In recent decades the technical capacity and performance of information and communication technologies, which massively expand data volumes and comprehensively network people and things, has increased enormously (Bell 1976; Castells 1996). Coupled with advances in robotics and sensor technology, this means that considerable improvements in performance are also expected in industrial production (Industry 4.0). In the services sector, important technical applications of artificial intelligence and algorithms may emerge.

Frey and Osborne (2013) calculated that 47 percent of jobs in the USA could be automated and thus eliminated. Further studies have questioned this high figure (Bonin et al. 2015); Lorenz et al. (2015) even forecast increases in employment. In the meantime, it is assumed that the changes are "likely to be of the order of magnitude known from the past" (Absenger et al. 2016, 7). The effect on employment figures is expected to be relatively small because job losses are likely to be absorbed by reallocation (Niebel et al. 2018). But regardless of how large or small the quantitative changes are, digital technologies will change the labour market significantly in *qualitative* terms, i.e. new occupational profiles will emerge and new skills will be required (Blien et al. 2019).

The possible replacement of human labour by technology – in contrast to the automation of the 1970s and 1980s – no longer relates only to industrial production, but also to intellectual work (Krings 2011; Gandini 2016). For example, software is already available today that can write (standardised) journalistic reports, and ever-improving automatic speech recognition technology also has the potential to replace much secretarial work, for example.[2]

How can social actors deal with these changes in the world of work? Could the potential decline in human labour actually be an opportunity to discuss and implement models of extended work? Some authors, such as Kurz and Rieger (2013, 284), believe this to be the case:

> It should no longer be a personal drama when an essentially boring, strenuous, health-sapping or dangerous job is done by machines. Creating the economic and social conditions that enable us to see our new symbiosis with machines as something positive, liberating and meaningful requires wide-ranging discussion of our societal goals and ideals.

However, new, visionary concepts of digital extended work have not been developed to date. The debate on digitalisation has so far focused on education and the need to equip employees for new technical requirements through changing occupational profiles, fields of activity and skills (Walwei 2016). Such measures should be seen as fundamentally positive. However, they remain stuck on old pathways; in other words, they are tied to the rationale of gainful employment (Ebert/Rahner 2017).

If one assumes, though, that digitalisation will release human labour, there may well be scope for activities that can be carried out alongside and outside gainful employment (in the sense of mixed work). This would require, first, at the social and political level, a change to the dominant model of work that recognises its plurality. At the same time, specific measures would have to be taken: these could include a financial credit at the beginning of adult life, or the promotion of cooperative ideas "in the digital age". Such approaches should be built on and taken further in the spirit of an expanded concept of work (Jürgens et al. 2018).

3.2 Working time

Labour and industrial sociologists have been discussing the consequences of flexible working hours intensively since the 1990s (Kratzer 2003). The flexibilisation of working hours has been based since the beginning on technical options – initially on information and communication technologies – and has expanded to the point of "permanent availability" through the use of digital technologies and mobile devices (Carstensen 2015, 187). The option of virtual work, i.e. not tied to either time or place, is spreading rapidly. This is often associated with the idea of a successful "work-life balance" through the flexible accommodation of the needs of both spheres – gainful employment and private life (Krings et al. 2010).

Academic research is divided on whether the positive or negative consequences of the growing dissolution of boundaries predominate. On the one hand, the focus may be on the negative health effects of the end of the "regulated 8-hour working day, of regulated breaks and prescribed maximum working hours" (Absenger et al. 2016, 8). On the other hand, flexible working hours can facilitate the reconciliation of family and career (Krings et al. 2010; for a critical view, see von Jorck/Schrader in this book, see also Hochschild 1997). Time flexibility is supposed to make it possible to reconcile work and private life in everyday life and also in different life phases (Corino 2018).

Relevant questions for concepts of extended work and digitalisation also arise from the analysis of working time, because the way working time is organised is of central importance when it comes to forms of extended work. In this context, flexible working hours are primarily discussed under the heading of "mobile work". There is also some discussion of restrictions on working hours, for example the "digital end of the working day" at VW[3] or the "right to be unavailable" which was recently the subject of political debate.[4] After the reduction of working hours had long been absent from collective bargaining negotiations and public debates (see Reuter in this book), it has now once again come to the fore, partly in light of the potential consequences of automation (Srnicek/Williams 2016). This is relevant for extended work, because working time is the basis for creating free time for the broader spectrum of activities such as family work, self-determined work, voluntary work or political participation (Coote/Maréchal 2018).

Today, the high demands on time and skills made by gainful employment are (still) reflected in a lack of time for family work. This is particularly evident in the care of the elderly (on care work and its demands, see also Hagedorn in this book). Care and care work (care and nursing care or professional nursing work) are poorly paid despite their increasing general orientation towards formal employment and the growth in outsourcing of private care work (Aulenbacher/Dammayr 2014, 10).

There are many different approaches to providing care services by means of digital technologies (e.g. care robots). However, the use of technology in a social field is always in part a transformation process that should be subject to a thorough technology assessment. For example, the use of new technologies often results in new objectives which would not have been conceivable without these technologies, and which can create new dependencies. The use of tablet computers in ambulatory care, for example, has simplified the documentation task for nurses, since the relevant vital data can be entered in a standardised form and are available in aggregated form for further work processes. At the same time, tablets are used to monitor the work process, which makes spontaneous and caring interactions between nurses and patients more difficult (Mol et al. 2010).

There is no doubt that digitalisation enables flexible working hours and creates the scope at the individual level for a variety of work forms. This is why it is important to link up with current debates on reducing working hours and to recognise the value of the time that can then be devoted to other people in the form of extended work. Such work can certainly be given technical support and may thereby be enhanced in value.

3.3 New digital forms of work

The third point to be addressed here is the emergence of new digital forms of work such as platform work (De Stefano 2016; Börner et al. 2017). Platform work can be divided into different types, which differ in many aspects (such as form and level of remuneration, qualifications required, whether purely virtual work or dependent on location and time). A key common feature is that the work is distributed via Internet platforms. A recently proposed typology distinguishes three types (Vandaele 2018):

1. "Online micro crowd work": one example of this is the Amazon Mechanical Turk platform, which distributes e.g. the task of describing images in online catalogues to the digital crowd.
2. "Online macro crowd work": it is carried out by highly qualified freelancers and may include IT services or design assignments, for example.
3. "Time-and-place–dependent on-demand work": examples of this include repair or cleaning services, delivery services (for example Lieferando) or mobility services (for example Uber).

Platform work currently raises many unanswered and fundamental issues such as the lack of workers' rights or the low remuneration of crowdworkers, and is relevant to the debate on extended work in two ways.

First, the evolution of crowd work highlights the lack of viable social security schemes for such new forms of employment and self-employment (see Kubon-Gilke in this book). Second, the scope for extended work can be inferred from the way work activities are distributed via the Internet: digital platforms can be used for the networking and communication of actors (examples are community hubs for mutual assistance, machines or tools, or the organisation of labour and/or the dissemination of technical blueprints for cooperative agricultural projects). (Digital) technology can also give rise to new forms of extended work, as envisaged in the concept of "high-tech self-providing", i.e. self-provisioning at the highest technical level (Schor 2010; Bergmann, 2019): using digital "commons", instructions are provided for specific technical applications such as prostheses or wind turbines, which can be (re)built at local level by lay people (Kostakis et al. 2018). In addition, the continuing interest in open workshops such as FabLabs or Bike Kitchens (Bradley 2018; Schneider 2018) shows that it is precisely through the inclusion of (digital) technology in self-determined work that new kinds of social innovation can emerge in which technology is the key to communitisation.

3.4 Interim conclusions

In all three fields of digital work there are potential links to extended work.

In terms of the *volume of work*, working time which is no longer required due to the digital transformation of the labour market could be used more for family, neighbourhood, hobbies or community engagement. Gainful employment would thus decline in importance, while at the same time a greater variety of activities would be possible (Nierling 2012).

With regard to *working time*, not only its flexibilisation, but also and more especially its reduction, or the integration of alternative working time arrangements into peoples' life courses, should be under discussion, so that the special demands of care work, in particular, can be met. This can create space for the many kinds of extended work, space which must be given social recognition and made accessible for individual life paths (Stronge/Harper 2019).

With regard to *new digital forms of work*, emerging platforms should not only be available for paid forms of work. Rather, the potential of digital networking should be tapped for extended work such as the coordination of urban gardening projects or the establishment of FabLabs (Mason 2015).

At this point it should be emphasised that extended work can also provide an alternative to increasingly virtual workspaces, for example by enabling manual, physical or social experience to be gained through manual or gardening work for oneself, or through care work. The trick – following Ivan Illich – should lie in not diminishing the valuable "analogue" elements of extended work through increasing virtualisation, but rather enriching them in a way that is oriented towards human needs (Illich 1973; Sennett 2008; Samerski 2018).

4 Challenges for forms of extended work in the course of digitalisation

Parallel to the debates on digitalisation, on "Industry 4.0" and artificial intelligence, other digital developments are currently spreading in numerous working environments. In view of the global ecological and economic crises, it is surprising that such strategies are still justified using arguments for enhancing economic performance and competitiveness. This means that the opportunities and potential for a humane and visionary design of socio-technical working environments remain unused. Rather, the conversion to digital work processes will be driven forward in accordance with the (classical) objective of increasing productivity. Experience to date shows that digitalisation intensifies gainful employment in particular and creates new insecurities, and that this results in high subjective follow-up costs (Muhic/Johanson 2014). If models of extended work are compared with current developments in digital working, it quickly becomes clear that they are not really compatible. A technical mindset predominates which appears to be incompatible with the goals associated with expanded forms of work.

In order to strengthen the concept of extended work, digital structural change should therefore not primarily be driven by technology – as has been the case up to now – but should be managed with human needs in mind, for example by creating space for self-determined forms of work that support and help shape technical innovations. In this way, digital technologies could enrich "analogue" extended work, for example through new networking possibilities, work arrangements that are more flexible in terms of time and place, or new digitally supported forms of community work (such as FabLabs or virtual platforms). The digital possibilities for flexible time management should also be used and developed much more to support extended work. For extended work can support a self-determined lifestyle, for example if it reduces working hours or enables new life courses.

Experience in recent years has shown that the world of work is in transition and that the total volume of work, working time models and forms of work are all changing, in many ways. These processes should be used more intensively to design and support extended forms of work. To help the social transformation towards a post-growth society, special attention should therefore be paid in future to ensuring that time and productivity gains are not "reinvested" exclusively in the sphere of gainful employment, as has been the case in the past. Rather, models should be developed that combine new technologies with social visions of an ecologically oriented and solidarity-based work society. This could result in the emergence of free spaces that could accommodate the diversity of meaningful human activity in a post-growth society.

Notes

* The authors wish to thank Philipp Frey for valuable comments on this chapter.
1 Examples of commodification are the consumption of food in restaurants instead of cooking it oneself or the commissioning of craftsmen instead of self-building.
2 One example is Google Duplex – a digital assistant that can make calls by itself.
3 This measure has been in place since 2011. It is based on the idea that no e-mails will be sent after normal business hours, i.e. between 18.15 and 7.00. One criticism of this measure is that it applies only to a small proportion of employees covered by collective agreements. However, Daimler and BMW have also subsequently launched initiatives aimed at restricting working hours.
4 Rosa (2018) even goes a step further at the level of social theory and calls for people to be "unavailable" as a counter-model to the alienated world of work and life in today's societies. In view of ubiquitous and technically generated accessibility, the issue here is the right of unavailability, a right that has a high emancipatory value.

Bibliography

Absenger, N., Ahlers, E., Herzog-Stein, A., Lott, Y., Maschke, M., Schietinger, M. (Eds.) (2016): *Digitalisierung der Arbeitswelt?* Ein Report aus der Hans-Böckler-Stiftung, Mitbestimmungs-Report, No. 24, Düsseldorf

Arbeitskreis Industrie 4.0 (2013): *Umsetzungsempfehlungen für das Zukunftsprojekt Industrie 4.0*, Abschlussbericht, www.bmbf.de/files/Umsetzungsempfehlungen_Industrie4_0.pdf (accessed 21.01.2021)

Aulenbacher, B., Dammayr, M. (2014): *Für sich und andere sorgen – Einleitung*, in: Aulenbacher, B., Dammayr, M. (Eds.): Für sich und andere sorgen. Krise und Zukunft von Care in der modernen Gesellschaft, Weinheim/Basel, 9–17

Baukrowitz, A., Berker, T., Boes, A., Pfeiffer, S., Schmiede, R., Will, M. (Eds.) (2006): *Informatisierung der Arbeit – Gesellschaft im Umbruch*, Berlin

Bell, D. (1976): *The Coming of Post-Industrial Society*, New York

Bergmann, F. (2019): *New Work, New Culture. Work We Want and a Culture That Strengthens Us*, Winchester, Washington

Blien, U., Ludewig, O., Rossen, A., Sanner, H. (2019): *Zu den Arbeitsmarktwirkungen des technischen Fortschritts*, in: Hagemann, H., Kromphardt, J., Sahin, B. (Eds.): Arbeit und Beschäftigung – Keynes und Marx, Marburg, 43–55

Börner, F., Kehl, C., Nierling, L. (2017): *Chancen und Risiken mobiler und digitaler Kommunikation in der Arbeitswelt*, Endbericht zum TA-Projekt, Berlin

Bonin, H., Gregory, T., Zierahn, U. (2015): *Übertragung der Studie von Frey/Osborne (2013) auf Deutschland*, Zentrum für Europäische Wirtschaftsforschung, Kurzexpertise Nr. 57

Bradley, K. (2018): *Bike kitchens – spaces for convivial tools*, Journal of Cleaner Production 197, 1676–1683

Brandl, S., Hildebrandt, E. (2002): *Zukunft der Arbeit und soziale Nachhaltigkeit. Zur Transformation der Arbeitsgesellschaft vor dem Hintergrund der Nachhaltigkeitsdebatte*, Opladen

Braverman, H. (1974): *Labor and Monopoly Capital: The Degradation of Work in the Twentieth Century*, New York

Carstensen, T. (2015): *Neue Anforderungen und Belastungen durch digitale und mobile Technologien*, WSI-Mitteilungen 3, 187–193

Castells, M. (1996): *The Rise of the Network Society, the Information Age: Economy, Society and Culture*, Vol. I., Cambridge

Coote, A., Maréchal, A. (2018): *When time isn't money: The case for working time reduction*, Green European Journal 17, 66–70

Corino, E. (2018): *Das Nacheinanderprinzip. Vom gelasseneren Umgang mit Familie und Beruf*, Berlin

De Stefano, V. (2016): *The Rise of the "Just-in-Time-Workforce": On-Demand Work, Crowdwork and Labour Protection in the "Gig-Economy"*, Geneva

Ebert, A., Rahner, S. (2017): *Warum das bedingungslose Grundeinkommen keine Antwort auf den digitalen Wandel ist*, in: Bundesministerium für Arbeit und Soziales (Ed.): Werkheft 04. Sozialstaat im Wandel, Berlin, 174–181

Fisher, E. (2008): *The Classes Workplace: The Digerati and the New Spirit of Technocapitalism*, Oxford

Frey, C.B., Osborne, M.A. (2013): *The Future of Employment: How Susceptible Are Jobs to Computerisation?* Oxford

Gandini, A. (2016): *The Reputation Economy: Understanding Knowledge Work in Digital Society*, London

Hochschild, A. (1997): *The Time Bind: When Work Becomes Home and Home Becomes Work*, New York

Huws, U. (2003): *The Making of a Cybertariat: Virtual Work in a Real World*, New York

Huws, U. (2013): *Working online, living offline: Labour in the internet age*, Work Organisation, Labour & Globalization 7(1), 1–11

Illich, I. (1973): *Tools for Conviviality*, New York

Illich, I. (1978): *The Right to Useful Unemployment*, London

Ittermann, P., Niehaus, J., Hirsch-Kreinsen, H. (2015): *Arbeiten in der Industrie 4.0. Trendbestimmungen und arbeitspolitische Handlungsfelder*, Düsseldorf

Jürgens, K., Hoffmann, R., Schildmann, C. (2018): *Let's Transform Work! Recommendations and Proposals from the Commission on the Work of the Future*, Düsseldorf

Kostakis, V., Latoufis, K., Liarokapis, M., Bauwens, M. (2018): *The convergence of digital commons with local manufacturing from a degrowth perspective: Two illustrative cases*, Journal of Cleaner Production 197, 1684–1693

Kratzer, N. (2003): *Arbeitskraft in Entgrenzung. Grenzenlose Anforderungen, erweiterte Spielräume, begrenzte Ressourcen*, Berlin

Krings, B.-J. (Ed.) (2011): *Brain Drain or Brain Gain? Changes of Work in Knowledge-based Societies*, Berlin

Krings, B.-J. (2018): *Digitalisiert, effizient & global? Die fortlaufende Technisierung der Erwerbsarbeit*, in: Hausstein, A., Zheng, C. (Eds.): Industrie 4.0/Made in China 2025. Gesellschaftswissenschaftliche Perspektiven auf Digitalisierung in Deutschland und China, Karlsruher Studien Technik und Kultur, Vol. 10, Karlsruhe, 165–181

Krings, B.-J., Nierling, L., Pedaci, M. (2010): *Out of control: Changes in working-time and strategies for work-life balance in Europe*, Work Organisation, Labour & Globalisation 4(1), 136–159

Kurz, C., Rieger, F. (2013): *Arbeitsfrei. Eine Entdeckungsreise zu den Maschinen, die uns ersetzen*, München

Lorenz, M., Rüßmann, M., Strack, R., Lueth, K.L., Bolle, M. (2015): *Man and Machine in Industry 4.0. How Will Technology Transform the Industrial Workforce Through 2025?* Boston Consulting Group, Munich

Mason, P (2015): *Post Capitalism: A Guide to Our Future*, London

Mol, A., Moser, I., Pols, J. (Eds.) (2010): *Care in Practice: On Tinkering in Clinics, Homes and Farms*, Bielefeld

Muhic, M., Johanson, B. (2014): *Cloud sourcing – next generation outsourcing?* Procedia Technology 16, 553–561

Niebel, T., Saam, M., Schulte, P. (2018): *The Sectoral Impact of the Digitisation of the Economy*, European Commission, Directorate-General of Communications Networks, Content & Technology, Brussels

Nierling, L. (2012): *"This is a bit of the good life": Recognition of unpaid work from the perspective of degrowth*, Ecological Economics 84, 240–246

Nierling, L. (2018): *Digitale Rationalisierung, digitale Entgrenzung und digitale Arbeitsteilung? Trends und Herausforderungen einer digitalen Arbeitswelt – sozialwissenschaftliche Perspektiven*, in: Hausstein A., Zheng, C. (Eds.): Industrie 4.0/Made in China 2025. Gesellschaftswissenschaftliche Perspektiven auf Digitalisierung in Deutschland und China, Karlsruher Studien Technik und Kultur, Vol. 10, Karlsruhe, 183–196

Noon, M., Blyton, P., Morrell, K. (2013): *The Realities of Work – Experiencing Work and Employment in Contemporary Society*, London

Poutanen, S.; Kovalainen, A.; Rouvinen, P. (2020): *Digital Work and the Platform Economy. Understanding Tasks, Skills and Capabilities in the New Era*, London and New York

Rammert, W., Schulz-Schaeffer, I. (2002): *Technik und Handeln. Wenn soziales Handeln sich auf menschliches Verhalten und technische Abläufe verteilt*, in: Rammert, W., Schulz-Schaeffer, I. (Eds.): Können Maschinen handeln? Soziologische Beiträge zum Verhältnis von Mensch und Technik, Frankfurt a. M., 11–64

Rosa, H. (2018): *Unverfügbarkeit*, Salzburg

Samerski, S. (2018): *Tools for degrowth? Ivan Illich's critique of technology revisited*, Journal of Cleaner Production 197, 1637–1646

Schmelzer, M., Vetter, A. (2019): *Degrowth/Postwachstum zur Einführung*, Hamburg

Schmiede, R. (Ed.) (1996): *Virtuelle Arbeitswelten. Arbeit, Produktivität und Subjekt in der „Informationsgesellschaft"*, Berlin

Schneider, C. (2018): *Opening Digital Fabrication: Transforming TechKnowledgies*, Karlsruhe

Schor, J.B. (2010): *Plenitude: The New Economics of True Wealth*, New York

Schwemmle, M., Wedde, P. (2012): *Digitale Arbeit in Deutschland. Potentiale und Problemlagen*, Bericht herausgegeben von der Friedrich Ebert Stiftung, Bonn

Sennett, R. (1998): *The Corrosion of Character. The Personal Consequences of Work in the New Capitalism*, New York

Sennett, R. (2008): *The Craftsman*, London

Srnicek, N., Williams, A. (2016): *Inventing the Future*, London

Stronge, W., Harper, A. (2019): *The Shorter Working Week: A Radical and Pragmatic Proposal*, Hampshire

Vandaele, K. (2018): *Will Trade Unions Survive in the Platform Economy? Emerging Patterns of Platform Workers' Collective Voice and Representation in Europe*, Brussels

Walwei, U. (2016): *Digitalization and Structural Labour Market Problems: The Case of Germany*, Geneva

Part 4

The socio-economic context

12 Social security in the post-growth society

Gisela Kubon-Gilke[*]

Summary

The financing of most social security systems is based on social security contributions from paid employment and on general taxation. If labour productivity increases or the proportion of the elderly in the population rises, this will result in pressure for economic growth if participation in social life is to be secured in the long term. A post-growth society therefore needs a re-structuring of social security. Two alternatives are presented in this chapter: first, a preventive social policy, e.g. through redistribution of wealth, state or employee investment funds and the promotion of cooperatives and workers' self-management; second, a change in the financing and entitlement basis, for example through an unconditional basic income, negative income tax or the inclusion of civil society activities not remunerated in monetary terms (e.g. timebanking models). The chapter analyses the extent to which the pressure for growth can be reduced by such alternative ways of providing social security.

> Only those orientations transcending reality will be referred to by us as
> utopian which, when they pass over into conduct, tend to shatter, either
> partially or wholly, the order of things prevailing at the time.
>
> (Mannheim 1991/1929, 173)

1 Introduction

As a rule, the central reference parameter of social security systems is earned income. They are financed from the income of individuals through social security contributions or (income) taxes, and they either guarantee a certain percentage of the individual's last net income or provide a universal basic livelihood for all at the same level, sometimes supplemented by a range of services designed to increase the opportunities for recipients on the labour market.

DOI: 10.4324/9781003187370-12

If income from capital and employment provides the basis for social order, then that order is at risk if production stagnates or declines because only production generates income, as the concept of national accounts shows. The debate about post-growth society is therefore also about how social security might be decoupled from earned income and thus from economic growth. However, fundamental reforms are very difficult to conceptualise and to implement politically, because the contingent nature of human value systems, motives and preferences tends to perpetuate the social security system (on change processes, see Lewin 1947).

To adhere to the status quo means failing to grasp the potential of alternative *social narratives* to point the way forward, if they are understood as implementable utopias in the sense of Karl Mannheim (1991/1929), which can support a reform process in the sense of Lewin (1947). Eduard Heimann (1980/1929), one of the leading social theorists of the first half of the 20th century, saw the period of transformation to a capitalist market society in the 19th century, with all its social problems, as the birth of new social ideas and *social narratives* and of the social movements they motivated. Actual and perceived injustices in terms of poverty and inequality provided the starting point in his view. They produced new social ideas and movements and put pressure on the political system. Measures such as social security, which alleviated social problems, were the outcome. According to Heimann's underlying theory, today's social and ecological problems could bring about something similar through new social-ecological ideas and corresponding social movements.

A post-growth society (PWG) will only become a "real", i.e. implementable utopia and coherent social structure if it is combined with concrete policies and programmes (such as an unconditional basic income or a solidarity-based citizens' insurance). Undesirable effects such as increased poverty and inequality at times of economic stagnation or decline must be taken into account. Only in this way can the system remain resilient and the democratic constitution of society be preserved.[1] The goals of sustainability and social justice provide the normative basis for a post-growth society (Seidl/Zahrnt 2010) and for other growth-critical concepts.

2 Competition between coordination systems

In transaction cost theory (see Kubon-Gilke 2018, Chapter 4), there are three ways to solve the allocation and distribution problem in society:[2] markets, hierarchy (central control) and reciprocity. In predominantly market-based economies, markets and hierarchies generally use money as a medium of exchange; reciprocal subsystems are based on reciprocity and are more likely to involve payment in kind or time. They also have a different social-psychological impact due to their underlying social norms and values (for a more detailed discussion, see Kubon-Gilke 2018, section 2). The theory is that – in the area of social security, too – the subsystems that best coordinate an economy based on the division of labour with comparatively low transaction costs will eventually predominate, in a kind of evolutionary process.

If, under market or hierarchy systems, costs are passed on to society and the environment to a greater extent than under reciprocal systems, then "system competition" will not necessarily result in the best system in terms of transaction costs prevailing. If such costs cannot be passed on thanks to internalisation, the market and hierarchy may nevertheless remain superior to reciprocity. Conversely, even under the current economic system, in which many costs are shifted from the market or state sector to the social and ecological level, reciprocal forms of coordination have been able to achieve transaction cost advantages in some areas, for example within households or local networks. Reciprocity systems also provide good arenas for social innovation.

3 Social security under different coordination systems

To date, social security in most capitalist countries has been based only on the monetarily controlled areas of market-mediated and state-directed production. This form of production and price-mediated or state-financed consumption (and only the corresponding form of production) lead to monetary income, which, in turn, provides the basis for social security contributions.

Those who were mainly active in reciprocally organised areas – such as housework, bringing up children, care and nursing of family members, voluntary work or neighbourhood assistance – and thus received little or no pay, are only covered partially and unsystematically in these social insurance systems: thanks to parental allowance regulations, family members who are employed and paying contributions, or pension credit periods while bringing up children, for example, or by claims to widows' or widowers' benefits. Tax-financed basic social security schemes complement these social insurance elements. If reciprocally organised activities increase in future, for example because the need for care for the elderly rises, then the question of how to provide social security for such people will become more pressing.

For example, the following situation may arise. If the average age of the population increases and healthcare costs rise, the proportion of reciprocally organised areas in the overall economy may well increase. In this case, even with a growing gross domestic product (GDP), it might become difficult to cover the costs of social security for pensioners from the contributions of wage earners alone, because the number of wage earners might have decreased. If GDP is not growing any more, the problem is exacerbated, and considerable social upheaval may result (see Höpflinger 2010). This makes it all the more important to think about reforms to the existing social security system, about possible supplements and about testing new and visionary approaches.

4 Alternative forms of social security in the post-growth society

Various reforms, innovations and additions to the current social security system are currently being discussed. In the spirit of prevention, they are intended to systematically reduce inequalities in opportunities, wealth and income, thus improving the scope for private self-provision and broadening the basis of social security. This would also reduce dependence on GDP growth.

In what follows, a selection of reform ideas will be presented and evaluated. Concepts such as citizens' insurance, a switch from a pay-as-you-go to a funded pension system,[3] shorter working hours, later retirement and various other proposals (e.g. the use of premium-based models or the promotion of healthy lifestyles in healthcare systems; see the proposals in Umweltbundesamt, 2018) are not examined in detail. Although in some cases they broaden the finance basis of social security, their aim is to reduce the need for social services and to partially decouple social security from its dependence on formal employment alone. However, it is only under certain specific conditions that such concepts can help to solve problems such as the decline in total wages in the course of digitalisation, rising unemployment or the growth of the low-wage sector, as they continue to rely on monetary income. Nor will this section address in detail the fundamental problem of the extent to which our current economic system, in general and irrespective of the type of social security it provides, is dependent on growth, and which immanent systemic crises may result from this (see Binswanger 2013; Witt 2018). Instead, a number of reform ideas will be presented which either broaden the finance basis of social security to a greater or lesser extent or have a preventive effect.

4.1 Preventive social policy

Redistribution of wealth. Wealth redistribution can be seen as a kind of preventive social policy, as a more equal distribution of wealth makes personal social security possible for poorer people too (see Kubon-Gilke et al. 2018, section 7.6.2). It is for reasons of social justice that Piketty, for example, argues for the introduction of a wealth tax or an increase in existing wealth taxes; and Rüstow proposed a progressive inheritance tax in the 1960s already. Atkinson proposes a redistribution of wealth through subsidised social housing. However, the question of how a (significant) tax on wealth affects economic development cannot yet be answered with certainty. Such a tax could promote growth through increased consumption or reduce it through a lower willingness to invest. Even if the former may result in greater environmental impact, the revenue from wealth taxes can be used to improve equality of opportunity and income.

Sovereign wealth funds derived from state enterprise and taxation. Proposals to equalise wealth and income through sovereign wealth funds as a form of preventive social policy have moved to the centre of economic theory discussions in recent years. Atkinson (2014) proposes, in addition to other measures, a sovereign wealth fund that would manage the income derived from a wealth tax and from state enterprise or government holdings in companies. Every citizen would receive a "minimum or guaranteed inheritance" on their 18th birthday, to finance their education, for example. Corneo (2014, 2015, 2016) goes even further: he suggests that the state should make much more use of state capital for entrepreneurial activities. The surpluses from business activities could be distributed to the population via a fund, or held and managed on behalf of the public, or invested elsewhere, and in this way contribute to wealth generation among poorer households.

Sovereign wealth funds and state enterprise also appear to be dependent on traditional economic activity and growth. However, Corneo wants his proposal to be understood to mean additionally that the state should orient its business policy towards other objectives, such as sustainability. All capital market investments also face the fundamental problem that there is currently a huge amount of money searching for investment opportunities all over the world. This situation could lead to serious problems on the capital markets, which, in turn, would endanger financial assets. Such proposals should therefore be examined very carefully.

Redistribution via CO_2 tax dividends. A CO_2 tax is seen as a sensible way of internalising the external costs of carbon dioxide emissions and reducing the consumption of carbon-based energy sources by making CO_2 emissions more expensive (on the restructuring of the tax system, see Köppl and Schratzenstaller in this book). There are various proposals for the distribution of the revenue raised: ecological tax reform is about making the tax system ecologically sound. The most common recommendation is to tax energy and raw materials more heavily and use the revenue to reduce the tax burden on labour as a factor of production in order to promote employment. In the ecological tax reform introduced in the Federal Republic of Germany in 1999, the revenue from the eco-taxes flows into the state pension scheme. Although the reduction in the ecological burden was small – due to the fact that energy tax rates remained at a constant and too low level – the eco-tax revenues provided long-term relief for the pension funds (DIW 2019). One criticism of this revenue-neutral reform (eco-taxes are balanced by reductions in pension insurance contributions and pension increases) concerns its negative distributional effects: as a proportion of net income, the eco-tax burdens affect poor households more than rich households, while poor households benefit less from the relief in pension contribution payments and pension increases. In the current discussions on developing the eco-tax into a CO_2 tax – mainly because of climate change – other or complementary uses for higher tax revenues are therefore under consideration, e.g. a social fund or an eco-bonus (payment of a certain amount to all residents) in order to avoid undesired distribution effects. Overall, the DIW (2019) concludes that the ecological tax reform introduced in Germany 20 years ago has had a disappointing impact in terms of environmental and climate policy. In terms of financial and social policy, it is judged to have been successful; in terms of distribution policy, to have shortcomings. In any next reform step, there is a strong case for allocating part of the tax revenue to social security and using the rest for distribution policy measures.

Promotion of cooperatives and of profit sharing in companies. Since John Stuart Mill, cooperative organisations have been talked of as a means of overcoming social inequalities. In the competition between different forms of enterprise, however, cooperatives only occupy a niche position in the capitalist corporate landscape. This may change in the course of digitalisation, insofar as major specific investments are made through creative work and no longer through capital. The promotion of such forms of enterprise can help prevent social hardship.

Basu (2017) emphasises that new production monopolies, for example due to network externalities or falling average costs as a result of digitalisation and an increased share for capital in total income, do not necessarily lead to income monopolies and greater income inequalities. He favours employee profit sharing as a means to reduce income and wealth inequalities, as such schemes spread capital income more widely. This can be seen as a watered-down version of a cooperative organisational form, in which co-determination rights are generally less pronounced, which alleviates some incentive problems.

4.2 Changes to the financing of and entitlement to social security, and institutional safeguards

Unconditional basic income and negative income tax. Both the basic income and negative income tax concepts are also financed by levies on monetary income. This results in a need for growth in order to finance a basic income that secures the livelihood of the individual, or to prevent the negative income tax requiring an excessively high transfer withdrawal rate (reduction of transfer payments with personal income). The financing problem is exacerbated if the proportion of older people in society rises and the upper age limit for formal employment cannot be raised any further.[4] Van Parijs (1995) provides an illustration of this argument in calculating that only a high income level (and thus a high level of production) will provide a sufficient tax base for a subsistence level monetary basic income. This can lead to political support for the continuation of existing production and consumption structures and thus of economic growth. Another idea is proposed by Bohnenberger (2020). For ecological reasons, she discusses tax-financed benefits directly at the level of goods and services.

> Four types of welfare benefits can be distinguished for UBV [Universal Basic Vouchers] along with different types of goods/services and for different target groups. *Quasi-currency vouchers* can be introduced to govern common-pool resources by rationing or restricting the right to use the resource. *Commons-innovation vouchers* are distributed to allow the emergence of new socio-ecological institutions and are hence applicable for club goods. There are no restrictions about to whom the vouchers are allocated. Finally, the distribution and use of private goods can also be managed through vouchers: *Needs vouchers* can be issued with a focus on a specific target group, to guarantee access to a certain amount of basic goods or services at given market prices. *Shift vouchers* are issued with emphasis on transforming the goods and services used.
>
> (Bohnenberger 2020, 7)

State guarantees and institutional requirements for occupational pension schemes. In many countries there is a demand for occupational pension provision, but little political support. It is true that it is primarily employees who benefit from occupational pension provision. However, occupational pensions could solve the essential dilemma of the statutory pension insurance system, i.e. that if the population ages, either the retirement age has to be raised, pensioners become steadily worse off or the pension insurance contribution rate has to be increased. It is important that such schemes allow entitlements to be transferred when changing jobs. This can be done using the Swiss model of pension funds. A similar approach is conceivable for company health insurance schemes, although in Germany some fundamental reforms in the health sector would be necessary. All these options expand the finance base for social security.

An additional pillar of social security. Traditionally, social security rests on the three pillars of traditional social insurance, occupational (old-age and health) care provision and state-supported personal asset formation or state-supported private pension contracts. Besides the carbon dioxide tax and other incentivising taxes, perhaps the most promising proposal for reforming social security to make it fit for a post-growth society involves extending these three pillars by adding in the reciprocally organised sectors of the economy. This would mean that all economic activities would contribute to social security. In practical terms, this can be done by promoting neighbourhood help or community support infrastructures such as residential communities for the elderly or multi-generational houses, or through timebanking schemes for volunteer work. The latter already exist in Switzerland, among other countries, in various forms (see Wehner et al. 2015; Wehner/Güntert 2017). In order to develop such timebanking associations, hitherto mostly privately organised, into an element of an additional pillar of social security, state guarantees for the acquired entitlements would be needed in order to create the necessary confidence in the systems. Other ways of incorporating the reciprocally organised economy will also require support from the state or from non-governmental social organisations.

In such an extension of the three-pillar model, the monetary-mediated pillars and those based on reciprocity must be coordinated: anyone who has been or is predominantly active in the area of reciprocity also needs money in order to live in the monetarily organised areas of an economy based on the division of labour. Conversely, anyone who has been or is predominantly active in the monetary sector also needs support in old age, which cannot be organised well or at all via markets or by the state.

Such an extension would correspond to a change from a pure basic *income* model to a comprehensive concept of basic *security* and would therefore not be limited just to provision for old age.

5 Conclusions

This chapter has argued that in all traditional systems – and also in many reform proposals – it is above all market-mediated or centrally controlled state production with monetary income which serves as the basis for social security. Since monetary income, under the system of national accounting, is generated only through production, and since GDP only includes goods and services that can be measured in prices or costs; and since these goods and services, together with some capital assets, also make up the entirety of the tax base, the area of reciprocal relations and economic activities is largely ignored. Although this area provides a wide range of informal forms of support to the social services, it is itself only insufficiently and unsystematically buttressed by the formalised system of social security based on regular gainful employment. Here it is important to consider which of these support services are integrated into and financed by the social security system and which should be financed directly by the state – and to what extent.

As long as social security depends on monetarily coordinated production, it will not be possible to entirely eliminate the pressure for growth if the proportion of older people in the population continues to increase and if healthcare costs continue to rise. A new social structure which has been transformed into some kind of realisable "utopia", one which incorporates – in the form of institutionalised timebanking accounts and other measures – the area of non-monetary labour alongside the traditional pillars, can reduce the pressure for growth, especially if supported by preventive measures such as the redistribution of wealth. However, this requires both state guarantees – above all to ensure in a mobile society that entitlements are transferable – and a direct link with the traditional elements of social security. Even in a post-growth society, social security and tax-financed social policy will play a central role as market-mediated services financed and coordinated by the state – perhaps with a different mix of corporate and management structures. R eciprocal services should, however, be incorporated to a greater extent, and systematically, and should also be financially supported.

Notes

* I would like to thank Alexa Köhler-Offierski, Willehad Lanwer, Remi Maier-Rigaud, Werner Sesselmeier and Aysel Yollu-Tok for constructive criticism and many helpful suggestions.
1 Eric Olin Wright (2017) discusses "real" utopias in detail, proposing among other things desirability, feasibility and accessibility as criteria for evaluating social alternatives (ibid.: 63ff.).
2 The allocation problem consists in finding solutions to the question of who should produce what, how, where, with what and when, in accordance with individual preferences and/or social values. The distribution question then follows when it comes to who should receive the goods and services produced. Transaction costs are the costs of the exchange itself: they include

the costs of negotiation, contracting and contract enforcement, but also inefficiencies in coordination.

3 Such a switch would further increase the dependence of the pension system on economic growth.

4 For different models of basic income, see e.g. Fischer (2016) and Van Paijs and Vanderborght (2017). See also UBI_interaktiv.de, an interactive documentation and discussion forum on unconditional basic income, where all major questions – not only about financing – are dealt with reference to the current literature.

Bibliography

Atkinson, A.B. (2014): *Inequality: What Can Be Done?* Cambridge

Basu, K. (2017): *Inequality in the twenty-first century*, in: Project Syndicate, December 15, 2017, www.project-syndicate.org (accessed 21.01.2021)

Benz, B., Huster, E-U., Schütte J.D., Boeckh, J. (2015): *Sozialpolitik und soziale Sicherung*, Informationen zur politischen Bildung Nr. 327/15, 23. Oktober 2015, www.bpb.de/izpb/214343/sozialpolitik-und-soziale-sicherung (accessed 21.01.2021)

Binswanger, H.C. (2013): *The Growth Spiral: Money, Energy, and Imagination in the Dynamics of the Market Process*, Berlin, Heidelberg

Bohnenberger, K. (2020): *Money, vouchers, public infrastructure? A framework for sustainable social benefits*, Sustainability 12(2), 596, 1–30

Corneo, G. (2014): *Kapitalsteuern und öffentliches Eigentum: Anmerkungen zum optimalen Umgang mit einer hohen Vermögenskonzentration*, Freie Universität Berlin, Fachbereich Wirtschaftswissenschaft, Discussion Papers 2014/27

Corneo, G. (2015): *Kapitalismus: Alternative in Sicht?* Aus Politik und Zeitgeschichte 65(35–37), 24–32

Corneo, G. (2016): *Öffentliches Kapital: Ein evolutionäres Programm für mehr Demokratie und Wohlstand*, ethikundgesellschaft 1, www.ethik-und-gesellschaft.de (accessed 21.01.2021)

DIW (Deutsches Institut für Wirtschaftsforschung) (2019): *20 Jahre Ökologische Steuerreform*, DIW Wochenbericht, 13

Fischer, U. (2016): *Das Bedingungslose Grundeinkommen. Drei Modelle*, Bundeszentrale für politische Bildung, Dialog: Die Netzdebatte, www.bpb.de/dialog/netzdebatte/223286/das-bedingungslose-grundeinkommen-drei-modelle (accessed 21.01.2021)

Heimann, E. (1980/1929): *Soziale Theorie des Sozialismus. Theorie der Sozialpolitik, mit einem Vorwort von Bernhard Badura*, Frankfurt a. M.

Höpflinger, F. (2010): *Alterssicherungssysteme: Doppelte Herausforderung von demografischer Alterung und Postwachstum*, in: Seidl, I., Zahrnt, A. (2010): Postwachstumsgesellschaft. Konzepte für die Zukunft, Marburg, 53–63

Kubon-Gilke, G. (2018): *Außer Konkurrenz. Sozialpolitik im Spannungsfeld von Markt, Zentralsteuerung und Traditionssystemen*, Ein Lehrbuch und mehr über Ökonomie und Sozialpolitik, 3. Aufl., Marburg

Kubon-Gilke, G. et al. (2018): *Gestalten der Sozialpolitik. Theoretische Grundlagen und Anwendungsbeispiele*, Marburg

Kubon-Gilke, G., Emanuel, M., Gilke, C., Kirchhoff-Kästel, S., Vilain, M. (2019): *Bits und Bytes: Markt ade? Wirtschaftliche und gesellschaftliche Konsequenzen der Digitalisierung und Folgen für eine humane Arbeitswelt*, Marburg

Lewin, K. (1947): *Frontiers in group dynamics. Concept, method and reality in social science; social equilibria and social change*, Human Relations 1(1), 5–41

Mannheim, K. (1991/1929) *Ideology and Utopia. An Introduction to the Sociology of Knowledge*, London

Seidl, I., Zahrnt, A. (Eds.) (2010): *Postwachstumsgesellschaft. Konzepte für die Zukunft*, Marburg

Sturn, R. (2011): *Die Natur der Probleme – Institutionen ökologischer Nachhaltigkeit*, in: Held, M., Kubon-Gilke, G., Sturn, R. (Eds.): Jahrbuch Normative und institutionelle Grundfragen der Ökonomik 9, 9–38

Umweltbundesamt (Ed.) (2018): *Gesellschaftliches Wohlergehen innerhalb planetarer Grenzen. Der Ansatz einer vorsorgeorientierten Postwachstumsposition*, www.umweltbundesamt.de (accessed 21.01.2021)

Van Parijs, P. (1995), *Real Freedom for All: What (If Anything) Can Justify Capitalism?* Oxford

Van Parijs, P., Vanderborght, Y. (2017): *Basic Income. A Radical Proposal for a Free Society and a Sane Economy*, Cambridge

Wehner, T., Güntert, S. (2017): *KISS Schweiz. Zeitvergütete organisierte Nachbarschaftshilfe*, Ein Evaluationsbericht, Züricher Beiträge zur Psychologie der Arbeit, Schriftenreihe des Zentrums für Organisation und Arbeitswissenschaft 1

Wehner, T., Znoj, H., Jochum-Müller, G., Lehner, H. (2015): *Die Zeitvorsorgen Oberwalden und St. Gallen*, in: Znoj, H. (Ed.): Anders Wirtschaften. Gespräche mit Leuten, die es versuchen, Zürich, 30–42

Witt, U. (2018): *Innovative expansion of capitalism and institutional destabilization*, Lecture at the Working Group on Evolutionary Economics of the Verein für Socialpolitik at the TU Dresden, unpublished folio set

Wright, E.O. (2017): *Envisioning Real Utopias*, London, New York

13 An employment-friendly tax system

Angela Köppl and Margit Schratzenstaller[1]

Summary

From a sustainability perspective, the current European tax systems are out of date. They are largely based on the taxation of labour, and many tax systems are still based on the assumption of a (usually male) primary earner in a standard employment relationship and a female additional earner. Not enough use is made of tax incentives to meet the major challenges of climate and environmental policy, and the redistributive power of tax systems has declined over the long term. In order to make European tax systems fit for the future, a fundamental restructuring is needed that shifts the tax burden away from labour income onto emissions and resource and energy consumption on the one hand and property and higher incomes on the other. More than in almost any other policy area, structural reforms to the tax system have the potential to address the various dimensions of sustainability simultaneously.

1 The challenges for future-oriented tax systems

Modern industrial societies are facing a number of major challenges if the goals of sustainable development and decarbonisation, as enshrined in various European and international agreements (Sustainable Development Goals (Kettner-Marx et al. 2018 and 2019) and Agenda 2030 for Sustainable Development (European Commission 2019), Paris Agreement, etc.), are to be achieved by 2050. These challenges range from demographic developments (migration and ageing), environmental problems and climate change, disruptive technological change (for example digitalisation) (Köppl/Schleicher 2018), declining growth rates, unemployment and increasing income and wealth inequality to an unequal distribution of paid employment and unpaid care work between men and women (Köppl/Schratzenstaller 2015a). Added to this are the

DOI: 10.4324/9781003187370-13

possible consequences of a serious sustainability policy which, in the course of structural change (for example in the areas of mobility and energy), might reduce economic performance and thus tax revenues, and of abandoning the growth paradigm and moving towards a post-growth society. Some of these challenges are directly interlinked with the extent and structure of (paid) work[2] and/or will have an influence on it in the future.[3]

Because of the sheer scale of taxation,[4] tax policy in the industrialised countries is an important lever on the path to more sustainable development in general[5] and a key factor in securing future employment in the long term. In 2019, taxes and social security contributions account for an average of 39.4 percent of GDP in the EU15 countries (the EU before the eastern enlargement) and 36.8 percent in the EU28. In Germany, the ratio is 40.7 percent of GDP, in Austria 42.5 percent of GDP.[6] Taxes on this scale influence economic activity through various channels, in proportion to the extent to which taxed individuals, households and firms respond to taxation in terms of their economic decision-making: not only with regard to production, consumption, investment and saving, but also with regard to the supply of and demand for labour by individuals and firms. Depending on the concrete design of the tax system, different effects on economic decisions and thus on sustainability are possible: taxation can promote or hinder sustainable development.

Against this background, this chapter first identifies sustainability gaps in existing tax systems, with a focus on the European Union (EU). In doing so, it focuses in particular on structural imbalances related to labour taxes. It then outlines possible strategies for a fundamental reform of European tax systems that could boost employment and at the same time help to achieve other objectives of a sustainability-oriented economic policy (in particular, social inclusion and ecological sustainability). The chapter also briefly discusses the relationship between the national and European levels.

2 Sustainability gaps in European tax systems

European tax systems have a number of structural deficits that can be described as sustainability gaps (Schratzenstaller et al. 2017). European tax systems are largely based on taxes and contributions on labour income. In 2018, on average 46.9 percent of total tax revenue in the EU came from labour taxes. The tax system in Germany, as in Austria, features a significantly above-average share of taxes on labour (Figure 13.1).

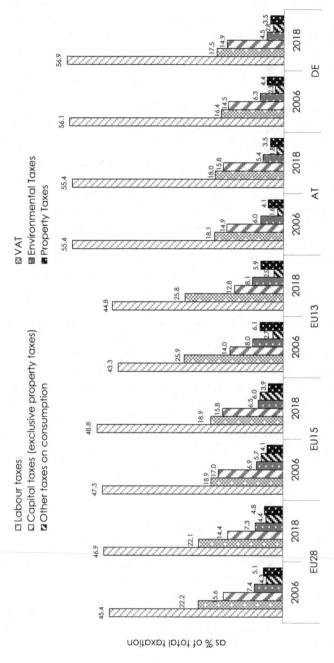

Figure 13.1 Structure of the tax systems in Europe, Austria and Germany (2006 and 2018)

On average in the EU15, labour income is particularly heavily taxed in the lower and middle income brackets. Table 13.1 shows the average personal tax rate in the EU15 and the OECD for different income levels. This average tax rate represents the total income tax and social security contributions paid by employees as a percentage of their total gross income. In 2019, the average tax rate in the "old" EU was 23.6 percent for an employee earning 67 percent of the average salary. As salaries increase, the rate rises, reaching 36.7 percent for employees earning 167 percent of the average salary. Labour income in the EU15 is thus taxed slightly higher than the average for the 36 OECD countries. The personal tax rates for Austria and especially Germany are significantly above the EU15 average.

Table 13.2 shows the personal marginal tax rate for different income levels on average for the OECD, the EU15, Germany and Austria. The marginal tax rate indicates the additional tax burden resulting from an increase in gross income by one unit. This rate increases on average in the EU15 and the OECD with increasing income. In Austria this rate is close to the EU15 average for three of the four income groups considered, in Germany it is significantly higher for all income groups. For the top income group (167 percent of average earnings), however, the marginal burden in these two countries falls below the values for lower gross earnings because of the maximum contribution base for social security.[7]

The high tax burden on labour income is problematic from an employment policy perspective. The average tax rate influences decisions on participation, i.e. the decision on whether to take up work; the marginal tax rate, however, affects decisions on the number of hours worked (Meghir/Phillips 2010, Keane 2010, Econpubblica 2011, Koskela 2002). A number of empirical studies have shown that the impact of taxes on labour supply is particularly strong for women with children, while for men the elasticity of labour supply is relatively low except among the low-skilled.[8] The high tax burden on low and middle incomes in Europe is therefore also an obstacle to gender equality in employment and ultimately to a more equal distribution of paid and unpaid work between women and men (Gunnarsson et al. 2017). Last but not least, the high tax burden on labour and thus the high labour costs in Europe are one of the obstacles to a transformation to a circular economy, in which labour-intensive services such as repair and recycling would play a major role (Köppl et al. 2019).

The contribution of environmental taxes to total tax revenue in the EU declined between 2006 and 2018 (Figure 13.1). A longer-term view shows that the contribution of environmental taxes to total tax revenue in Austria in 2018 was slightly higher than in the mid-1990s

Table 13.1 Average personal tax rates for the EU15, OECD, Germany and Austria in 2019

	Average personal tax rate 2019 on a gross income at the following percentage of the average							
	67%	100%	133%	167%	67%	100%	133%	167%
	Taxes on employees (tax and social contributions as % of gross income[1])				*Change 2000/2019*			
OECD	21.4	25.9	28.9	31.2	−1.1	−0.4	−0.6	−0.5
EU15	23.6	29.6	33.6	36.7	−2.6	−1.3	−1.1	−0.5
Germany	34.4	39.3	42.0	43.4	−2.5	−3.9	−4.9	−5.4
Austria	27.7	33.2	36.9	38.1	2.0	2.3	2.2	1.8

Source: OECD (2020) (Taxing wages).
[1] Average full-time gross wages/salaries of employees.

Table 13.2 Personal marginal tax rate for the EU15, the OECD, Germany and Austria 2019

	Personal marginal tax rate 2019 on a gross income at the following percentage of the average							
	67%	100%	133%	167%	67%	100%	133%	167%
	Taxes on employees (tax and social contributions as % of gross income[1])				*Change 2000/2019*			
OECD	32.5	36.1	39.6	40.2	0.5	−1.5	−0.1	−0.4
EU15	38.5	42.9	48.1	49.2	0.2	−2.2	0.9	1.5
Germany	46.6	52.1	51.7	44.3	−6.4	−7.2	−6.2	−7.2
Austria	43.3	48.2	48.2	36.9	2.8	7.0	0.2	−1.6

Source: OECD (2020) (Taxing wages).
[1] Average full-time gross wages/salaries of employees.

(Figure 13.2). In Germany, the proportion increased between 1998 and 2003 as a consequence of the environmental tax reform, but has since fallen well below the 1995 level. In both countries the contribution of environmental taxes in 2018 was significantly below its peak in the mid-2000s.

Finally, it is striking that the proportion of overall tax revenue raised from wealth-related taxes in Germany and Austria is significantly below the EU average (Figure 13.1). However, such taxes only play a minor role in European tax systems (Krenek/Schratzenstaller 2018).

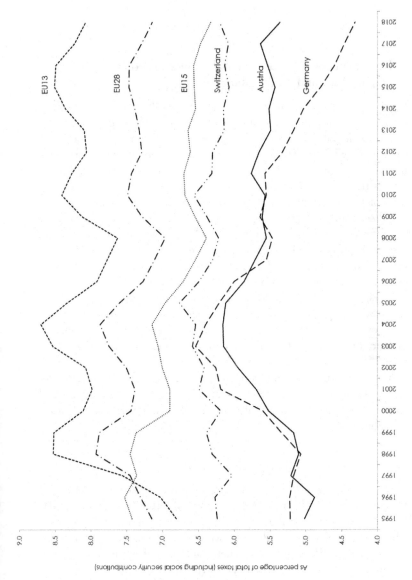

Figure 13.2 Environmental taxes in the EU, Germany, Austria and Switzerland (1995–2018)

These data show that European tax systems, including the German and Austrian systems, display a number of sustainability gaps (Gunnarsson et al. 2019): high and in some cases rising labour taxes, tax obstacles to gender equality in the labour market, low and declining environmental tax incentives and a tax system which is becoming less progressive.

3 Key elements of a tax system designed to promote employment and sustainability

Making tax systems more employment-friendly and sustainability-oriented requires a comprehensive approach combining a significant reduction in labour taxes with a greater role for environmental and wealth-related taxes.[9] A key element of such a fundamental restructuring of tax systems, in which labour income would be taxed significantly less, is the use of alternative sources of tax revenue: first, to compensate for the loss of revenue from the reductions to income tax and to social security and perhaps other wage-related contributions.[10] Second, however, because such a change can make the overall tax system more sustainability-oriented, i.e. more employment-friendly (3.1), more environmentally sustainable (3.2) and more socially inclusive (3.3). However, environmental taxes also entail a fiscal risk: if these taxes have the desired incentivising effects, it means that less use is made of the taxed resource. As a result, tax revenues from this resource will decline over time. This effect can be counteracted over a longer period of time if the reform of the tax system towards environmental taxation includes a gradual increase in the tax rates on environmental resources and if environmental taxation is also extended to cover resources previously untaxed. In the long term, however, it must be borne in mind that designing a tax system that delivers stable tax revenues will involve new challenges.

3.1 Reducing the burden on labour income

A reform of European tax systems to promote employment must first reduce the high tax burden on labour income (Köppl/Schratzenstaller 2015b). This reduction must be focused on lower and middle incomes, which bear a high tax burden and where the labour supply reacts particularly sensitively to changes in net wages (including changes brought about via taxes and social security contributions).

In countries such as Germany and Austria, where the social security systems, following the Bismarckian model, are primarily financed by employers' and employees' social security contributions, such a reduction cannot be achieved solely by lowering the personal income tax, because those on lower incomes pay little or no personal income tax anyway because of the personal tax-free allowance.[11] However, above the de minimis threshold,[12] social security contributions are payable, which account for the bulk of the overall tax burden in the lower and middle income brackets. In order to make the tax systems more employment-friendly, therefore, social security contributions in the lower and middle income brackets must be reduced as well as the personal income tax. In order to compensate for the loss of revenue, the social security systems must be financed to a greater degree from general tax revenues.

Digitalisation is another reason for considering a shift in the financing basis for social security towards a greater reliance on taxation (Schratzenstaller 2018). Digitalisation is expected to lead in many cases to job losses and to some degree of precarisation, and thus to a reduction in the significance of regular formal employment subject to social security contributions. This belief, also known as the "erosion thesis", holds that digitalisation is eroding the financing basis for the social security system. Even if it is not possible at present to make a serious forecast as to whether, to what extent and at what speed the financing base will actually erode in this way, these possible future developments provide an additional argument for looking for financing alternatives for the welfare state other than labour income.

In order to remove tax barriers to female employment, and thereby indirectly to contribute to a more equal distribution of unpaid work, tax provisions that support an unequal distribution of paid and unpaid work should be removed in addition to the general reduction of the tax burden for lower and middle incomes. For example, many European tax systems have regulations that support a traditional intra-family division of labour, such as the joint tax assessment of married couples or tax relief for sole earners or households with a second earner contributing a relatively small part of the overall household income (Gunnarsson et al. 2017). In Germany, for example, the system of splitting income within married couples for tax purposes ("Ehegattensplitting") should be reviewed, as should various regulations in Austria (such as non-contributory co-insurance in health insurance, the deduction for sole earners or tax relief on overtime pay; for details see Schratzenstaller/Dellinger 2018b).

3.2 Making more use of environmental taxes

Environmental taxes are a core element of a sustainability-oriented restructuring of European tax systems. In recent decades, and up to the present day, environmental taxes have been discussed and implemented mainly in relation to energy and climate change. This discussion is embedded in a broader debate on climate policy instruments at the centre of which are two disputes: should reductions be achieved through prices or quantity limits, and are market-based instruments or regulatory measures preferable? As early as 1974, Martin L. Weitzman showed that the question of whether environmental taxes or emissions trading are the better instrument cannot be answered unequivocally. His argument is that the same cost and marginal cost information would be required by each for the correct quantity or price signal to be set. Weitzman further argues that it depends on the precise course of assumptions regarding costs and benefits whether price or quantity instruments are preferable. He argues, though, that it is possible to give preference to one of the two instruments for other reasons. These reasons include political acceptance and administrative requirements (Weitzman 1974).

There are similar arguments in the controversy over economic versus regulatory instruments: here, too, the answer is inconclusive. For example, regulatory standards are more likely to help achieve a climate-friendly building stock than environmental taxes. To sum up, it could be concluded with regard to choosing adequate climate policy instruments that it is not so much a question of choosing the best instrument, but rather of a suitable mix of instruments that combines their different advantages so as to achieve the most effective climate policy.

The ideas proposed for an employment-friendly tax system in the relevant literature emphasise the importance of embedding environmental taxes in an eco-social tax reform. The revenues generated should be used to reduce other, less sustainability-oriented taxes (such as those on labour), to invest in improving the quality of the environment or to offset undesirable distributional effects (e.g. by paying an eco-bonus). In this way, revenues from environmental taxes do not flow into the general budget but are to be earmarked. The choice of alternative uses, or combinations of alternatives, for the revenues from environmental taxes depends on political preferences.

There is a broad consensus in economics that it makes sense to tax environmentally harmful activities in order to set an incentivising price signal against overuse of environmental resources. This applies to climate-related taxation as well as to other environmental problems.[13] It is often not possible to estimate in advance how effective environmental taxes will be in terms of incentive effects. An ex-post evaluation by the German Institute for Economic Research 20 years after the 1998 ecological tax reform leads to a sobering assessment of the environmental effects (Kemfert et al. 2019). This is related to the fact that the price signal was not sufficiently high to bring about a lasting change in behaviour. The scope for tax rates which are sufficiently high to achieve such a change is limited due to issues of political acceptability. This strengthens the argument that environmental taxes should be embedded within a broader mix of instruments.

Greening the tax system must essentially be based on three pillars. The first pillar consists of a systematic reform of environmentally harmful subsidies (Kletzan-Slamanig/Köppl 2016), such as can be found in all European tax systems. Examples are the preferential tax treatment for diesel, something which cannot be justified from an environmental point of view but exists in almost all EU countries (Kettner-Marx/Kletzan-Slamanig 2018, Nerudová et al. 2018), and the preferential tax treatment for company cars (European Commission 2018). Tax privileges which are clearly environmentally harmful, such as the "diesel privilege" or the total tax exemption for kerosene, should be abolished. The removal of tax exemptions, such as the commuter allowance or tax exemptions for energy-intensive companies, which could lead to competitiveness problems or other economic or social problems must be cushioned by means of transitional regulations, supportive industrial and innovation policy measures, an expansion of public transport and similar measures.

The second pillar of a greening of the tax system consists of positive tax incentives that encourage environmentally desirable behaviour, for example in the transport or housing sectors. This also includes tax incentives to promote the transformation to a circular economy, such as the tax incentives for repair services in Sweden (Köppl et al. 2019).

The third pillar involves increasing existing environmental taxes and introducing new ones. The pricing of CO_2 emissions plays a particularly important role here (Baranzini et al. 2017). Like the dismantling of environmentally harmful tax breaks, which also generates additional tax revenues, it should be integrated into a structural shift within the overall tax system. Such a structural eco-social tax reform can help to reconcile environmental goals with social and employment policy concerns. Specifically, the additional tax revenues – for example from wider taxation of the use of resources – should be used to reduce taxes on labour in order to achieve a "double dividend" (Maxim et al. 2019) in the form of a simultaneous improvement of the environment and increased employment. In addition, targeted investments should be made in climate policy measures to enable more climate-friendly behaviour in general. Care must be taken to ensure that those on low incomes, who are particularly hard hit by certain environmental tax increases, are also given support. If this is not possible through tax relief measures, then increases in social transfers will be necessary. Having a variety of different options for the redistribution and use of eco-tax revenues is important for broad public acceptance (Carattini et al. 2019, Timilsina 2018, Klenert et al. 2018).

One of the options discussed for a redistribution of additional environ-mental tax revenues is that of an eco-bonus.

A greening of the European tax systems must on the one hand be integrated into a broader mix of instruments (including taxes and regu-latory measures as well as research policy) in order to be as environmen-tally effective as possible (Stiglitz 2019a), but on the other hand it has to directly address transport as the second largest cause of CO_2 emissions. A gradual raising of mineral oil taxes and the elimination of the "diesel privilege" would be important elements. Also worthy of discussion are a use-dependent road pricing and an extension of the HGV toll to the overall road network. For the transport sector in particular, it can be argued that it is necessary to invest simultaneously in low-carbon infra-structure, since the transport infrastructure shapes individual mobility decisions. In addition, the introduction of a cross-sectoral CO_2 tax that reflects the emission intensity of fossil fuels should be considered. In connection with the aim of promoting the transition towards a circular economy, resource taxes must play a greater role than in the past: espe-cially because digitalisation and the hardware required for it are asso-ciated with a growing demand for resources such as rare earths, which are linked to considerable environmental, social and political problems (especially in the countries where they are mined, the crisis and war regions in Africa) (Schratzenstaller 2018). Taxes on waste can also help the implementation of the circular economy strategy (European Com-mission 2018).

3.3 Greater use of taxes on wealth and capital income

Ultimately, higher taxes on wealth and on higher incomes are an ele-ment of tax reforms to make tax systems more employment-friendly and socially inclusive. At the nation-state level, inheritance and gift taxes are one option for limiting growing wealth inequality. Such taxes are also considered to be comparatively conducive to growth and employ-ment (European Commission 2018). There is also scope for greater tax-ation of capital income. Almost all EU countries have dualised their income tax systems in recent decades, and in some cases tax capital income at much lower rates than labour income: whereas in 2018 the top tax rate applicable to labour income was 39 percent on average in the EU, the average tax rate on capital income was, at 19 percent, only half as high (Stiglitz 2019b).

In addition to these conventional taxes on wealth and capital in-come, there has recently been increasing discussion of taxing "robots" (i.e. automated machines and production processes) and their owners (Schratzenstaller 2018). This could compensate for any erosion of labour income and thus of the financing of social security or wider public budgets. A "robot tax" would very probably slow down technical progress. Some welcome this effect, as it would give the economy more time to adapt to the economic and social effects of digitalisation; others see it as problematic, as it would hinder innovations that increase welfare and competitiveness (UNCTAD 2017). Moreover, the implementation of value added based employer contributions or a robot tax would face similar challenges and problems to those more generally associated with the taxation of corporate profits and capital income due to intense international tax competition and the multiple opportunities for multinational companies to minimise their taxable profits.

3.4 The European level

Finally, designing European tax systems for sustainability requires the involvement of the European level. Intensifying cooperation on tax matters would make it possible to make greater use of certain financing alternatives that cannot be used to full effect at present because of tax competition and tax avoidance, and thereby to reduce the tax pressure on labour income. Three approaches are particularly relevant here (see Stiglitz 2019b). First, setting effective minimum tax rates in the area of environmental and energy taxes, which would impose effective barriers on the race to undercut competitors. This would include the long overdue revision of the EU Energy Tax Directive, but also minimum tax rates for a CO_2 tax, as proposed by the European Commission as long ago as 2011 (European Commission 2011). The amendment of the Energy Tax Directive for sectors not subject to EU emissions trading was rejected by the member states, but remains necessary.

Second, in order to counteract the further erosion of corporate taxation, an EU-wide harmonised corporate tax base with a minimum tax rate should be introduced. Declining corporate taxation is one reason for the long-term shift in the tax burden onto labour income, as empirical research shows (Loretz/Schratzenstaller 2019).

Third, replacing part of the national contributions used to finance the EU budget with tax-based own resources could make it possible to effectively implement taxes that are difficult to enforce on a national basis (e.g. taxes on air travel, financial transactions or assets) (Schratzenstaller/Krenek 2019). This would create leeway for the EU member states to reduce taxes on labour in return.

4 Concluding remarks

From a sustainability perspective, the existing European tax systems are out of date. They rely heavily on the taxation of labour, and many tax systems are still predicated on a (usually male) main wage earner engaged in a standard employment relationship and a (usually female) second earner. Tax incentives as a means of addressing the major challenges in climate and environmental policy are underused, and the contribution of tax systems to the achievement of distributional policy objectives has declined over the long term. In order to make European tax systems fit for the future, a fundamental restructuring is necessary, with a shift in the tax burden away from labour income and towards emissions and/or environmental and energy consumption on the one hand and wealth and higher income on the other. Structural reforms to the tax system, more than in almost any other policy area, have the potential to address the various dimensions of sustainability simultaneously.

Notes

1 We are indebted to Andrea Sutrich for careful research assistance.
2 Such as migration, unemployment and the unequal distribution of paid and unpaid work between men and women.
3 Such as digitalisation, migration and ageing.
4 Tax and taxation here include social security contributions.
5 On the design of tax systems for sustainability, see Schratzenstaller et al. (2017).
6 In Switzerland, the tax ratio is 28.1 percent. However, it is not comparable with other countries, among other things because parts of the health and pension insurance systems are run privately, i.e. membership in an insurance scheme, and thus contributions are obligatory, but the contributions go into the private rather than the public sector. They therefore do not appear in the tax ratio. For this reason, no figures on Switzerland are included below.
7 The contributions assessment limit is a fixed ceiling on the amount of gross income on which insured persons pay social security contributions.
8 For an overview of empirical results on the extent of labour supply elasticity and the influence of taxes on labour supply, see Schratzenstaller/Dellinger (2018a, b) and the literature cited therein.
9 In its regular analyses of the tax policies of the EU member states within the framework of the European Semester, the European Commission has also been recommending for years that steps should be taken in this direction (see e.g. European Commission 2018).
10 In Austria, these include local community tax, which is based on wages, and contributions to the family benefit equalisation fund and housing construction subsidies.
11 The basic income tax allowance exempts the first EUR 11,000 of income in Austria and the first EUR 9,409 in Germany from tax.

12 This is a wages threshold above which social security contributions become due. In Austria currently around 460 euros, in Germany 450 euros per month.

13 A wider discussion of environmental taxes in the EU can be found in European Environmental Agency (2016).

Bibliography

Baranzini, A., van den Bergh, J. C.J. M., Carattini, S., Howarth, R. B., Padilla, E., Roca, J. (2017): Carbon pricing in climate policy: Seven reasons, complementary instruments, and political economy considerations, WIREs Climate Change, 8: e462, https://doi.org/10.1002/wcc.462

Carattini, S., Kallbekken, S., Orlov, A. (2019): How to win public support for a global carbon tax, Nature 565(7739), 289–291

Econpubblica (2011): The role and impact of labour taxation policies, Università Bocconi, Centre for Research on the Public Sector, Milano

EEA (European Environmental Agency) (2016): Environmental taxation and EU environmental policies, EEA Report No 17

European Commission (2011): Communication from the Commission to the European Parliament, the Council and the European Economic and Social Committee on Smarter Energy Taxation for the EU: Proposal for a Revision of the Energy Taxation Directive 2003, Brussels

European Commission (2018): Tax policies in the European Union 2018 survey, Luxembourg, ec.europa.eu/taxation_customs/sites/taxation/files/tax_policies_survey_2018.pdf (accessed 21.01.2021)

European Commission (2019): Towards a sustainable Europe by 2030, Brussels, ec.europa.eu/commission/sites/beta-political/files/rp_sustainable_europe_30-01_en_web.pdf (accessed 21.01.2021)

European Commission (2020): Taxation trends in the European Union, https://ec.europa.eu/taxation_customs/business/economic-analysis-taxation/taxation-trends-eu-union_en (accessed 21.01.2021)

Gunnarsson, Å., Nerudová, D., Schratzenstaller, M. (2019): About fair tax, Intereconomics 54(3), 133

Gunnarsson, Å., Schratzenstaller, M., Spangenberg, U. (2017): Gender equality and taxation in the European Union, Directorate-general for Internal Policies, Policy Department C – Citizens's Rights and Constitutional Affairs, Study for the EMM Committee, Brussels

Keane, M.P. (2010): Labor Supply and Taxes: A Survey, Sydney

Kemfert, C., Schill, W.-P., Wagner, N., Zaklan, A. (2019): Umweltwirkungen der Ökosteuer begrenzt, CO_2-Bepreisung der nächste Schritt, DIW Wochenbericht 86(13), 215–221

Kettner-Marx, C., Kletzan-Slamanig, D. (2018): Energy and carbon taxes in the EU. Empirical evidence with focus on the transport sector, WIFO Working Paper 555

Kettner-Marx C., Kletzan-Slamanig, D., Köppl, A., Littig, B., Zielinska, I. (2018): Monitoring sustainable development. Climate and energy policy indicators, WIFO Working Paper 573

Kettner-Marx, C., Kletzan-Slamanig, D., Köppl, A., Littig, B., Zielinska, I. (2019): *Monitoring sustainable energy development: A cross-country comparison of selected EU members*, WIFO Working Paper 575

Klenert, D., Mattauch, L., Combet, E., Edenhofer, O., Hepburn, C., Rafaty, R., Stern, N. (2018): *Making carbon pricing work for citizens*, Nature Climate Change 8, 669–677

Kletzan-Slamanig, D., Köppl, A. (2016): *Subventionen und Steuern mit Umweltrelevanz in den Bereichen Energie und Verkehr*, Wien

Köppl, A., Schleicher, S. (2018): *What will make energy systems sustainable*, Sustainability 10(7), 2537

Köppl, A., Schratzenstaller, M. (2015a): *The Austrian tax system – status-quo*, WIFO Bulletin 20(5), 55–71

Köppl, A., Schratzenstaller, M. (2015b): *The Austrian tax system – perspectives for reform*, WIFO Bulletin 20(6), 72–79

Köppl, A., Loretz, S., Meyer, I., Schratzenstaller, M. (2019): *Effekte eines ermäßigten Mehrwertsteuersatzes für Reparaturdienstleistungen*, Wien

Koskela, E. (2002): *Labour taxation and employment in trade union models: A partial survey*, in: Ilmakunnas, S., Koskela, E. (Eds.): Towards Higher Employment: The Role of Labour Market Institutions, Helsinki, 63–86

Krenek, A., Schratzenstaller, M. (2018): *A European net wealth tax*, WIFO Working Paper 561

Loretz, S., Schratzenstaller, M. (2019): *Der EU-Vorschlag zur Harmonisierung der Körperschaftsteuer. Auswirkungen für Österreich*, WIFO Monthly Reports 92(1), 61–71

Maxim, M., Zander, K., Patuelli, R. (2019): *Green tax reform and employment double dividend in European and non-European countries: A meta-regression assessment*, International Journal of Energy Economics and Policy 9(4), 342–55

Meghir, C., Phillips, D. (2010): *Labour supply and taxes*, in: Mirrlees, J., Adam, S., Besley, T., Blundell, R., Bond, S., Chote, R., Gammie, M., Johnson, P., Myles, G., Poterba, J. (Eds.): Dimensions of Tax Design, The Mirrlees Review, Oxford, 202–274

Nerudová, D., Dobranschi, M., Solilová, V., Schratzenstaller, M. (2018): *Sustainability-oriented future EU funding: A fuel tax surcharge*, Fair Tax Working Paper 21

OECD (2020): *Taxing Wages 2020*, Paris

Schratzenstaller, M. (2018): *Auswirkungen der Digitalisierung auf den öffentlichen Sektor – ein erster Überblick*, Wirtschaftsdienst 98(11), 799–804

Schratzenstaller, M., Dellinger, F. (2018a): *Regelungen im österreichischen Abgabensystem mit gleichstellungspolitischer Relevanz*, WIFO Monthly Reports 91(2), 121–137

Schratzenstaller, M., Dellinger, F. (2018b): *Genderdifferenzierte Lenkungswirkungen des Abgabensystems auf das Arbeitsangebot*, WIFO Monthly Reports 91(2), 105–120

Schratzenstaller, M., Krenek, A. (2019): *Tax-based own resources to finance the EU budget*, Intereconomics 54(3), 171–177

Schratzenstaller, M., Krenek, A., Nerudová, D. et al. (2017): *EU taxes for the EU budget in the light of sustainability orientation – a survey*, Jahrbücher für Nationalökonomie und Statistik 237(3), 163–189

Stiglitz, J.E. (2019a): *Addressing climate change through price and non-price interventions*, NBER Working Paper 25939

Stiglitz, J.E. (2019b): *Rewriting the rules for the European economy*, FEPS – Foundation for European Progressive Studies, Brussels

Timilsina, G. (2018): *Where is the carbon tax after thirty years of research?* World Bank Working Paper 8493

UNCTAD (2017): *Trade and Development Report. Beyond Austerity: Towards a Global New Deal*, New York, Geneva

Weitzmann, M.L. (1974): *Prices vs. Quantities*, Review of Economic Studies, 41, 477–491

14 Work in low- and middle-income countries

Georg Stoll[*]

Summary

Most of the contributions to the debate on a post-growth society are of European or (North) American origin, and tend to focus on their own economic, political, social and cultural context – while contributions to this debate from the Global South are rare. Here, the focus is more on questions of social justice and international dependencies. Despite numerous possible common points of reference, the strands of discourse on the question of what kind of society we want to live in in the face of globally relevant ecological and social conditions remain largely unconnected. This chapter highlights differences in the living and working worlds for people in the Global South and addresses the role of economic growth in the North and South. This perspective can also complement and stimulate reflection on productive activity [work] in the post-growth society.

1 The faces of work

"How are things with you?" – when young people who have not seen each other for a while meet in Brazil, they sooner or later come around to the topic of work. "Tem emprego?" – "Have you got a job?" – is the usual question, meaning a contractually agreed employment relationship with social security. If this question is answered in the negative – one in three young people in Brazil is unemployed – the next question is: "Tem trabalho?" – "Have you got work?", which means any (legal) activity that provides the necessary livelihood if you are not supported by the family solidarity network.

This difference between formal work (with legally regulated and protected minimum standards and legal entitlements) and informal work (without such protection) is an existential one for most people in low-income countries and for many in middle-income countries,[1] and all

DOI: 10.4324/9781003187370-14

the more so the lower the income is. In these countries, regulated and protected working conditions are the exception rather than the rule, unlike in the early industrialised high-income countries with their high levels of material prosperity and workers' rights acquired over the course of industrialisation. For those in informal employment, this means no guaranteed minimum income, no protection against short-term loss of employment, no defined safety standards in the workplace, no entitlement to days off or paid annual leave, no or insufficient access to social security systems and generally no trade union organisation. However, these features are all integral to decent work according to internationally recognised standards such as those of the Universal Declaration of Human Rights or the International Labour Organization (ILO).[2]

The ILO estimates that more than 60 percent of the total number of those employed worldwide are in informal employment.[3] Who are these two billion people? They are rural small farmers and plantation workers; women working without fixed contracts in the households of the middle and upper classes in India, Brazil or Germany; young people unable to enter the official labour market; workers in the informal mines of Africa or on the big construction sites of the Middle East; street vendors in the cities; refuse sorters who dismantle imported electronic waste; migrants and refugees trying to find an economic niche in their host countries; workers in companies supplying the textile and electrical industries; people who have lost their jobs in conflict regions and now have to secure their livelihoods under conditions of endemic violence and destroyed infrastructure. For these people, informality is a synonym for poverty. For it means not only precarious living conditions, but also daily social marginalisation. Those who work informally or live in an informal settlement (both usually go hand in hand), and those without an employment contract or official work card and no official address are constantly exposed to discrimination as second-class citizens.

1.1 Global data on informal employment

For statistical purposes, the ILO uses a strict definition of "*work*" as a generic term as well as definitions of sub-categories.[4] "*Informal employment*" – one of the sub-categories – is complex, and blurred at the edges: it includes both paid and self-employment, producing or providing goods and services for third parties. "*Paid employees*" are engaged in informal work if their employment relationship is not subject to national labour legislation, income taxation, social protection or legal rights to notice, paid holidays or sick leave and the like. The payment of social security contributions by the employer or the employee's entitlement to paid annual leave and sick pay are decisive indicators. "*Own-account workers*" are engaged in informal work if they are part of the informal sector, i.e. if they carry out their economic activities in a personal or family business without a separate legal identity independent of the owners, or in a private household, and do not have a complete set of accounts and/or are not registered under national legislation. "*Contributing family members*" whose work is not solely for their own needs are always considered to be informally employed.[5]

If we look at the phenomenon of informal employment through these statistical lenses, the following picture emerges:

Regional distribution: Informal employment is particularly widespread in Africa (86 percent of total employment), the Arab states (69 percent), and Asia and the Pacific (68 percent) (for comparison, the Americas: 40 percent, Europe and Central Asia: 25 percent).[6] But this could be a derivative phenomenon depending on per capita income, since there is a clear link with the following factor:

Distribution by income group: Whereas almost 70 percent of the working population in low- and middle-income countries are in informal employment, this share is only 18 percent on average in high-income countries. The country with the lowest share is Luxembourg (1.2 percent), the country with the highest Burkina Faso (94.6 percent).[7]

Sectors: By far the largest share of informal workers is found in agriculture. Globally, the figure there is 94 percent, and even in the so-called developed countries it is still 59 percent. Industry follows with 57 percent (high-income countries: 16 percent) and the service sector with 47 percent (high-income countries: 18 percent). Informal work in the agricultural sector is especially marked in Africa and Asia.[8]

Level of education: The lower a person's educational attainment, the greater their likelihood of working in an informal employment relationship. This correlation can be demonstrated in all regions. Globally, the range extends from 24 percent (with tertiary education) to 94 percent (without educational qualifications). However, education does not by any means guarantee a formal employment relationship in low-income and newly industrialised middle-income countries. Almost two-thirds of those with a secondary education and even one-third with a tertiary education do not find formal employment in these countries.[9]

Age: Two age groups stand out statistically. Among both the youngest (15–24 years) and the oldest (65 years and older) more than 77 percent are in informal employment, while in all other age groups the maximum is 63 percent. This correlation applies to a greater or lesser degree in all regions.[10]

Sex: Here the situation is more complex. There are 740 million women among the two billion who are informally employed. The proportion of 68 percent of men employed in the informal economy contrasts with 58 percent among women. However, this picture is largely determined by China and Russia. In the majority of countries (56 percent), proportionally more women than men are employed informally. This is particularly true in Africa, South Asia and Latin America. The ILO draws attention to an additional aspect however: the proportion of women is especially high among contributing family members – a group which is considered to be particularly vulnerable, because not only do they have no social protection but, as a rule, no personal remuneration is even paid.[11]

Informal work in the formal sector: A good quarter of all employees working informally are in the formal sector, i.e. in publicly owned companies, non-governmental organisations or private companies that keep proper accounts and are registered with national tax and social security authorities.[12] This is an astonishing finding, as it shows that many companies subject to the legal requirements of the formal sector employ people under conditions of largely unprotected informal work. It is not clear from the statistics to what extent they take advantage of loopholes in the law or violate it in doing so.

Even if statistics on informal work cannot reflect the reality experienced by each and every worker,[13] they provide a clear overall picture: most people in low-income countries and large sections of the population in middle-income countries work in conditions that make a mockery of their human right to adequate and secure employment. Statistics and studies on the "working poor",[14] on child labour[15] and on labour rights[16] complement and confirm this picture.

People who work under such conditions usually do so not of their own free will, but for lack of better alternatives. A lack of qualifications may play a part, but above all there is a lack of sufficient opportunities for good employment. The only reason why this is not reflected in even higher unemployment rates is that social security systems are inadequate and consequently unemployed people do not register with employment offices or are not registered in any other way. Neither the public sector nor the private sector is in a position to offer even remotely sufficient employment with minimum social standards. There are regular employment relationships of that kind, mainly in public administration and in larger companies, but only for a minority who themselves are often under pressure: from rationalisation in the companies, and, in the public sector, from scarce public revenues and from international economic, trade and development policies favouring privatisation and liberalisation.

The basic pattern is usually the same everywhere: people who find themselves in a predicament accept exploitative conditions because the market offers them no better alternative and neither the law nor the state protects them sufficiently. However, this basic pattern also involves the demand side, i.e. all those who use and benefit from such informal employment and services. They include other poor people living in conditions of informality in the immediate environment, but above all members of the middle classes and, at the end of international value creation chains, consumers looking for cheap products and companies looking to produce and buy goods at the lowest possible cost. Exploitative conditions extend to forced labour, child labour, sexual exploitation and human trafficking, which are internationally outlawed but nevertheless widespread.[17] Even without these extreme forms of crime, the proliferation of informal and precarious work shows that global markets benefit from this type of employment and that policy-makers in North and South cannot or will not effectively restrict it.[18]

But there are also positive sides to the informal sector: an enormous energy of initiative, creativity and flexibility is evident in the diversity of informal work. Even if these qualities have arisen out of necessity, they represent important resources not only for individual economic activity and satisfaction, but also for the economic potential of society as a whole. The drama of those working in the informal economy is that these potentials are impeded and for the most part do not yield benefits for themselves but for others.

The army of informal workers and "working poor" makes indispensable contributions to the functioning of the formal economy and of society as a whole. This applies both nationally and internationally. What would cities look like without the work of rubbish collectors? How much would food cost without the labour of plantation and seasonal workers? Who would serve, supply and guard the aspirant middle classes, clean their households and enable them to do their well-paid formal work? Who would care for the old and sick if there were no poorly paid migrants? These altogether positive contributions come at the expense of the informal workers and their social environment.

2 Sustainable livelihoods through economic growth – a dilemma in which ecological and social objectives are in conflict

Precarious work as described above can be observed as a mass phenomenon in those countries in which low per capita income and low state revenues leave virtually no financial scope for a lasting and comprehensive assurance of decent living conditions for the entire population. If one takes the threshold value of a maximum of 1,035 US dollars per capita income for the World Bank category of low-income countries, this means that even if gross national income were distributed completely evenly, the populations of these countries would still live between absolute poverty (1.9 US dollars per day, i.e. 693.5 US dollars per year) and moderate poverty (3.1 US dollars per day, i.e. 1131.5 US dollars per year)[19] – despite the fact that they are working hard to make a living. Under such conditions, significant economic growth is a necessary, though not sufficient, condition for effective poverty reduction. Accordingly, political and economic strategies revolve around the question of how this growth can be achieved and distributed. Questions of global ecological sustainability, or even development without growth, are generally not up for debate in these contexts.[20]

The overall economic situation of many middle-income countries enables them in principle to combat poverty through social and distributional policies. Higher per capita income is reflected in a growing middle class who increasingly demand a stronger voice in politics, but also in a marked increase in environmental pollution and resource consumption. Individual critical voices from science, civil society and politics are therefore questioning the path of catch-up development in the well-worn tracks of the rich industrialised countries.[21] However, even in the middle-income countries, economic growth enjoys high credibility as a path to eradicating poverty and increasing prosperity. As in low-income countries, per capita income in most newly industrialised countries is still at a level where it correlates strongly with indicators of general life satisfaction.[22]

Increasing economic growth and productivity lies at the core both of national economic policy strategies and of the policy recommendations made by multilateral and bilateral cooperation partners such as the

World Bank. The underlying theory is that the increased integration of the economies of low- and middle-income countries into global markets should ensure access to raw materials and cheap labour and also sales markets for the companies of the high-income countries. At the same time, low- and middle-income countries will be given more opportunities to export raw materials, semi-finished and finished goods and services, thus creating more jobs, with higher qualifications, in the formal economy while also ensuring sufficient income and consumption opportunities for their growing populations. "Inclusive growth" is the slogan, one which can be found in speeches by politicians such as Indian Prime Minister Narendra Modi[23] as well as in the 2030 Agenda for Sustainable Development ("Promote sustained, inclusive and sustainable economic growth, full and productive employment and decent work for all").[24]

In order to ensure that economic growth is truly inclusive, i.e. that the entire population gets its fair share, policies to increase the share of formal economic activity and employment usually accompany the economic growth agenda. The intention is that new jobs should be in the formal sector and the existing informal employment relationships should be converted into regular forms of paid employment or self-employment. The eighth Sustainable Development Goal, for example, aims to combine these objectives in subgoals 8.1 ("Sustain per capita economic growth..."), 8.2 ("Achieve higher levels of economic productivity...") and 8.3 ("... encourage the formalization and growth of micro, small and medium-sized enterprises...").

Civil society actors and non-governmental organisations (NGOs) who support informal workers are usually sceptical about whether formalisation is a promising way to achieve decent work for all. They mistrust their governments' promises to provide adequately regulated jobs and complain that public programmes are focused narrowly on regular work, neglecting the potential of informal work as well as the opportunities already available to improve conditions for informal workers. For example, the Parliamentary Liaison Office of the South African Catholic Bishops' Conference deplores the fact that although the informal sector will have helped 2.9 million people to earn their living in 2018, the government's National Development Plan does not contain any concrete proposals for the development of this sector.[25] In India, NGOs work for the adoption of occupational health and safety regulations, for example for construction workers and domestic workers in informal employment, and subsequently support them in claiming their rights. In São Paulo, Brazil, the Centro Gaspar Garcia de Direitos Humanos carries out social assistance, legal aid and political lobbying for street vendors and rubbish collectors, who are often at risk of violence, displacement and homelessness. What all these examples have in common is that they start with the existing working conditions and the people potentially affected and demand the implementation of promises made by the government, but do not wait for them to be fulfilled.

But if economic growth in low- and middle-income countries could be made socially inclusive, and all those seeking employment could have access to decent work, this would exacerbate the ecological problems. Under the current political and economic conditions, the growth required to raise living standards and provide social security in many countries will increase environmental pollution and resource consumption. This can be described as a dilemma for development policy: in the same proportion as economic growth reduces poverty and enables people to earn a sustainable and sufficient living from their work, so the overloading of ecological systems and cycles, which is already threatening us today, will increase further.[26] If one accepts the International Labour Organization's estimate that some 1.2 billion jobs worldwide – 40 percent of global employment – are directly dependent on ecosystem services, and most of these jobs are in Africa, Asia and the Pacific region,[27] then it is evident that exceeding environmental sustainability thresholds will very quickly lead to serious social consequences (e.g. the loss of housing and livelihoods, or land and resource conflicts). The desire to create decent living and working conditions on a global scale through sustained economic growth obviously ends in a blind alley over the long run.

3 Options for resolving the dilemma

What options does this dilemma leave us with? At this point, we would like to outline three possible pathways.

3.1 Sticking with the two-tier world society

A first option is to maintain the prevailing global conditions of exploitation. The unsustainable production and consumption patterns of the early industrialised high-income countries (and now also of some middle-income countries, or of some groups within their populations) could be made somewhat less environmentally harmful through technical efficiency measures, but would not have to be reduced to an ecologically compatible per capita level. This is because the global sustainability limits would be met under this option by setting off the excessive ecological footprint of some countries against a sufficiently small footprint for others – at the cost of sacrificing global justice, of course. In terms of work, this option means that enough people would continue to be willing to take up low-paid and insecure work in order to survive, and that these people would be kept at a sufficient distance from the beneficiaries of this model. As cynical as such a model of a two-tier world society may sound, it is very close to both past and present reality. And the more or less blatant defence of this model can be observed right now in the political mainstream.

3.2 *Green growth*

A second option is described using terms such as "green economy" (UN),[28] "green growth" (OECD)[29] and "sustainable growth",[30] and is often associated with the concept of "sustainable development". This approach is the favourite among the policy planning and programming community. It sets out to reconcile global ecological sustainability with decent living and working conditions for all, without having to break with the paradigm of an economy geared towards continuous growth. With regard to work, this model is based on the gradual improvement of working conditions and on a sufficient number of jobs in ecologically sound sectors of the economy. The key strategy of this option is to decouple economic growth from the consumption of natural resources and sink capacities. This decoupling is to be achieved primarily through technical measures of resource efficiency, recycling and the use of short-term renewable biological raw materials, especially in the energy sector.

The problems of this approach are well known. The necessary decoupling would have to ensure compliance with pollution limits in all areas of the global ecology (the "planetary boundaries")[31] – which, given the current overload in terms of greenhouse gas emissions or loss of biodiversity, would require not only an end to but actually a reversal of existing trends. The idea that this can be achieved cannot be ruled out in principle, but it has not yet been historically proven on a global scale.[32] The ILO has recently addressed the question of whether its goal of achieving decent work for all is compatible with environmental sustainability, given the links between work, the economy and resource consumption. It answered this question in the affirmative by referring to the decoupling described above, while admitting that globally only relative decoupling, not absolute decoupling, has been achieved so far.[33] The International Labour Organization sees support for its optimism in the fact that, between 1995 and 2013, 23 countries worldwide succeeded in reducing both their production-related and their consumption-related CO_2 emissions despite an increase in their per capita income over the same period, i.e. in achieving absolute decoupling, at least regionally.[34]

What is not mentioned, however, is that these countries, whose emissions savings were more than offset globally by emissions increases in other countries, are for the most part countries with already very high per capita emissions (including Germany) or former Eastern Bloc countries undergoing accelerated restructuring of their economies. These regional success stories cannot therefore support the thesis of the feasibility of global absolute decoupling. Despite the political popularity of this approach, considerable doubts remain as to whether the existing growth-based economy is compatible with ecological sustainability and social inclusion on a global scale under the label of a "green economy".[35]

3.3 System change through social-ecological transformation

The third option is a strategy that addresses the root causes of the current dilemma between ecological sustainability and socially just economic development. At the core of this strategy is the diagnosis that the globally dominant capitalist economic system, which requires for its functioning and expansion the most comprehensive and unregulated markets possible and which is inherently linked to an unchecked growth dynamic, is the decisive cause both of the disruption and destruction of the natural foundations of life and of the displacement of large population groups into living and working conditions that are unfit for human beings. Because nature and human labour are treated as marketable goods (commodities) in this economic system, they are subject to the remorseless dynamic of a return-optimised valorisation of capital. Their value (and thus also the value of life) is measured on the basis of pricing mechanisms according to prevailing supply and demand.

Advocates of the third option do not seek only to make the most of what is possible within the existing system (option one), nor do they believe in sufficient corrective potential inherent in the system to be able to protect nature and people effectively against exploitation (option two). They are striving for a fundamental system change, a social-ecological transformation. Even if the objectives, pathways and ideas for this change do not add up to a clear master plan due to the widely differing starting points, a number of common elements can be clearly identified, such as liberation from the economic growth dogma (post-growth society), strengthening participation and democratisation, strengthening local economic cycles, freedom from foreign control (decolonisation), opening up the narrowly restricted relationship with nature of Western modernity, the protection of the global commons, decent living and working conditions for all.[36] Nevertheless, the option of fundamental social-ecological change remains dependent on continuous dialogue processes in order to take account of the diversity of actors and their contexts and to provide the necessary space for the participation required.

4 Social-ecological transformation and strategies for the organisation of work

What points of contact, possibilities for action and requirements for the organisation of work under the specific conditions outlined above in low- and middle-income countries are given by option three?

4.1 Resistance to existing conditions of exploitation

The fact that decent living and working conditions on the one hand and ecological sustainability on the other hand can conflict with each other is related to the fact that they can be played off against each other in an economic system that treats nature and labour as tradable market goods. Resistance to this system is therefore aimed both at the exploitation of people and at the exploitation of nature. Labour is a crucial interface between human being and nature. Often, however, resistance is still articulated separately, either as resistance to the destruction of natural habitats or as resistance to human rights violations.[37] No matter how effective existing resistance is, in order to pool the transformative forces, it would be better to identify exploitative labour relations on both dimensions (human and natural) – and not only where they conspicuously coincide, such as in numerous forms of extractivism in Latin America, Asia and Africa. Civil society organisations working in the areas of human rights, better working conditions and ecological sustainability should therefore talk to each other and work together more often. This applies at both national and international levels, since conditions of dependency and exploitation in the extractive sectors in particular are organised at an international level.[38]

4.2 Labour productivity – not at any price

In a growth-oriented economy, increasing labour productivity is considered one of the key levers for increasing the competitiveness of companies and national economies. For countries with a rapidly growing labour force, however, this is a double-edged sword: they would have to buy their competitiveness with high unemployment (open or hidden, for example in informal employment) or achieve very high growth rates. An alternative is to support labour-intensive sectors and companies that are less exposed to international competition, as long as this does not lead to unacceptably high prices for basic goods for daily consumption.[39] From an ecological perspective, too, such a relativisation of labour productivity seems sensible. This is because, in international comparisons, labour in regions with high labour productivity is very material- and greenhouse gas-intensive, while regions with a large subsistence sector have significantly lower labour-related material and greenhouse gas intensities.[40] The macroeconomic calculation of labour productivity (gross domestic product divided by the number of hours worked by people in employment) shows how closely this concept is linked to the model of the growth economy: work is equated with gainful employment and is only recognised as productive to the extent that it contributes to gross domestic product.

4.3 Strengthening local economic and political structures

The local level has a special role to play in the necessary social and ecological adaptation of work. The specific needs, potentials and starting conditions of those affected can be better taken into account. The externalisation of ecological costs, for example through long trade routes, can be reduced. And last but not least, participation, education and management of common goods as well as civil society control of public actors can be more easily achieved at this level. Strengthening local structures without losing sight of global connections is therefore an important strategy for a social-ecological orientation of the economy and society, especially with regard to work. Urban community gardens, or improving marketing opportunities for small farmers in the urban periphery are examples of how work can secure income and make valuable social and ecological contributions.[41] In addition to the local political level, locally rooted companies and civil society groups are particularly important in this area.

Cities and districts, villages and individual communities also make up the local area where traditional economic and living patterns, often in tension in different ways with a "modern" Western lifestyle, remain prevalent. In these tensions, alternatives can be discerned which call into question the claims of such a lifestyle to represent an exclusive key to progress and the good life.[42] Probably the most prominent example of this are the traditional Andean ideas and practices which have found their way into international discourse under the term "buen vivir". The speed at which the often conflict-laden confrontation between tradition and modernity takes place makes it difficult for those affected to bring the potential of their own traditions into a critical and fruitful dialogue with the new, which presents itself under the claim of modernity.[43] Yet such an exchange would be of great value not only for those affected, but for the search for a differentiated post-growth agenda that is viable for everyone. The same applies to the creative potential so often visible in the alternative approaches people develop under the difficult working conditions of the informal economy. Building on this potential and at the same time harnessing the know-how and technological possibilities of a modern knowledge society to develop forms of work that meet the social and ecological requirements would be an important task for education, economic and social policy.

4.4 Differentiated post-growth strategies

Even if the concept of a post-growth society[44] as a proposed solution to global structural problems also claims global validity in principle, it is clear that its implementation must take into account the different contexts of high-, middle- and low-income countries and their interdependence.[45] Adapting a model from Munasinghe (2011), high-income countries have the responsibility and the opportunity to reduce their ecological footprints below the threshold for global sustainability as quickly as possible with the help of appropriate post-growth strategies – and at the same time to open up additional scope for resource use for low-income countries. While this latter group will temporarily need high growth rates to achieve decent living and working conditions, they could, through responsible policies and with the support of rich countries from the outset, ensure that this growth is concentrated in sectors that are socially useful and ecologically sound. Finally, middle-income countries should use their scope for financial and political flexibility to advance their own social development without creating ecologically damaging path dependencies.[46]

4.4.1 Post-growth strategies for low-income countries

For countries with low per capita incomes, it follows that economic policy should not blindly follow the employment-through-growth approach with regard to labour. Three important correctives would appear to be appropriate:

–   Dependence on sectors exporting primary goods should be reduced. Although these sectors, with their large ecological footprints, can generate quick revenues, they have limited scope for value creation and are highly dependent on foreign markets.[47] As a complementary strategy to the necessary reduction in global resource use, this rectification will also help to make the economy more resilient to the expected job losses in these sectors.

-   Economic growth should not be encouraged at the nationally aggregated level, but only selectively (and slowed down as well). In this context, particular importance should be attached to those domestic sectors of the economy which are labour-intensive and play a special role in providing citizens with basic goods and services.

-   In general, priority should be given to labour-intensive sectors and companies over capital-intensive ones. Given the comparatively low capacity of the formal sector to create jobs, this means, especially for low-income countries with a growing labour force, that more political attention should be paid to supporting the informal sector.[48] This entails improving working conditions for informal micro-enterprises (legal protection, access to credit and consultancy, reducing bureaucracy, combating corruption, etc.), gearing vocational training to the skills requirements of informal economic activities and, finally, building up sufficient social security not tied to formal employment relationships.

4.4.2 Post-growth strategies for middle-income countries

In newly industrialised countries with medium per capita incomes, the focus of an appropriately adapted post-growth agenda with regard to work will to some extent be different. While the high importance of primary goods exports also applies to many middle-income countries, most of them are at the same time importers of primary goods and exporters of services and industrial finished and semi-finished goods. As industry and the service sector grow, so do the numbers employed in these sectors. The higher per capita incomes compared with low-income countries has led to the formation of growing middle classes. However, the unequal distribution of income and wealth still means that a high proportion of the population lives in poverty.[49] Thus, the recommendations for improving the working conditions of micro-entrepreneurs and employees in the informal sector and for political incentives for the selective promotion of ecologically sound economic fields remain valid for middle-income countries as well. In addition, two further fields of action suggest themselves:

-   Middle-income countries should also use their comparatively greater financial leeway to explore and pursue new paths of economic and social development that enable prosperity for all within ecological boundaries. Modern technologies can be combined with traditional practices that also offer employment opportunities. Examples might be the use of locally available and ecologically safe building materials in modern construction methods for housing in growing cities, or shared electric taxis in an IT-supported logistics network. Such initiatives need financial and political support in order to survive in the current competitive regime, which significantly encourages social and ecological externalisation (in the above examples: the cement industry and the conventional car industry). Without a change in this regime, such innovative initiatives will hardly be able to extend beyond niche markets.[50]

–   If the fast-growing middle classes in the newly industrialised countries follow the consumption patterns of people in the early industrialised countries, resource shortages will become even more acute and more striking. In addition to the necessary (and ethically dictated) departure from resource-intensive consumption and lifestyles in the high-income countries, the question of what kind of consumption these new middle classes are striving for therefore plays a central role. To address such a question in society is not an easy political task in countries where for the vast majority their rise into the middle class was only very recent and is closely linked to an increase in material consumption opportunities.[51] Governments court their middle classes, and exporting companies from high-income countries do their bit to boost consumption of their products in newly industrialised countries as domestic markets become tighter. But consumption is closely linked to work. Material consumption demands require correspondingly high incomes, which are generated primarily through employment. While the goal of maximising these incomes further promotes the externalisation of social and environmental costs in production processes as mentioned above, traditional forms of subsistence, community and care work are falling behind. Since a public debate on these issues is hardly to be expected from politics and business, civil society actors have a particular responsibility here.

5 Conclusion

Creating differentiated and complementary strategies for the organisation of work in low-, medium- and high-income countries which meet the objective of a global post-growth society serving to reconcile people with each other (social justice) and with nature (respect for natural boundaries and cycles) will require cooperation across a wide range of policy areas. Above all, however, such strategies will depend on the creativity and participation of all those who, in their precarious working conditions, belong to the majority of the global workforce, but who are also, through their work, caught up and entangled in the globally prevailing model of an economy which is evidently incapable of guaranteeing either ecological sustainability or the fulfilment of human rights for all.

Notes

* I would like to thank all those who have contributed to this chapter through their valuable comments: Aravind Unni from the Indo-Global Social Service Society (representing numerous Misereor project partners) and my colleagues at Misereor, Almute Heider, Astrid Meyer, Anselm Meyer-Antz, Thorsten Nilges, Regina Reinart, Steffen Ulrich and Markus Zander. However, this text does not claim to represent official positions of Misereor; the responsibility lies solely with the author.

1 In what follows, I will primarily use the terms low-income countries, middle-income countries and high-income countries instead of the terminology of "developing countries", "emerging economies" and "developed countries" respectively as generally used by the International Labour Organization (ILO) and other UN organisations. Although the ILO's country classification is identical to the World Bank's classification into low-, middle- and high-income countries (see ILO 2018b, 76), its terminology suggests that the level of development of these groups of countries is linked to per capita income.

2 UN 1948, Art. 23–25; UN 1966, Art. 6–10; ILO 2008, for example p. 2 with the four elements of the ILO's "Decent Work" agenda: employment, social protection, social dialogue and rights at work.

3 ILO (2018b), 13. According to the ILO definitions, "employed" persons are all persons who are at least 15 years old and work at least one hour per week for pay. This includes "employees" as well as "own-account workers" and "employers", but also "contributing family members" who work in the business of a relative, even if they do not receive individual payment for it; ILO (1982), No. 9.

4 ILO (2013), 2–9. Work is defined as follows: "Work comprises any activity performed by persons of any sex and age to produce goods or to provide services for use by others or for own use" (ibid, 2).

5 ILO (2018a), 1–2; ILO (2018b), 7–11.

6 I am using here the ILO's geographical groupings of countries: ILO (2018b), 75.

7 Ibid., 23, 98, 102. In the "Developed Countries" (= high-income countries) category, Africa and the Arab states do not appear.

8 Ibid., 23, 26.

9 Ibid., 25.

10 Ibid.

11 Ibid., 20f., 25.

12 Ibid., 16, 23.

13 In the practical reality of workers' and job seekers' lives, there are often considerable grey areas and transitions between "formal" and "informal" work; see Diaz et al. (2018).

14 ILO (2018c), 8, 65. The "working poor" are people who live in poverty despite (formal or informal) employment. In low-income countries, 68 percent of the working poor live in households with a daily per capita income of less than 3.1 US dollars (purchasing power parity), with 40 percent actually living in absolute poverty (less than 1.9 US dollars). For middle-income countries, the shares are 22 percent (less than 3.1 US dollars) and 7 percent (less than 1.9 US dollars).

15 ILO (2017a), 9. Of the world's 152 million child labourers (under 15), 72 million live in sub-Saharan Africa (almost one in five children in this region) and 62 million in the Asia-Pacific region.

16 ITUC (2018). Of the 70 countries in the lowest places in the International Trade Union Confederation's ratings for the status of labour rights, only four are high-income countries: Qatar, Saudi Arabia, the United Arab Emirates and the United States of America. Certainly, in the first three of those countries, migrants from developing and newly industrialised countries are particularly affected by the violation of internationally recognised labour rights.

17 Estimates for forced labour are around 25 million people (40 million if forced marriages are included), with the main concentration in Asia (ILO 2017b, 18f.). The number of detected and reported cases of human trafficking is estimated at just under 25,000 in 2016 (UNODC 2018, 21). Fifty-nine percent of the cases involve sexual exploitation (of the women who are victims of human trafficking, 83 percent are sexually exploited), 34 percent involve forced labour (82 percent of all male victims of human trafficking have to perform forced labour); ibid., 28f. However, this figure is likely to be subject to considerable statistical inaccuracies due to a probably large number of unreported cases. On child labour, see endnote 16.

18 A more differentiated analysis would have to distinguish more clearly between national and international conditions and dynamics with regard to the phenomenon of informality, as already presented and discussed in de Soto (1989) and Altvater/Mahnkopf (2002).

19 Andy Sumner draws attention to this important difference between low- and middle-income countries (Sumner 2012).

20 This and the following observations are based on discussions that Misereor regularly holds with its civil society project partners in Africa, Asia and Latin America as part of the ongoing project dialogue. The partner organisations' interest, particularly in low-income countries, is focused on two main areas: income-generating measures at local level and strengthening economic and political participation at national level. Questions of ecological sustainability, however, usually only play a role if they are perceived as direct and immediate local issues.

21 Authors such as Ashish Kothari and Vandana Shiva from India or Alberto Acosta (Ecuador) and Eduardo Gudynas (Uruguay) are examples. In 2007, Ecuador's (failed) initiative to forego oil production in the Yasuní National Park, a global biodiversity hotspot, in exchange for financial compensation, caused a political stir.

22 See Wilkinson/Pickett (2009). The results of the World Values Survey (http://www.worldvaluessurvey.org/WVSContents.jsp) also show a close

relationship between economic development and life satisfaction, although it is not possible from this to conclude the existence of a monocausal relationship.

23 For example, in the *Hindustan Times* of 15 July 2018, or in a promotional YouTube article of 1 October 2018 entitled "Inclusive Growth is our tribute to Mahatma Gandhi: PM Modi".

24 Although there is no general definition of inclusive growth, two characteristics can be identified in the use of the term by organisations such as the World Bank, the IMF, the OECD and the UN: all social strata and groups must benefit from economic growth and all must have the opportunity to contribute to it. As the OECD puts it on its website: "Inclusive growth is economic growth that is distributed fairly across society and creates opportunities for all" (www.oecd.org/inclusive-growth).

25 SACBC (2018).

26 This correlation is demonstrated particularly clearly by the example of China. While most of the global reduction in absolute poverty in the past two decades can be attributed to China's economic development and the associated increase there in per capita income, over the same period China has risen to become the largest emitter of CO_2 and now also exceeds global sustainability limits for per capita emissions.

27 ILO (2018d), 19–21. Examples given in the text include agriculture, fisheries, forestry and tourism.

28 See www.unenvironment.org/explore-topics/green-economy: "We promote the transition to economies that are low carbon, resource efficient and socially inclusive".

29 See www.oecd.org/greengrowth: "Green Growth means fostering economic growth and development, while ensuring that natural assets continue to provide the resources and environmental services on which our well-being relies".

30 See Sustainable Development Goal 8 of the 2030 Agenda for Sustainable Development: "Promote sustained, inclusive and sustainable economic growth, full and productive employment and decent work for all".

31 On the concept of "planetary boundaries" see Rockström et al. (2009). In order to deliver on the promise of an economic growth that is compatible with sustainability, it is not enough to reduce resource intensity in a given proportion (relative decoupling). Rather, the reduction must be large enough not only to slow down the momentum of environmental pressure but also to keep it within absolute limits (absolute decoupling). To achieve this, it must be able to offset both the effect of rising global per-capita income and the effect of the growing world population on resource use.

32 Tim Jackson uses the example of carbon intensity and concludes that even in the best-case scenario, carbon intensity would have to fall ten times more than the average since 1990 if the targets of the IPCC's Fourth Assessment Report on limiting global warming are to be met (Jackson 2009). Funke et al. (2016, 5) ignore these calculations in their critique of Jackson and use only the argument that the fact that an absolute decoupling of CO_2 emissions from economic growth has not been possible in the past does not mean in principle that it will not be possible in the future.

33 ILO (2018d), 13, 16.

34 Ibid., 13f.
35 See Brand (2012) in the run-up to the Rio+20 summit conference.
36 See for example Acosta/Brand (2018), Castillo et al. (2015) and Kothari (2016).
37 Temper et al. (2018) do not mention labour in their analysis of the role of "environmental justice movements" advocating radical transformations towards sustainability. Barth et al. (2019), however, following Karl Polanyi, explicitly emphasise the parallels and connections between work and nature with respect to a socio-ecological transformation.
38 One example is the import of hard coal from South Africa, Colombia and Russia to Germany to compensate for the ending of domestic production. These imports not only contribute to global CO_2 emissions, but also result in environmental destruction and human rights violations in the producing countries (Misereor 2018).
39 For this reason, Braun (2010, 124f.) advocates state support in developing countries for traditional crafts rather than for industry.
40 ILO (2018d), 17f.
41 For example, the Brazilian civil society organisation AS-PTA supports the production and marketing of healthy food in local markets (aspta.org.br/2013/09/projeto-alimentos-saudaveis-nos-mercados-locais/). The formation of regional nutrition councils is important in this context, and has meanwhile been adopted in several other countries such as Germany.
42 The importance of local communities for social-ecological change, and the tension between tradition and modernity in which these communities find themselves were consistent motifs in the civil society dialogue forums that Misereor conducted as part of a three-year project on a "Global Common Good" 2012–2015 (Stoll 2015, 264–266).
43 See for example the touching case of a local indigenous Adivasi population in the Odisha state of India which finds itself under threat of losing its traditional livelihood and way of living through the government-driven forced introduction of cotton cultivation (for export) at the expense of the existing pristine forest vegetation (https://youtu.be/uRWq1NhtQhk).
44 According to Seidl/Zahrnt (2014), the central requirements of this concept can be summarised as follows: no general policy of growth promotion; the restructuring of growth-dependent and growth-driving systems and institutions with the aim of achieving independence from growth; limiting environmental use in line with the sustainability goals.
45 Ibid., 17; see also Acosta/Brand (2018), 118–121, Gudynas (2011), 8f.
46 This ideal-typical conception of a differentiated post-growth strategy is based on an optimistic assessment of the quality and governance capacities of political institutions which is by no means undisputed.
47 In Latin America, in particular, this topic is intensively discussed in the extractivism debate; see Kruip et al. (2019), Acosta/Brand (2018), Brand (2015). The latter two also address the links to the more European-based post-growth/degrowth debate.
48 Fourie (2013) illustrates this using the example of South Africa. See also Braun (2010), 124–136.
49 Fourteen percent in the lower middle-income countries (in the low-income countries in comparison, it is 42 percent). In absolute figures, however, almost two-thirds of those in extreme poverty in the world today live in middle-income countries; World Bank (2018), 29.

50 Scherhorn (2011), Hoffmann (2015).

51 Ramakrishnan (2020); Herry Priyono (2015); Fernandes (2009); see also the ongoing research project of the German Institute for Development Policy on consumption and lifestyle patterns of the new middle classes in Ghana, Peru and the Philippines (www.die-gdi.de/veranstaltungen/middle-classes-preferences-attitudes-and-environmental-impact/).

Bibliography

Acosta, A., Brand, U. (2018): *Radikale Alternativen. Warum man den Kapitalismus nur mit vereinten Kräften überwinden kann*, München

Altvater, E., Mahnkopf, B. (2002): *Globalisierung der Unsicherheit*, Münster

Barth, Th. et al. (2019): *Transformation of what? Or: The socio-ecological transformation of working society*, IHS Working Paper, 1

Brand, U. (2012): *Green economy – the next oxymoron? No lessons learned from failures of implementing sustainable development*, Gaia 21(1), 28–32

Brand, U. (2015): *Degrowth und Post-Extraktivismus: Zwei Seiten einer Medaille?* Working Paper Nr. 5 of the DFG-KollegforscherInnengruppe Postwachstumsgesellschaften

Braun, H.-G. (2010): *Armut überwinden durch Soziale Marktwirtschaft und Mittlere Technologie. Ein Strategieentwurf für Entwicklungsländer*, Münster

Castillo, O.L. et al. (2015): *Reflections on the global common Good. Systematization of an intercultural dialogical research process*, in: Reder, M. et al. (Eds.): Global Common Good. Intercultural Perspectives on a Just and Ecological Transformation, Frankfurt, New York, 243–259

De Soto, H. (1989): *The Other Path*, London

Diaz, J.J. et al. (2018): *Pathways to formalization: Going beyond the formality dichotomy*, IZA Discussion Paper, 11750

Fernandes, L. (2009): *The political economy of lifestyle: Consumption, India's middle class and state-led development*, in: Lange, H., Meier, L. (Eds.): The New Middle Classes, Dordrecht, 219–236

Fourie, F. (2013): *Reducing unemployment: Waiting for high growth? Waiting for Godot?* Econ 3x3, March 12, 2013

Funke, F. et al. (2016): *Wirtschaftswachstum aufgeben? – Eine Analyse wachstumskritischer Argumente*, MCC Working Paper, 1

Gudynas, E. (2011): *Überholter Mythos. Die Suche nach grundlegenden Veränderungen, die über die Entwicklungsidee hinausführen, hat in Lateinamerika Hochkonjunktur*, in: Misereor (Ed.): In den Grenzen von morgen. Für ein neues Verhältnis von Entwicklung, Wirtschaftswachstum und Umwelt, Welt-Sichten-Dossier, 9, 7–9

Herry Priyono, B. (2015): *Nachzügler im Konsumdelirium. Indonesiens Mittelschichten und ihre Vorbilder – ein Realitätstest für die Streiter um globale Nachhaltigkeit*, in: Misereor (Ed.): Baustellen einer Postwachstumsagenda. Nachhaltige und gerechte Entwicklung ohne Wachstumszwänge, Welt-Sichten-Dossier, 3, 21–23

Hoffmann, J. (2015): *Rahmenbedingungen für nachhaltigen Wettbewerb. Der ökologische, soziale und kulturelle Raubbau ist ohne veränderte Spielregeln nicht aufzuhalten*, in: Misereor (Ed.): Baustellen einer Postwachstumsagenda. Nachhaltige und gerechte Entwicklung ohne Wachstumszwänge, Welt-Sichten-Dossier, 3, 10–12

ILO (1982): *Resolution Concerning Statistics of the Economically Active Population, Employment, Unemployment and Underemployment, Adopted by the Thirteenth International Conference of Labour Statisticians (October 1982)*, Geneva

ILO (1998): *ILO Declaration on Fundamental Principles and Rights at Work and Its Follow-up* (second edition with Annex revised 2010), Geneva

ILO (2002): *Resolution Concerning Decent Work and the Informal Economy*, Geneva

ILO (2008): *ILO Declaration on Social Justice for a Fair Globalization*, Geneva

ILO (2013): *Resolution concerning statistics of work, employment and labour underutilization*, 19th International Conference of Labour Statisticians, Resolution I, Geneva

ILO (2017a): *Global Estimates of Child Labour: Results and Trends 2012–2016*, Geneva

ILO (2017b): *Global Estimates of Modern Slavery: Forced Labour and Forced Marriage*, Geneva

ILO (2018a): *Informality and non-standard forms of employment* (Prepared for the G20 Employment Working Group Meeting February 20–22, Buenos Aires), Geneva

ILO (2018b): *Women and Men in the Informal Economy: A Statistical Picture*, Geneva

ILO (2018c): *World Employment Social Outlook 2018: Trends*, Geneva

ILO (2018d): *World Employment Social Outlook 2018: Greening with Jobs*, Geneva

ITUC (2018): *ITUC Global Rights Index. The World's Worst Countries for Workers*, Bruxelles

Jackson, T. (2009): *Prosperity without Growth*, London

Kothari, A. (2016): *The search for radical alternatives. Key elements and principles*, CounterCurrents.org, 3 November 2016

Kruip, G. et al. (2019): *Neo-Extraktivismus in Bolivien. Chancen, Risiken, Nachhaltigkeit*, Forum Sozialethik, 20

Misereor (Ed.) (2018): *Kohleausstieg – weltweit. Argumente für eine globale Energiewende*, Welt-Sichten-Dossier 5

Munasinghe, M. (2011): *Addressing sustainable development and climate change together using sustainomics*, WIREs Climate Change, 2, 7–18

Ramakrishnan, A. et al. (2020): *Keeping up with the Patels: Conspicious consumption drives the adoption of cars and appliances in India*, Energy Research & Social Science, 70, 101742

Rockström, J. et al. (2009): *Planetary boundaries: Exploring the safe operating space for humanity*, Ecology and Society 14(2), 32

SACBC (2018): *Southern African Catholic Bishops' conference – parliamentary Liaison office: The informal sector: Creating jobs*, Briefing Paper 470, December 2018

Scherhorn, G. (2011): *Die Welt als Allmende: marktwirtschaftlicher Wettbewerb und Gemeingüterschutz*, Aus Politik und Zeitgeschichte 61(28–30), 21–27

Seidl, I., Zahrnt, A. (2014): *Postwachstumsgesellschaft. Die Emanzipation von Wachstumszwängen dient dem Gemeinwohl – auch in Schwellen- und Entwicklungsländern*, in: Misereor et al. (Eds.): Weltgemeinwohl. Neue Ansätze zu Postwachstum und globaler Gerechtigkeit, Welt-Sichten-Dossier 12(1), 13–17

Stoll, G. (2015): *Views from civil society practitioners*, in: Reder M. et al. (Eds.): Global Common Good. Intercultural Perspectives on a Just and Ecological Transformation, Frankfurt, New York, 261–268

Sumner, A. (2012): *Where will the world's poor live? An update on global poverty and the new bottom billion*, Center for Global Development Working Paper 305

Temper, L. et al. (2018): *A perspective on radical transformations to sustainability: Resistances, movements and alternatives*, Sustainability Science 13(3), 747–764

UN (1948): *Universal declaration of human rights*. Adopted and proclaimed by General Assembly resolution 217 A (111) of 10 December 1948, New York

UN (1966): *International covenant on economic, social and cultural rights*, Adopted and Opened for Signatures, Ratification and Accession by General Assembly Resolution 2200 A (XXI) of 16 December 1966, New York

UNODC (2018): *Global Report on Trafficking in Persons 2018*, Vienna

Wilkinson, R., Pickett, K. (2009): *The Spirit Level: Why More Equal Societies Almost Always Do Better*, London

World Bank (2018): *Piecing Together the Poverty Puzzle. Poverty and Shared Prosperity 2018*, Washington

Conclusion

15 The prospects for practical action

Irmi Seidl and Angelika Zahrnt

Summary

Our social and economic system needs to be rebuilt if it is to be set free from its dependence on growth. This is the only way to overcome the various crises in which we currently find ourselves. Diminishing the role of formal employment and the further extension of meaningful activities must play a central role in such a rebuilding process. There are numerous possible starting points and courses of action, and these can be related to four groups of actors: individuals, civil society, businesses and the state.

1 Introduction

Retaining jobs – and creating new ones – is a key argument in the call for economic growth – and this is true globally. But the planet can no longer cope with the high levels of resource consumption and emissions that accompany high levels of economic activity. The reports on global warming, biodiversity loss and other environmental damage are becoming increasingly dramatic, with many countries in the South being particularly affected.

Decoupling economic growth from environmental use is not on the horizon, which means that the climate neutrality agreed upon in Paris in 2015 most probably cannot be achieved in case of ongoing growth. In addition to the ecological crises, social inequalities and new challenges such as digitalisation and the Corona pandemic are increasingly calling the existing social and economic system into question.

Work will play a central role in the necessary restructuring of the social and economic system: the opportunities for formal employment and other meaningful activity, the relevant conditions and meaningfulness, the significance for individual and societal well-being.

DOI: 10.4324/9781003187370-15

The 14 chapters of this book analyse how work can be configured differently, what changes are needed to its context and conditions, and, above all, how the dominance of formal employment can be scaled back so that individuals and society are no longer so totally dependent on it and so that its negative effects in the ecological sphere can be reduced.

This concluding chapter summarises possible starting points and courses of action for individuals, for civil society, for businesses and for the state. These starting points can facilitate a shift away from the fixation on formal employment and economic growth in order to enable the development of an economic and social system that is not dependent on growth and operates within the ecological boundaries.

2 The individual

Depending on our financial circumstances, work situation and personal values, we can influence how much formal employment we want, how much importance formal employment should have in our lives, how much time we want to devote to other forms of meaningful activity (self-determined work, care work, volunteering, etc.) and how we can create our own time wealth. In so doing, we can pursue the goal of greater independence from both formal employment and professional status and of achieving reduced financial dependence, greater resilience to economic crises, more varied social relationships and greater personal satisfaction through a mix of formal employment and other (unpaid) activities. Compared with formal employment, voluntary work more often provides a greater sense of meaning and autonomy. For such a portfolio of activities, it makes sense for an individual to acquire a wide range of qualifications and skills.

When choosing a job, important criteria may include how meaningful the work is and what the working conditions are like – whether reduced hours or flexible working time are possible, whether the company is open to the idea of sustainable work and products, and whether there is sufficient scope for personal life and meaningful activity alongside formal employment.

A modest lifestyle oriented towards sufficiency can make people less dependent on earned income – as can being meaningfully active, e.g. by producing one's own food, DIY, carrying out repairs and sharing. Time for such activities can be created by reducing formal work. If they take place in the context of exchange systems and if there are relevant organisational structures (e.g. repair cafés, repair advice services), more people can take part in them.

An individual's consumption practices influence the working conditions and incomes of other people, and needs can be met more precisely and appropriately through the co-creation of consumer products (collaborative consumption). In this way, the overall level of consumption can be reduced.

Another possible starting point for redressing the balance between formal employment and other forms of meaningful activity is to get involved directly in labour policy – as an entrepreneur, at the workplace or through trade unions. Possible relevant areas of influence are working hours and conditions, job content and product design. Political engagement in processes of change is possible both in the area of formal employment and in the development of structures for voluntary work, self-determined work, care work, etc.

It is possible to try to alter the strong link that currently exists between formal employment and social security both by political means and by diversifying one's own social security arrangements – through social innovations such as intergenerational housing, timebanking or ensuring lifelong affordable housing, e.g. in alternative, cooperative housing projects.

Because the present-day dominance of formal employment often seems fixed and immovable to us, it is instructive to take a look back into history to see that in other eras, completely different understandings of work and different emphases prevailed.

3 Civil society

A large proportion of all work beyond formal employment is carried out within civil society structures, such as political engagement, work in voluntary social or environmental associations, or in the public services (first aid, fire protection or civil defence organisations, etc.). There are several reasons why an increase in such civil society work would be a good thing: changes in the world of work (demographic change, transition to greater flexibility, reduction of working hours, etc.) are creating increasing opportunities for volunteering. At the same time, there is a greater social need for such work (demographic change, desire for participation and engagement). Volunteering can provide personal fulfilment and offer professional skills development.

In order to enable the expansion and professionalisation of voluntary work, new or enhanced organisational structures might be conceivable, such as job centres for volunteering, volunteering placements for long or very short periods of time, international volunteer exchanges, timebanking and electronic organisation platforms. Some voluntary work could also be financially compensated and linked to basic social security.

4 Business

Alongside the state and other non-profit organisations, businesses are the largest providers of formal employment. In a post-growth society, the role of formal employment should be scaled back in relation to other activities, and at the same time structures enabling such other activities should be expanded. What can businesses contribute to this? They can offer reduced and more flexible working hours, or make them the norm; they can support the use of a limited proportion of working hours – whether paid or not – for other activities, e.g. for voluntary work (as is already the case today for the volunteer fire service), care work, sabbaticals, pro bono work. Employees must not suffer any resultant detriment in terms of social security.

Companies can work together with business associations, works councils and trade unions to formulate regulations on how to reduce working time and make it more flexible. In addition, companies can establish high-quality and satisfactory working conditions, not the least benefit of which could be a reduction in compensatory consumption and thus a reduction in employees' dependence on earned income. Businesses can also choose suppliers who provide good working conditions and they can restrict their business relations to their local area, which can improve the quality of trading relations with suppliers and consumers and thus also improve working conditions.

As far as product design and production are concerned, businesses should basically develop and manufacture sustainable products that are useful and durable. They can involve their employees and consumers in this process, and together they can encourage shared forms of use.

Finally, companies can develop business models that do not require them to constantly increase labour productivity; this means they do not have to produce either in greater numbers or more cheaply or else to lay off employees. At the macroeconomic level, this reduces the pressure for economic growth to ensure a sufficient number of jobs.

5 The state

The state essentially shapes the framework conditions for formal employment and for other meaningful activity. One factor that is not sufficiently taken into account in this context is the tax system. The state can reduce taxes and social security contributions on earned income, thereby making work "cheaper". As a result, workers can reduce their working hours because more is left in their pay packets, and/or businesses can hire more people or escape some of the pressure on them to constantly increase labour productivity. The current high level of taxes on labour is the result of a historical evolution and of globalised neoliberal policies that favour lower taxation of companies and capital and higher taxation of labour. This trend has adverse distributional effects, leads to high environmental consumption due to the fact that resources are hardly taxed at all and drives pro-growth policies. This is because companies react to "expensive" labour by increasing labour productivity, which in turn increases macroeconomic pressure for further economic growth in order to create new jobs. Such interconnections have so far been discussed principally in the context of ecological tax reform proposals. But this discussion should increasingly include their implications for work.

Additionally, the state is called upon to develop the social system in such a way that the strong link between social security and formal employment – which is also the result of a historical process – is weakened and the social system is no longer financed primarily through taxes on labour, which also makes labour "more expensive". In parallel, it can expand essential public services (public health, education, old-age provision) and thus make social security less dependent on formal employment.

The state also creates the framework within which businesses operate, e.g. through taxation, subsidies and company law. It can cut back the financial incentives for new investments and technical progress which constantly drive up labour productivity. It can promote non-profit enterprises as well as ones which provide many jobs, i.e. which are comparatively labour-intensive.

The state can also create new, labour-intensive employment and promote and support it through appropriate framework conditions. In view of the ecological and social crises, this will have to be targeted above all at the social services sector, green sectors (the energy transition, the circular economy, etc.) and agriculture. A Green Deal must thus also address the employment issue and contribute to alleviating the demand for growth.

The state has a role to play in orienting training and education of the population towards a broad range of meaningful activities and in promoting creativity and initiative in those activities. This applies to all areas of education.

Finally, the state can also pursue policies geared towards sufficiency and promote structures and activities that reduce consumption and make it more sustainable. Such a statement may sound inappropriate at present in view of the current economic collapse induced by the Corona pandemic, from which society – according to current political discourse – is expected to escape via increased consumption. But it remains true that wasteful material consumption must be drastically reduced if we are to remain within the planetary boundaries. This in turn will reduce dependence on earned income.

6 Conclusion

Formal employment is an integral part of our complex socio-economic system today. The livelihoods of countless people, their social security, their opportunities for meaningful activity and often their identity are tied to it. However, both formal employment and the socio-economic system as a whole are undergoing radical change. The main causes are the multiple ecological crises together with digitalisation. While constant economic growth, driven by the argument that it is needed to create jobs, can no longer be maintained and extended around the globe for ecological reasons, digitalisation is fundamentally changing both the need for formal employment and its content.

Where these changes will lead, and what political responses they will trigger, can only to a limited extent be foreseen. What is indisputable, however, is that the changes have to lead to good work for all; they must improve for everyone their individual prospects of leading a good life, participating in society and realising their potential. There also needs to be a certain level of material and social security and a structure for the delivery of essential public services. On this foundation, people can then develop as individuals and engage in economic activity within the planetary boundaries.

Such a prospect presupposes that the importance of formal employment decreases and that other meaningful activity is able to take up more time and space. Perhaps we will not work less in the future, but rather differently: engaging in multiple activities, working less intensively but more collaboratively and doing more unpaid work, all of which can nevertheless contribute to securing our livelihoods.

There are already numerous ideas and strategies around for how society can develop in this direction, but there are also many open questions, as the 14 chapters in this book demonstrate. The preceding remarks show that there are already possibilities for practical action today that can pave the way for a post-growth society which is no longer centred on formal employment, but widens the space for diverse, life-serving and meaningful activities.

Index

Note: **Bold** page numbers refer to tables; *italic* page numbers refer to figures and page numbers followed by "n" denote endnotes.

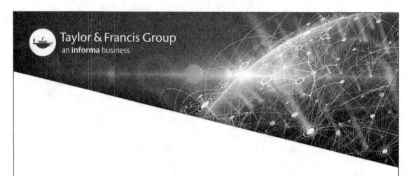

Printed in the United States
by Baker & Taylor Publisher Services